World Histories From Below

World Histories From Below

Disruption and Dissent, 1750 to the Present

*Edited by Antoinette Burton
and Tony Ballantyne*

BLOOMSBURY ACADEMIC
LONDON • NEW YORK • OXFORD • NEW DELHI • SYDNEY

BLOOMSBURY ACADEMIC
Bloomsbury Publishing Plc
50 Bedford Square, London, WC1B 3DP, UK
1385 Broadway, New York, NY 10018, USA

BLOOMSBURY, BLOOMSBURY ACADEMIC and the Diana logo are
trademarks of Bloomsbury Publishing Plc

First published in Great Britain 2016
Reprinted 2018, 2019

Cover design: Sharon Mah
Cover image © Afro American Newspapers / Gado / Getty Images

A catalogue record for this book is available from the British Library.

Library of Congress Cataloging-in-Publication Data
Names: Burton, Antoinette M., 1961- | Ballantyne, Tony, 1972-
Title: World histories from
below: disruption and dissent, 1750 to the present / edited by Antoinette Burton and
Tony Ballantyne.
Description: London; New York: Bloomsbury Academic, an imprint
of Bloomsbury Publishing Plc, 2016. | Includes bibliographical references and index.
Identifiers: LCCN 2015048001| ISBN 9781472587640 (hardback) |
ISBN 9781472587633 (paperback) | ISBN 9781472587657 (PDF) |
ISBN 9781472587664 (ePub)
Subjects: LCSH: World history—Textbooks. | Social history—Textbooks. |
Dissenters—History—Textbooks. | Social conflict—History—Textbooks. |
Revolutions—History—Textbooks. | Social change—History—Textbooks. |
BISAC: HISTORY / General. | HISTORY /
World. | HISTORY / Social History.
Classification: LCC D21 .W925 2016 | DDC 909.08–dc23 LC record available at
https://lccn.loc.gov/2015048001

ISBN: HB: 978-1-4725-8764-0
PB: 978-1-4725-8763-3
ePDF: 978-1-4725-8765-7
ePub: 978-1-4725-8766-4

Typeset by RefineCatch Limited, Bungay, Suffolk
Printed and bound in the United States of America

To find out more about our authors and books visit
www.bloomsbury.com and sign up for our newsletters.

In loving memory of Mark Leff:
historian
rabble rouser
friend and
champion of everything from below

CONTENTS

ILLUSTRATIONS

Figures

Tables

CONTRIBUTORS

Clare Anderson is Professor of History at the University of Leicester. Her research centers on the history of incarceration and penal colonies, and their intersections with other modes of confinement and coerced labor, with a focus on South and Southeast Asia, the Indian Ocean and Australia. Her publications include: *Convicts in the Indian Ocean* (Macmillan, 2000), *Legible Bodies* (Berg, 2004), *Subaltern Lives* (Cambridge University Press, 2012), and (with Madhumita Mazumdar and Vishvajit Pandya) *New Histories of the Andaman Islands* (Cambridge University Press, 2016). Clare is currently working on a global history of penal colonies, spanning the Atlantic, Indian Ocean and Pacific worlds. She tweets about her work @ sysgak.

Tony Ballantyne is a Professor of History and Pro-Vice-Chancellor Humanities at the University of Otago, where he also is the Director of the Centre for Research on Colonial Culture. He has published widely on the cultural history of the modern British Empire and his most recent sole-authored book is *Entanglements of Empire: Missionaries, Maori and the Question of the Body* (Duke University Press, 2014). He has also worked collaboratively with Antoinette Burton on modern world history, co-editing *Bodies in Contact: Rethinking Colonial Encounters in World History* (Duke University Press, 2005) and *Moving Subjects: Gender, Mobility and Intimacy in an Age of Global Empire* (University of Illinois Press, 2007), as well as co-authoring *Empires and the Reach of the Global, 1870–1945* (Harvard University Press, 2012).

Antoinette Burton is Professor of History and Bastian Professor of Global and Transnational Studies at the University of Illinois, Urbana Champaign, USA. She is the author, most recently, of *The Trouble with Empire: Challenges to Modern British Imperialism* (Oxford, 2015) and co-editor, with Dane Kennedy, of *How Empire Shaped Us* (Bloomsbury, 2016). She has collaborated extensively with Tony Ballantyne on books and collections that bring empire and world history into the same frame of analysis. She currently directs the Illinois Program for Research in the Humanities and is Principal Investigator of the Andrew W. Mellon Foundation Project "Humanities without Walls" (http://www.iprh.illinois.edu/programs/hww.html).

Eileen Ford is Associate Professor of History at California State University, Los Angeles. She specializes in Latin American history, the history of childhood and youth, cultural history and more recently, global history. Currently she is working on a book project on the history of childhood in post-revolutionary Mexico City.

Durba Ghosh is Associate Professor of History and affiliated with Asian Studies and Feminist, Gender, and Sexuality Studies at Cornell University. She teaches and researches modern South Asian history, which includes the nations of the Indian subcontinent. She focuses on the history of colonial governance and law, gender, sexuality, and (increasingly) the tensions between security and democracy. She is the author of *Sex and the Family in Colonial India: The Making of Empire* (2006) and with Dane Kennedy, the co-editor of *Decentring Empire: Britain, India and the Transcolonial World* (2006) as well as over a dozen chapters and articles in volumes such as the *Archive Stories* (also edited by Antoinette Burton), the *Oxford Handbook of the History of Terrorism*, the *American Historical Review*, *Gender and History*, and *Modern Asian Studies*.

Nancy J. Jacobs is an Associate Professor in the Department of History at Brown University and a fellow of the Institute for Environment and Society there. Her research has probed the nexus of environmental and social history. She is author of *Environment, Power, and Injustice: A South African History* (Cambridge University Press, 2003) and *Birders of Africa: History of a Network* (Yale University Press, 2016). She has also produced a curricular resource: *African History through Sources: Colonial Contexts and Everyday Experiences* (Cambridge University Press, 2014). The second volume of that set, on sub-Saharan Africa, is in preparation. Her research interests are now turning toward topics in animal history.

Danielle Johnstone is a curriculum designer and research assistant. Her research interests focus on experiences of injustice in sub-Saharan Africa.

Christopher Kelly is a graduate student pursuing a PhD in the Department of Earth, Environmental, and Planetary Sciences at Brown University, where he is also affiliated with the Institute for Environment and Society. He was a 2014 National Science Foundation Graduate Research Fellowship recipient, and in 2013 received a US Fulbright award to Durban, South Africa. Chris's research probes the geologic record to interrogate past climate change on the scale of millions to hundreds of years ago. In particular, his work focuses on locations likely to be susceptible to future anthropogenic climate change for natural and/or socio-economic reasons. Two ongoing research projects focus on climatic reconstructions from the Pacific Ocean offshore of the Baja peninsula, Mexico, and Sulawesi Island, Indonesia. Moving forward, he is most interested in the interplay between climate change and human history, combining proxy work and historical archives. He is also passionate about redressing contemporary inequities in STEM education amongst underrepresented groups.

Mary Jo Maynes is a Professor of History at the University of Minnesota. She is a historian of Modern Europe with interests in comparative and world history. Her work explores the social and cultural history of the family, gender and generational relations, class dynamics, and personal narratives. Her books include *The Family: A World History* (Oxford, 2012), co-authored with Ann Waltner; *Telling Stories: The Use of Personal Narratives in the Social Sciences and History* (Cornell, 2008), co-authored with Jennifer Pierce and Barbara Laslett; *Secret Gardens, Satanic Mills: Placing Girls in European History* (Indiana, 2004), co-edited with Birgitte Søland and Christina Benninghaus; and *Taking the Hard Road: Life Course and Class Identity in French and German Workers' Autobiographies of the Industrial Era* (North Carolina, 1995). She has recently co-edited special issues of *Social Science History* on "Temporalities and Periodization in Human History: Conversations across the Disciplines of History and Archaeology" (2012), with Ann Waltner, and *Gender & History* on "Gender History across Epistemologies" (2012), with Donna Gabaccia. She is currently a co-editor of *Gender & History*.

Heather Streets-Salter is Department Chair and Director of World History Programs at Northeastern University in Boston, Massachusetts. She received her PhD in History from Duke University in 1998. She is the author of *Martial Races: The Military, Martial Races, and Masculinity in British Imperial Culture, 1857–1914* (Manchester University Press, 2004), *Traditions and Encounters: A Brief Global History* (McGraw-Hill, 2006) with Jerry Bentley and Herb Ziegler (now in its fourth edition), *Empires and Colonies in the Modern World* (Oxford University Press, 2015) with Trevor Getz, and *Southeast Asia during the First World War* (Cambridge University Press, 2016). Her next project is called *The Chill before the Cold War: Communism and Anti-Communism in Colonial Southeast Asia in the Interwar Period*.

Ann Waltner teaches Chinese and world history at the University of Minnesota. She has published widely in the fields of Chinese gender, kinship and religion. Together with Mary Jo Maynes, she is the co-author of *Family: A World History* (Oxford, 2012). In addition to her conventional work as a historian, she writes scripts and performs spoken word with the early music ensemble Sacabuce. She is currently devising an online course on the eighteenth-century Chinese novel *Dream of the Red Chamber* in conjunction with the San Francisco Opera production of an opera based on the novel.

Keywords:

"World History," "Below," and "Dissent and Disruption"

Antoinette Burton and Tony Ballantyne

Robert Nesta "Bob" Marley is a global icon: his music can be heard in all corners of the world as it circulates through radio, on CDs and on old cassettes and albums, as well as through online music streaming services and on iTunes. Portraits of Marley grace t-shirts, posters, and flags from his Caribbean homeland to villages and cities in Asia and Africa, and in university towns across the globe. As the most influential recording artist of reggae, an electrifying live performer, a staunch advocate for the downtrodden, and a passionate messenger of Rastafarianism, Marley not only embodied Jamaican "livity" (righteous living), but articulated a powerful set of messages. His music addressed both the pain of exploitation and the promise of redemption, urging his listeners forward, suggesting that they had to seize their own freedom and cast off those who exploited them, the "downpressors." Marley believed that liberty would not be won through violence, but rather through love, God's grace, and the power of song.

Bob Marley was optimistic about the ability of ordinary people to bring about change, suggesting that the big tree (the rich and the powerful) would be brought down by their own hands:

We are the small axe, sharp and ready,
Ready to cut you down

Revolutionary power lay with ordinary people; they had the power to seize their own liberty, not just in a political sense, but at a psychological and cultural level as well. The lyrics of Marley's famous "Redemption Song" reworked an influential speech by the great Jamaican political leader and key proponent of pan-Africanism, Marcus Garvey:

> Emancipate yourselves from mental slavery;
> None but ourselves can free our mind.

Bob Marley's stress on the possibility of redemption and his vision of Zion—a Rastafarian utopia that offered freedom, peace and unity in counterpoint to the Babylon of modernity's materialism—has had a great appeal. His music offered a promise of both black liberation and a kind of multiracial redemption, a vision that has had a particular appeal to the disenfranchised, oppressed and marginal, from Polish workers to the inhabitants of South Africa's townships, from Native American reservations to Maori and Pasifika peoples in New Zealand. As a consequence the reggae popularized by Bob Marley was localized and reworked by musicians in a range of contexts, from Brazilian samba reggae, to the strong Maori and Polynesian traditions of reggae in New Zealand, and to the efforts to reinvigorate traditional roots music and local identities in the Polish Tatras.[1]

We begin with the global reach of Bob Marley because his vision, his work, and his influence encapsulate some of the rich possibilities that are opened up by thinking about world history from below and his career embodies many of the central ideas developed in this volume. "World history" is, of course, a distinct approach to the past that focuses on the encounters, exchanges, and entanglements that link human communities, exploring shifting patterns of connection and interdependence. Although this analytical vision recognizes the importance of nation-states in the modern world, scholars of world history do not see nation-states as natural and clearly-bounded entities that order our apprehensions of the past. Rather, they are committed to examining the forces and processes that bring communities into contact and interdependence, tracing the "bundles of relationships" that draw disparate people and places into various forms of connection.[2] For a history of our contemporary world, the circulation and reworking of Bob Marley's music offers one important perspective on both the movement of cultural artefacts (like vinyl LPs, cassettes, CDs, and MP3 files) and the mobility of ideas, such as Marley's stress on the need for self-assertion, the pursuit of political rights, and a quest of spiritual redemption. These kinds of cross-cultural linkages and entanglements are nicely captured in the impact of Marley's visit to New Zealand, when he was formally welcomed in a pōwhiri (ritual of welcome) by Maori in 1979 and where his music helped catalyze a range of new political and cultural visions.[3] They remind us that, in addition to goods and people and ideas, a broad spectrum of radical symbols and referents—like the iconography of Bob Marley himself—have circulated widely and have had the capacity to generate all kinds of engagements with structures of power, whether local, regional, transregional or global.

The other element of our title, "from below," stresses the importance of thinking about the past through the experiences and perspectives of the downcast, the marginal, and the exploited. Drawing particularly from a tradition of work inaugurated by E. P. Thompson's landmark *The Making of the English Working Class* (1963), which demonstrated the centrality of an insurgent working class in shaping modern Britain, we make the case here that world histories should do more than simply take account of ordinary people or common protest. They should be alive to the ways in which such subjects have driven global processes and shaped the direction and the character of connectivity at many scales. Thompson's influential book, which cast its shadow on half a century of history of ordinary people and circumstances, argued for just such agency, stressing the need to look beyond political and economic elites, and to explore the aspirations and sensibilities of everyday people who were caught up in the momentous changes wrought by modernity. In keeping with this impulse to revision the past from the "bottom up," or from "below," in this volume our authors reckon with the histories of peasants and urban workers, colonized communities and indigenous peoples, the enslaved, indentured, and coerced, the ordinary men, women, and children whom we might think of as constituting the "people," the "masses," the "working class." Beyond the supportive roles they played in the making of modernity, capitalism, and other signifiers of the global, we argue that the challenges they posed as well as the conformities they embraced played a significant role in the making of the very conditions of what we think of as "global" history.

Thinking about and through the "below" also points to the importance of the geographical angle of vision the authors in this volume bring to bear, as they recognize the importance of grounding our understanding of the history of the modern world in an expansive analytical range that recognizes the impact of what has been variously figured as the "non-West," the "Global South," or the "Third World." This is important because for a very long time, and often still, world history has tended to reinforce narratives about the "rise of the West." The stories often told imagine that the energy, creativity, and influence has stemmed from western Europe and North America; that the world we have ended up with in the twenty-first century is a predominantly Westernized one; and that "others" whose histories arise along the way are easily incorporated into a seamless account of globalization's past, as well as its ascendant future. Marley's music is, again, a powerful counterpoint to that narrative. It owed so much to his upbringing in Kingston Jamaica's Trenchtown neighborhood, and it exemplifies the kinds of energetic, disruptive visions that have been generated from "below"—in his case, emanating from an incredibly rich outpouring of reggae that came from that neighborhood's "tenement yards" (shantytowns) and casting a hugely influential shadow on late twentieth-century global music and culture. In this volume, we are not only committed to understanding the particularities and significance of the histories of the Caribbean, South America, Africa, Asia, and the Pacific. We are also interested in the possibilities that thinking through the "below" might offer for analyzing, and right-sizing, the place of European and North American histories in the making of the modern world. Foregrounding the experience of workers, women, indigenous peoples, migrants and religious and racial minorities in these societies casts important light on how these regions laid claim to the global modern, at what cost, and to whose benefit. If world history is typically the horizontal view, emphasizing connections, encounters, and various forms of interdependence, the approach from below reminds us of the vertical axis of power relations and the considerable force these exerted during the extended moment of global consolidation we consider here (1750–present). It's these dynamic, even kinetic, terrains we seek to make visible as the grounds that have given momentum to globalization in its many forms and antecedents.

Of course, writing world history from below requires us to think through those two important keywords in our subtitle: "dissent" and "disruption." In this volume we stress the importance of struggles of various kinds—from slave rebellions to nationalist campaigns, from millenarianism to labor movements, from anti-colonial rebellions to political pamphleteering—in shaping the modern world's economic routines, political structures, and cultural patterns. One of the key things that E. P. Thompson's work underlined was the ability of the oppressed, exploited and marginal to conjure up new visions, to articulate their aspirations, to fight for their hopes, to be active participants in the making of society. To be sure, Thompson recognized that this agency operated within significant constraints and within highly unequal social relationships. This understanding of the ability of ordinary people to contextualize the social order is an important departure point for this volume. We draw inspiration from Karl Marx's famous observation that people "make their own history, but they do not make it just as they please; they do not make it under circumstances chosen by themselves, but under circumstances directly encountered, given and transmitted from the past."[4] In other words, in struggling to shape the social and political order, those at the bottom of society were not only pushing against the interests of the elite; they were also working within and pushing against the limits that the weight of the past imposed. Rather than seeing the emergence of modernity as a gradual unfolding of liberty, rationality and freedom, this volume suggests that social and political change was the product of conflict and contest—that it has developed not in a smooth progressive curve but rather in an irregular, unpredictable and lumpy manner.[5] Similarly, the geographical patterns of modernization and modernity have been and remain patchy and fundamentally uneven despite many advocates of globalization imagining the world as flat, smooth and seamless. In that sense, we give global capital its due but we don't understand it as hegemonic. We illuminate spaces and moments that exhibit its vulnerability to rifts and fissures, even and especially when the forces that drive it ultimately "win"—that is, remain in place, if reworked and recast by those who push up against it.

So, effectively, this volume brings world history into dialog with the tradition of a materialist social history that was committed to thinking the "bottom up" or from "below" not merely as vectors but as force fields that might register historical continuity and change, sometimes simultaneously. There are, we recognize, significant divergences between these ways of thinking about the past. Social history has generally operated within the analytical frame of the nation, as scholars have attempted to understand the development of community within the context of national economies and political structures. Conversely, world history has embraced more expansive geopolitical structures, especially focusing on the institutions and processes that linked the Mediterranean, Atlantic, Indian, and Pacific Ocean worlds, and has consistently focused on cross-cultural dynamics. While world history narratives have certainly acknowledged the importance of slavery, migration and religion, the major textbooks in the field are often focused on powerful elites and the periodizations those actors make visible. Or, when narratives of the global recognize ordinary people, they touch down only briefly on their struggles and on the dissent and disruptions they caused, in order to move quickly back to the main narratives of the hegemony of imperial dynasties or modern nations and economic, scientific, and material "progress."

Our approach is to ask students to imagine a world history narrative in which agitators, rebels, strikers, insurgents and unorthodox visionaries of all kinds are at the center—and, in the process, to think about history-making itself as a potentially revolutionary task across a broad range of actors, decades, and polities. These folks were radical not simply because they were rising up from below or striking at the root of power, but because they were more often than not mobile—literally, on the move. That rootless energy made them cosmopolitan in their repertoires and ready to appropriate forms and images across a range of movements and causes, as the global circulation of the French revolutionary Phrygian cap testifies. In order to capture the fast-moving character of these histories, and their irreverence for national boundaries, each chapter below follows the broad chronology of the mid-eighteenth century to the contemporary moment thematically so that we can appreciate the interconnections between them and the specific timelines of each globalizing form, whether revolution or religion or the Anthropocene itself. Bringing a variety of thematic approaches to the problem of world histories from below into conversation offers productive possibilities, presenting students of the global an opportunity to explore the various spaces and unstable terrains in which the struggles over the nature of modern life have played out.

As with historians who have tried to track a history of common people in the wake of Thompson, we recognize that from below does not mean beyond the sweep of power. And as witnesses to the most recent spate of revolutions in a global age, the Arab Spring of 2011, we know that "popular" rebellions are complexly intertwined with forces both above and below. And we see that their radical afterlives may be precarious and short-lived because "the above" does not readily give way. In placing struggle and conflict at the center of the accounts of the modern world offered in this volume, we recognize that the "below" was always in tension and dialog with the "above": hereditary elites, the economically dominant, the state and other powerful institutions. In thinking about the past from below we are committed to tracing the interrelations between diverse and often competing interest groups and social collectives. And in exploring the histories of dissent and disruption that have shaped the modern world, we focus not only on "successful" rebellions, revolutions, and social movements but also pay close attention to how resistance was subverted, misfired, or dissipated, recognizing the importance of what Thompson called the "blind alleys, lost causes, and the losers themselves."[6] Thompson himself was committed to charting the full range of social experiences and political strategies of the working-class in a time of far-reaching social change and upheaval: not a neat story of progress and advancement won, but rather an attempt to recover workers from the "enormous condescension of posterity," which tended to forget those who resisted the industrial order through strategies that failed or that appear ill-chosen to later generations.[7]

Dissent and disruption are the main foci of this book. But we see resistance co-existing with a range of strategies that ordinary people adopted in the face of unequal power relationships. So some of the chapters in this volume also stress the importance of conformity, consent and "deep deference" that were often important elements of the responses of much of the population to the operation of power, an important point recognized by Thompson in his later work.[8] Then as now, these tensions make for discomfiting reading and even politically volatile conclusions. They are the very stuff, in other words of the kind of rigorous historical thinking and struggle over the meanings of the past that world histories from below have the capacity to generate in an age skeptical of the value of such engagements. We hope students will range the radical histories in this book alongside whatever they already know about the global past, take issue with our arguments and vigorously debate the implications of the evidence we have gathered here. For it is not enough merely to be a witness to world histories and their frictions. To truly understand them, we must be ready, willing and able to enter into the fray.[9]

Two important caveats follow. First, to begin as we do with the 1750s is to recognize that the eighteenth-century age of revolutions was consequential to the way that world histories unfolded and that the "modern global" was imagined and lived. Yet it is also to acknowledge how ostensibly new forms of political, cosmological and economic expression were built on a variety of early modern and pre-modern traditions. As we have argued elsewhere with respect to the periodization of modern empires, the tendency to launch genealogies of globalization without regard to longstanding patterns of circulation, connection and exchange dating as far back as late antiquity reproduces the fetish of the European modern.[10] Missing out on the earliest forms of the global runs the risk of exceptionalizing post-Columbian new world orders. It can also downplay significant "non-Western" antecedents of mobility, interregional connection and, of course, violence and friction in "from below" across translocal spaces as well. We intend 1750 not as any kind of inaugural moment of globality but as shorthand for the ways that modern forces and those who sought to grapple with them across the globe were rooted in longer, deeper patterns. It's a sign, in other words, of the long—rather than the short—run-up to global forms in the present. Second, as will be clear to readers of each essay, we are keen to underscore the role of women, of gender and of sexuality in the making of world histories from below wherever possible. Here we must extend and improve upon Thompson's vision, since despite his sympathy for Joanna Southcott, his "below" did not much attend to women. Our determination to make a difference in this regard stems in part from our longstanding commitment to foregrounding bodies in contact and bodies in motion in narratives of colonial and global history. It is also the outgrowth of a concern that women, like non-elites more generally, tend to rise episodically to the sightline of globalization genealogies (when they appear at all) only to sink again below the weight of "big" phenomena like capital, migration, war, conquest. Women were makers of all kinds of dissent and disruption—sometimes "behind the scenes" but often on the battlements. They were out in front in many of the world's modern economic, social, and confessional revolutions. As for gender and sexuality, anxiety about these systems of representation, work, reproduction and labor were the motors of tremendous large-scale change. Such change might begin at the level of the household, to be catalyzed by forces—political, ecological—well beyond its purview. It might take flight as a kind of transnational anti-colonial brotherhood with all the affective registers and homosocial contours that such formations entailed. The wide array of histories from below—that commitments to centering women, gender, and sexuality can materialize—is evident from three generations of work in the field. This is true despite the considerable archival limits such a commitment continually poses. We urge students to take their indispensability seriously as they debate the limits and possibilities of a world history from below that is as capacious as possible in its vision of who counts as a maker of the global and its frictions.

We also encourage students to seriously debate the question of space-time as they think about the period this book covers. It is unquestionably true that the distances between spaces were spectacularly reduced by the acceleration of all kinds of transport and by the rapidity with which people, goods and ideas might circulate and be connected by the middle of, say, the nineteenth century. Yet integration on a global scale remained patchy and uneven, in part because of the actors who hoped to profit most from an interdependent world. The drivers of capital and empire, for example, were equally determined to control the levers of that mutual dependence, often in the interest of racist and heteronormative missions that relied on the subjugation of women and workers of all kinds. If these conditions were ripe for dissent and disruption, they could also isolate and alienate people who labored in the interstices of above and below; they might be spanners in the works or they might simply be subjected to the depredation of globalizing forces well, if not completely, beyond their control. In sum, "world histories from below" approaches challenge triumphalist narratives of a relentlessly integrative colonial modernity. But we do not replace it with a history of revolutionary triumphalism either. As the chapters that follow demonstrate, the frictions and striations produced by non-elites, whether dissenters or not, created an unmanageable terrain for global governors rather than a radically reworked world of radical equality or indigenous sovereignty in any simplistic way. Those who stood in the way of the smooth operation of global forces could be mowed down as easily as they could be incorporated, if not more so. Ours is not a utopian history, then. What it does is re-center marginalized actors and backlight some of the very real challenges to the story of global hegemony that tends to undergird views of today's globalization phenomenon.

Last but not least, *World Histories from Below* reminds all students of the global that narratives which transcend the nation or any other apparently bounded unit of analysis must be generated collaboratively. In our volume we have two essays written jointly, one by M. J. Maynes and Ann Waltner on revolutions, and the other by Nancy Jacobs, Danielle Johnstone, and Christopher Kelly on the Anthropocene. The latter is a particularly important reminder not just of the art of collaboration that can and must undergird global history writing, but of the urgency of interdisciplinary work as well. Their essay models how scholars in ecological sciences, history, and contemporary social science can, together, map the complex unfolding of planetary history through the archive of the carbon cycle and other repositories of climate knowledge. These, in turn, are indispensable to an appreciation of what thinking through global systems and their effects means today, and for the future. Work like theirs, which draws on multiple forms of disciplinary training yet tries to narrate shared findings and claims is remarkable though not especially rare, as new approaches to the deep histories of epidemiological and other medical/scientific phenomena illustrate.[11] Rooted literally and figuratively in the geography furthest down, the earth itself, this kind of work directs world histories from above and below in new exciting directions. Do such approaches allow history to be as predictive of what is to come as it is diagnostic of the past? It is hard to say but it is worth pondering nonetheless. Meanwhile, we hope students of global history at all levels will pursue such innovative collaborative models in their own thinking and teaching so that the kinds of dissent and disruption we seek to materialize here will have big, consequential futures.

Notes

1 David Walsh, "Rez Riddims: Reggae and American Indians," in *American Indians and Popular Culture: Media, Sports, and Politics*, ed. Elizabeth DeLaney Hoffman (Santa Barbara: Praeger, 2012); Timothy J. Cooley, *Making Music in the Polish Tatras: Tourists, Ethnographers, and Mountain Musicians* (Bloomington: Indiana University Press, 2005), especially 169–173; Eric A. Galm, *The Berimbau: Soul of Brazilian Music* (Jackson: University Press of Mississippi, 2010), 70.

2 Eric Wolf, *Europe and the People Without History* (Berkeley: University of California Press, 1982), 3.

3 Robbie Shillam, *The Black Pacific: Anticolonial Struggles and Oceanic Connections* (London: Bloomsbury Academic, 2015).

4 Karl Marx, "The Eighteenth Brumaire of Louis Bonaparte," in *Karl Marx: Selected Writings*, ed. Lawrence H. Simon (Indianapolis: Hackett, 1994), 187.

5 William H. Sewell Jr., *Logics of History: Social Theory and Social Transformation* (Chicago: University of Chicago Press, 2005), 9, 226.

6 Thompson, "Preface" [1963], *The Making of the English Working Class* (London: Penguin, 1980), 12.

7 Thompson, "Preface" [1963], *The Making of the English Working Class*, 12.

8 Thompson, "Postscript" [1968], *The Making of the English Working Class*, 917.

9 We are grateful to Alison Light's *Common People: The History of an English Family* (London: Penguin, 2014), for some of these insights.

10 Tony Ballantyne and Antoinette Burton, *Empires and the Reach of the Global, 1870–1945* (Cambridge, MA: Harvard University Press, 2012), pp. 13–14.

11 See Monica Green, ed., "Pandemic Disease in the Medieval World: Rethinking the Black Death," special inaugural issue of *The Medieval Globe* 1 (2014).

1

Modern Political Revolutions:

Connecting Grassroots Political Dissent and Global Historical Transformations[1]

M. J. Maynes and Ann Waltner

In the fall of 2014, the streets of Hong Kong filled with protesters. The movement that came to be called Occupy Central had originated in 2012, around the same time as Occupy Wall Street and other Occupy movements aiming to reclaim urban spaces associated with the interests of global capitalism. But the Occupy Central movement took on a particular urgency in July 2014 when the government of the People's Republic of China issued a white paper asserting its authority to restrict political autonomy in Hong Kong. Protesters set up tent cities in the business and government district known as Central, and in the working-class neighborhood of Mong-kok. In those encampments, protesters attempted to imagine a utopian future for Hong Kong.

Protesters came from virtually every walk of life. They wrote slogans, which they posted on walls, sometimes using Post-It notes (a tactical novelty), sometimes using big character posters (a more familiar protest tradition). They established lending libraries. Carpenters built makeshift desks so that students, an important presence in the movement, could study while they participated in the encampments. They showed solidarity with other protest movements across the globe, for example by raising their arms in the "Don't shoot!" stance popularized by recent protests against the police killing of Michael Brown in Ferguson, Missouri. The movement was firmly rooted in local political conditions, but the protestors' ideas and their repertoires drew on and fed into transnational flows. This essay will examine connections linking local and grassroots revolutionary movements with global flows of people, ideas, and repertoires of collective action throughout the modern era.

Our analysis begins in the eighteenth century; the revolutions associated with Western political modernity surely involved such global flows. Even contemporaries recognized that the events of the French Revolution held ramifications beyond French borders. For example, the Swiss-born journalist Jacques Mallet du Pan observed in 1793 that "the revolution, being cosmopolitan, so to speak, ceases to belong exclusively to the French."[2] Based on observations like this one, R. R. Palmer placed the French Revolution in transatlantic history in his path-breaking study, *The Age of the Democratic Revolution: A Political History of Europe and America, 1760–1800*, published in two volumes in 1959 and 1964. He argued that the French Revolution had to be understood as part of series of political and intellectual transformations occurring on both sides of the Atlantic. Although Palmer's study focused mostly on the activities of political elites, he was nevertheless aware of grassroots forms of activism in far-flung corners of the transatlantic world. "A Negro at Buenos Aires," he noted, for example, "testified that Frenchmen in the city were plotting to liberate slaves in an uprising against the Spanish crown. In the High Andes, at the old silver town of Potosi . . . the governor was horrified to discover men who toasted liberty and drank to France."[3] Still, Palmer ignored the Haitian Revolution, not to mention earlier uprisings elsewhere in the Atlantic world.

With the publication in 1962 of *The Age of Revolution: 1789–1848*, Eric Hobsbawm took the history of these revolutions in further new directions. Based on ideas first suggested by Karl Marx, Hobsbawm's "dual revolution" thesis explored specific connections between political rebellion in Europe and the economic dislocations that accompanied early industrial capitalism. Moreover, Hobsbawm also anticipated later developments in global history by suggesting connections between revolutionary ideas and events in Europe and contemporaneous or subsequent revolutions elsewhere in the world— not just in the Americas, but beyond. Still, as David Armitage and Sanjay Subrahmanyam note in their introduction to *The Age of Revolutions in Global Context, c. 1760–1840* (2010), even Hobsbawm, for all of his expansive thinking, now appears, like Palmer, "strikingly Eurotropic, if not quite Eurocentric." Only recently has the turn toward global history encouraged the exploration of provocative comparisons and previously invisible connections that are moving us closer to "viewing the Age of Revolutions as a . . . global phenomenon."[4]

Starting with a global reframing of "the age of revolutions," this essay will focus on select revolutionary moments from the mid-eighteenth century to the early twenty-first that hold particular significance in terms of global dynamics. We presume a broad working definition of "revolution," keeping in mind the difficulties entailed by both the changing meanings of the word and concept as understood and used by contemporaries over this long period and by the varying resonances of the term in different historiographies.[5]

Drawing on the work of Charles Tilly, we include under the term "revolutions" a continuum of political movements and processes that result in "forcible transfers of power over states" and "a forcible break in sovereignty." We are mainly concerned with what Tilly terms "great revolutions" such as the Chinese or the Russian Revolution—that is, transfers of power that involve deep social rifts in the polity and substantial power transfers among contending groups in society, rather than more limited and "top-down" events such as military coups or civil wars that did not challenge political institutions or the nature of political legitimacy per se.[6] In particular, given the nature of this volume, we will emphasize revolutions that involved notable political challenges "from below"—calls for a new relationship between "the people" and their rulers—although the political visions behind revolutions, the definitions of peoplehood in whose name they were carried out, and forms of revolutionary activity varied widely. We will investigate the operation and flow of specific "repertoires" of grassroots collective action; akin to theatrical performance, these repertoires of collective protest are the set of actions based on "available scripts within which [participants in political contention] innovate."[7] Repertoires include such actions as burning a landlord's castle, posting demands, carrying a banner on a march, or occupying a symbolic space. Finally, we will not limit ourselves to successful revolutions; we will also include cases where revolutionary situations did not result directly in regime change, such as the Taiping Rebellion in China or the 1848–49 revolts in Europe.

Placing political revolutions in global-historical context involves two somewhat distinct analytic projects. The first involves identifying roughly simultaneous but localized revolutionary activities in different regions of the globe and investigating global-scale processes (such as market development or imperialism or war) that might have fed into these spatially distant activities. The second involves tracking specific global flows—of ideas, people, and political practices—that have connected grassroots movements with one another across the globe and across time. Although the point here is to locate modern political revolutions in global history, it is nevertheless important to keep in mind the local historical particularities of individual revolutionary situations as well as the global dynamics through which we are re-framing them.

Global 1789

The transatlantic flows of individuals, ideas, and tactics that fed into late-eighteenth-century revolutions were complicated and multi-directional. The political principles at play in the American Revolution crisscrossed the Atlantic. Historians have long been aware of the role of the movements of Europeans and Americans of European descent in constructing transatlantic revolutionary discourses.[8] For example, the Declaration of the Rights of

Man and Citizen passed by the revolutionary French National Assembly in August of 1789 resembled the American Bill of Rights approved by the US Congress in September of the same year. The Marquis de Lafayette, who played a prominent role in both revolutions, wrote an influential draft for the Assembly committee charged with coming up with the Declaration. He consulted with Thomas Jefferson during the process of writing it. In a July 9, 1789 letter to Thomas Jefferson, Lafayette asked for Jefferson's "observations" on "[his] bill of rights" before presenting it to the National Assembly.[9] The writing of documents such as constitutions and petitions became a staple tactic of subsequent revolutions in the Atlantic world and beyond, as were practices involving the election of representatives to revolutionary assemblies.

Transnational intellectual and political connections at the grassroots have played a less visible role in historical narratives. According to Peter Linebaugh and Marcus Rediker, sailors and slaves who met and talked on shipboard and in port cities helped to construct a grassroots "revolutionary Atlantic" beginning in the mid-seventeenth century. Jane Landers has reconstructed the political activities of "Atlantic creoles"—men of African descent, some of them former slaves—who traveled widely through the southern Atlantic and Caribbean world, spreading political messages as they did so. Juan Bautista Whitten, for example, was born in West Africa in the late 1750s and taken slave there; his "remarkable career ... spanned the course of the American, French, Haitian, and Latin American revolutions as well as the eventual abolition of the Atlantic slave trade."[10]

The Revolution in the French Caribbean colony of Saint-Domingue (later renamed Haiti) is perhaps the best illustration of elite and grassroots connections that crossed the Atlantic. In the year before the outbreak of the French Revolution, the Society of the Friends of Blacks began meeting in Paris as part of an international effort to eliminate the slave trade. The roster of its members included leading intellectuals and politicians; its president, the Marquis de Condorcet, would later play an important role in the revolutionary National Assembly. The Society's agenda grew out of concerns over slaveholding in colonies like Saint-Domingue. The vast majority of the population of the colony's half-million residents (about 90 percent) were enslaved people of African origin. The remaining 10 percent were either whites or free people of color (*gens de couleur*). Each of these groups was positioned differently in terms of French colonial rule, and so the political upheavals in Paris presented each with different opportunities and strategies.

Those upheavals, of course, had much to do with internal conditions in the metropole. The fiscal problems faced by the French state in the late 1780s (which led King Louis XVI to call a meeting of the Estates General for the first time in over 150 years) were rooted in France's inegalitarian social structure and taxation system. But the situation was exacerbated by the huge state debt contracted primarily as a result of military and naval expenditures occasioned by colonial rivalries between France and England in the Americas and in South Asia. In terms of global processes, it is clear that French colonial ambitions and activities played a significant role in setting up a revolutionary situation, and thus in launching the events that would soon bring down the monarchy. Moreover, inequalities specific to colonial arenas were on the agenda.

Global 1789: Events in France

The process of electing delegates to the Estates General brought people in metropole and colonies together in the midst of a widening food crisis that evoked mobilization and political experimentation from below. The early years of the revolution saw the invention of new forms of political action and the re-purposing of old ones. Under the surveillance of Parisian popular crowds, the Estates General was transformed into a new entity—a "National Assembly"—that would soon challenge royal sovereignty. The Assembly in turn would face challenges as it took up questions of citizenship involving various and competing claims by groups of elites, peasants, workers, and women in the metropole, and also by slave-owners, people of color, and enslaved people in the colonies.

Assemblies of people in the streets of Paris and elsewhere, many wearing the red bonnets (understood to be a symbol of slave emancipation in ancient Rome) and cockades manifesting support for the Revolution, took on symbolic and sometimes actual power. They occupied public spaces as a way of laying claims to political rights, or marched in support of or opposition to a particular political faction. In October 1789, for example, a largely female crowd marched from Paris to Versailles to bring the royal family back to Paris where revolutionaries could more easily keep an eye on it (Figure 1.1). The significance of this "women's march" exemplifies how the openness of revolutionary situations can bring new historical actors and innovative applications of older forms of collective action; this women's march drew upon the "food riot" as a pre-existing form of protest and turned it into a form of direct action that undermined the monarchy. Newly empowered actors like the women of 1789 would begin to question the full meaning of the emerging Revolutionary principles of liberty, equality, and fraternity. Who was included among the equal? Men and women? People of color? Slaves? Who could be a citizen?

Global 1789: Haiti

The white ruling elite of Saint-Domingue got involved in these debates in early 1790 while electing representatives to the National Assembly in Paris. But they had been preceded in late 1789 by a delegation of free *gens de couleur* who went to Paris seeking political equality with whites (although they did not express solidarity with the enslaved). Then, even as the Assembly

FIGURE 1.1 *The women's march to Versailles, France, 1789. Contemporary print depicting the October 1789 march led by Parisian women to the Versailles palace to bring the royal family back to Paris. One of the women carries a pole topped by the Phrygian bonnet symbolizing emancipation and also an image of the scales of justice. Credit: DEA / G. Dagli Orti.*

was meeting for the first time, a massive slave revolt was launched in the colony. The slave rebellion emerged in a milieu where print culture played a marginal role; still, new ideas of equality circulated among the rebels and were expanded explicitly to claim racial equality.[11] In October 1789 the royal governor of Saint-Domingue reported that slaves "considered the new revolutionary cockade . . . a 'signal of the manumission of the whites . . . the blacks all share an idea that struck them spontaneously: that the white slaves kill their masters and now free they govern themselves and regain possession of the land.'"[12]

In April 1792, the National Assembly in Paris decreed equality among white citizens, *gens de couleur*, and free blacks.[13] In the face of the slave insurrection in Saint-Domingue, in 1794 the Assembly passed a decree abolishing slavery in France and its colonies. This emancipatory move had been anticipated by the decision in June of 1793 by the French commissioner in Saint-Domingue to emancipate insurgent (male) slaves willing to fight for the new French Republic, thus constructing what Elizabeth Colwill has termed "a gendered pathway to emancipation" in the colony.[14]

Although events in Saint-Domingue and France continued to be closely intertwined, the process of revolution in each place was distinct. Emerging from the slave revolt under the leadership of the ex-slave general Toussaint Louverture, the political model followed in Haiti evoked authoritarian kingship more than the republican alternative that briefly followed the overthrow of monarchy in France. Moreover, under Toussaint's rule and that of his successors, distinctive gendered ideals of citizenship were built into family law. The encouragement of formal marriage bonds (formerly uncommon or impossible among the enslaved) was seen as necessary to supply the army with male recruits and also to discipline the labor force—comprised of both male and female plantation workers—required by the plantation economy as it moved from enslaved to free labor.[15]

In 1799, Napoleon's seizure of power in France had direct consequences in Saint-Domingue: Napoleon sent French forces to discipline Toussaint's quest for political autonomy. An 1802 French law that revoked the 1794 abolition measure sparked further hostilities. Toussaint was captured and imprisoned, but the rebels still defeated the French force and Haitian independence was declared in 1804. Despite the war with Napoleonic France, the coat of arms of the new Haitian state featured a red Phrygian bonnet that tied it symbolically to the iconography of the French Revolution (Figure 1.2).

HAÏTI

FIGURE 1.2 *Coat of arms of Haiti, 1807. The palm tree is topped by the symbolic Phrygian bonnet popularized by the French Revolution. The symbol was doubly resonant in Haiti: formerly the French colony of Saint-Domingue, it became an independent state in 1804 as a result of a revolution by its enslaved people. Credit: public domain.*

The Haitian slave revolt was not widely imitated. Despite fears in the US, events in Haiti did not trigger slave rebellions to the north. Part of the explanation for the relative quietude among North American enslaved people might stem from the different family and gender systems in place on plantations there. In some regions at least, slaveholders' tacit acceptance of informal slave marriages may have introduced some of the elements of stability that the new legislation in Saint-Domingue aimed for. As Deborah Gray White suggests, "powerless North American male slaves were more easily manipulated [than their Caribbean counterparts] because their spouses and children could be held hostage and compelled to answer for their transgressions."[16]

The political possibilities raised by the Haitian and French Revolutions were not lost in Latin America, but they were transformed. Within a few decades, the Spanish Empire in the Americas was dissolved by political movements that overthrew Spanish rule and established independent states. The creoles who led these movements were made cautious by events in Haiti and also by insurrections of indigenous peoples in Peru and elsewhere, but the influence of the revolutionary Atlantic was apparent. Like Haiti, many of these newly founded states acknowledged at least symbolic links to France through references in national crests and flags to French Revolutionary symbols.

Global 1789: Java

If in the New World the age of revolutions toppled European empires, in Southeast Asia, European imperial ambitions actually expanded; in some areas imperial control became more entrenched and institutionalized, as is made clear in Peter Carey's analysis of Java.[17] Java and other islands in the eastern Indian Ocean had been central to European colonial projects since the sixteenth century because of their position vis-à-vis the lucrative spice trade; their strategic importance was enhanced by growing interest in such colonial products as coffee, sugar, and indigo.

At the time of the French Revolution, Java was overseen by the Dutch East India Company through a form of indirect administration that, similar to the approach of the British in India, relied on local princes who cooperated with concessionary company authorities. When, in 1795, the Dutch monarchy was replaced by a republic allied with Republican France, the deposed Dutch king turned Java and other Dutch East India territories over to the British to keep them out of the hands of France's revolutionary rulers. A series of devastating wars followed among various competing European colonial powers.

After Napoleon's defeat, control of Java returned to the Dutch in 1816, and the form of rule was more direct and exploitative than ever before. Agricultural production and land control were increasingly dominated by European demand for colonial products. Taxes become more oppressive under a system in which tax collection was put into the hands of Chinese tax collectors who brought growing revenues into colonial state coffers while bringing violence and insecurity to the indigenous peasantry and to travelers. Tollgates where travelers were forced to stop for searches and payment of tolls also became sites of new trades such as prostitution and opium sale. New forms of political opposition that emerged in this situation—resulting in a series of insurrections between 1825 and 1830 under the leadership of the millenarian prince Dipanagara—pitted popular indigenous and Islamic forces against foreigners (both Europeans and their Chinese agents). Despite the defeat of Dipanagara's forces, the anti-colonial insurrection brought together alliances and oppositions that would in the course of the following century birth modern Indonesian nationalism.[18] In contrast with the New World insurrections that drew on the discourses and iconography of the French revolution, the Javanese rebels were explicitly anti-European. Nevertheless, the insurrection in Java was arguably a last manifestation of "Global 1789."

Revolts of the mid-nineteenth century

The middle decades of the nineteenth century witnessed major revolts in several world regions—Europe and China and India—but in contrast with the revolutions of "Global 1789" there was no shared vision or set of tactics or symbols that moved across these disparate regions. Certainly the revolutionary moment was transnational *within* Europe; for example, the striking new element of the popular revolutionary repertoire—the urban barricade that demarcated the battle lines between revolutionary forces and defenders of the old order—spread across Europe with unprecedented speed between February and June of 1848 (Figures 1.3 and 1.4).[19] But rebels in China and India in the following decade developed distinctive visions and tactics in launching their revolutions. Global processes linked these various rebellions, especially the economic disruptions associated with industrial capitalism and imperialism, which were global in scope. Nevertheless, the forms of protest these processes evoked were particular to each world region.

Revolts of the mid-nineteenth century: Europe

Europe's 1848 revolts were both political and social in nature. The boundary lines drawn by Europe's rulers after the defeat of Napoleon in 1815 defied principles of popular sovereignty. The crowned heads of Europe formed a "Holy Alliance" determined to resist encroachments against monarchial power. But liberal political visions, awakened and then disappointed by the French Revolution, did not disappear as much as go underground.

C'est l'Drapeau d'la France... tirez donc.

FIGURE 1.3 *Barricade, Paris, France, 1848. Building barricades as lines of demarcation between revolutionaries and government troops became widespread in European cities in 1848. Here Parisian insurgents defend the tricolor flag and the revolutionary tradition it symbolized. This image also circulated on handkerchiefs! Credit: DEA / G. Dagli Orti.*

The decades following Napoleon's defeat were also marked by subsistence crises that accompanied the re-orientation of Europe toward trans-regional markets and the techniques of industrial capitalism. These crises reached an acute stage in the 1840s; in 1847 blight destroyed much of the potato crop that had become the dietary staple of poor peasants in Ireland and across northern Europe. In Ireland the potato famine caused a million deaths and twice that number of refugees; on the Continent, around 100,000 more died. This famine of the late 1840s, superimposed on a structural crisis of longstanding, was the last straw.

Once again, the signal for revolt came from France. Unrest came to a head over a seemingly minor issue—a political banquet. Banquets were a favorite form of expression of political protest in the conservative post-Napoleonic regime that suppressed open opposition. Banquets held in the fall and winter of 1847 featured toasts "to the downfall of the government" or "the death of the king." A huge banquet was planned in Paris for February

Die Barrikade an der Kronen- und Friedrichsstraße am 18. März 1848.
Von einem Augenzeugen. Kolorierte Lithographie von G. Nordmann

FIGURE 1.4 *Barricade, Berlin, Germany, 1848. Barricade fighting spread with unprecedented speed across Europe in 1848, aided in part by images such as this "eyewitness lithograph" of a Berlin barricade erected in March. Credit: Ullstein Bild.*

1848, but the Parisian police refused its organizers a permit. To everyone's surprise, this police action generated an enormous grassroots protest on the part of Parisians. Mass demonstrations in the streets were met with violent repression. Barricades—the form and symbol of neighborhood defense and revolutionary street fighting of this era—were erected in many neighborhoods. In confrontations with government troops, dozens of protesters were killed. King Louis Philippe, sensing that this assault was the result of growing resentment against his rule, agreed to abdicate in favor of his grandson. But it was too late to save the monarchy. Opposition leaders proclaimed the foundation of the Second French Republic on February 24, 1848.

News of events in Paris spread across Europe and spurred further revolt. On March 7, Fasching Tuesday celebrations in Germany took on a political dimension. Fasching, the day before the beginning of Lent, was often celebrated in European folk culture as a "festival of inversion" when the poor pretended for a day to be rich or men dressed as women. In 1848 the pretense became real. Eight hundred peasant men armed with axes and cudgels attacked the office of a rent collector in Boxberg in Baden and burned his books and contracts. Within a few days, peasant revolt had become general in southwestern Germany.[20]

On the same Fasching Tuesday in Berlin, a group of citizens met in a public "people's meeting" (*Volksversammlung*) to make their demands known. This meeting issued a set of demands to King Frederick William of Prussia: freedom of the press, freedom of speech, rights of association and assembly, equal political rights for all. Added to these was the specifically nationalist "calling of a united parliament for all of Germany." On March 18, a peaceful crowd was demonstrating in favor of an all-German constitution when the king ordered the army to clear the streets. The soldiers fired on the crowd, killing several people, and the peaceful assembly turned into a battle. For the first time ever, barricades went up in the streets of Berlin. In the street fighting between the Prussian troops and the citizenry of Berlin, over 200 civilians (mainly artisans, students, and unskilled workers) were killed and many more wounded.

The king was so taken aback by these developments that he did the unprecedented—he ordered the garrison removed from the city on March 19. Prussia, the great bastion of monarchy, capitulated at least temporarily to the forces of revolution. In capitals all over Europe similar events were transpiring, the closest thing Europe would ever to see to a general revolution. In Vienna, in Milan, in Palermo, in Rome, in Budapest, in Prague, and in many other places, the old order was seemingly toppled almost without resistance. Revolutionary ideals and tactics, of which the barricade is the most visible illustration, were spread by a network of men "who traveled ready to fight across Europe."[21]

The unfolding of revolutionary programs made clear the competing agendas that had brought people into the streets. Among the mainly middle-class men who took on leadership roles, some were committed to a fully parliamentary form of rule whereas others were satisfied with a more moderate form of constitutional monarchy. Artisans who wanted to defend their crafts against competition from factory goods and peasants who were losing their lands and livelihoods staked out alternative claims that threatened the property rights and faith in the market that animated many middle-class liberal reformers. And even some of their wives and daughters began to watch the revolution and think about their place in German society and politics. Louise Otto, later a founder of a democratic women's movement in Germany, launched her public career in 1848 by issuing a statement on behalf of women:

> I am writing this address not despite the fact that I am a weak woman, but because I am one. I recognize it as my most sacred duty to lend my voice to represent before you all those who don't have the courage to do it for themselves ... Gentlemen, as you occupy yourselves with the

greatest task of our times—the organization of labor—you must not forget that it is not enough to organize men's work only, but that you must also organize the same for women . . .[22]

For those deliberating in Paris and Frankfurt and other sites of revolution, these competing visions could not be disguised; dissent within the forces of revolution continued as monarchial forces re-grouped. Then, in June 1848, a different kind of signal came from France. In the "Bloody June Days" in Paris, the revolutionary coalition split apart as middle-class liberals, organized into national guards units, attacked the barricades staffed by their former allies from the handicraft classes, launching a period of counter-revolution across Europe. By 1851, strongholds of revolution had been re-captured by monarchial forces. Eventually, liberal parliamentary monarchies or democracies would become the dominant political form of organization in Europe, but the social conflicts would remain unresolved. Forms of anti-government popular protest popularized in the era around 1848—barricades and urban street confrontation, petitions and placards proclaiming to represent the voice of the people, and mass rallies in urban squares—have continued to resurface at moments of political contest even into the present (see Figure 1.5 and Figures 1.7 to 1.11 later in this chapter).

FIGURE 1.5 *Barricade, Paris, France, 1968. On May 11, 1968, in the Latin Quarter of Paris, students in revolt stood behind a barricade and fought against police forces throughout the night. Credit: Keystone-France/Gamma-Keystone.*

Revolts of the mid-nineteenth century: China

Other world regions also experienced uprisings in the middle of the nineteenth century, the most extensive of which were the Taiping Rebellion (1850–64) and the Indian Rebellion of 1857. Concern over the ineffectiveness of authorities in the face of economic dislocation marked these rebellions in Asia as they did in Europe. Moreover, we can see in the Asian rebellions a similar revolutionary process of cross-class alliances building and breaking down as the revolutions progressed. But the Asian rebellions, not surprisingly, were directly embedded in the politics of imperialism.

As had been the case of early nineteenth-century Java, the opium trade was at the center of major market developments resulting from European imperialist expansion in the eastern Indian Ocean. In Java, popular protest had targeted Chinese opium merchants who were acting as agents of Dutch colonialism. The opium trade, and European commerce more generally, also figured in the dynamics of rebellion in China and India.

The British East India Company had long been encouraging Indian peasants to produce opium; British and Indian merchants sold this opium in China in order to acquire tea and other commodities such as porcelain and silk.[23] The Chinese government resisted this mercantile strategy by proclaiming prohibitions against the sale of opium. In 1839 Lin Zexu, an official who had been commissioned by the Daoguang Emperor to end the opium trade, confiscated and destroyed 20,000 chests of opium. British retaliation was swift; British troops attacked and defeated the Chinese army. The 1842 treaty that ended the war created so-called treaty ports in China where Europeans had trading rights and privileges of extraterritoriality; the opium trade continued unabated.

The increase of opium production in India and tea production in China led to the reorientation of agricultural production in rural areas of both India and China. The British demand for tea especially affected agricultural production in Fujian province in southeastern China, where increased production of tea for the market led to a reduction in production of food crops necessary for subsistence.[24] Furthermore, the establishment of treaty ports after 1842 led to dislocations among dockworkers in Canton, which had from 1757 until 1842 been the only Chinese port where foreigners could trade.

These economic disruptions and the ineffective response by the Qing Dynasty fueled the Taiping Rebellion. The Taiping Rebellion was in this sense a response to imperialism, but ironically it drew ideological inspiration from another global import: Christianity. Christianity, or an interpretation of it that first intrigued and then appalled the European missionaries who had brought it to China, was at the core of the Taiping ideology. Hong Xiuchuan, the so-named Heavenly King of the Taipings, had visions that he was the younger brother of Jesus Christ. Other leaders of the rebellion also claimed visionary authority to justify their power.

The Taipings circulated critiques of the ruling dynasty and promoted egalitarian views, most notably a land law that aimed to redistribute all of the land in the realm equally and to both men and women. Although the land law was never put into effect, it marked the Taipings as social radicals on questions of gender relations as well as in terms of class and political relations. Taiping leaders, here anticipating later revolutionaries, saw gender hierarchy as a key support of the Chinese political order. Hong and many other Taiping leaders were Hakka people with a distinctive language and customs under which women were less subservient. Women, often wives or daughters of male leaders, assumed some leadership roles in the rebellion.

The Taiping mobilized a wide variety of tactics in making their revolution and spreading word about it. Leaders preached and performed religious ceremonies to win converts. Taiping leaders used the printed word as an important way of communicating revolutionary ideas (Figure 1.6). By 1847, each household in areas controlled by the Taipings was required to have a copy of a nine-page document entitled "Book of the Regulations of Heaven" (*Tian tiao shu*). By 1853, the publications of the Taipings were so

FIGURE 1.6 *Taiping Bible, China 1853. This book contains accounts of the visions at core of the Taiping ideology. The Taipings used printed texts like this one as a way of recruiting converts. The words across the top read "Newly printed in the second year of the Taiping Heavenly Kingdom." Credit: Sovfoto.*

numerous that one observer reported that "the oxen bearing them sweat and the house in which they are stored is full to the rafters."[25] Taiping rebels destroyed Confucian, Buddhist, and Daoist images and wrote slogans on temple walls advocating their version of Christianity. They also adopted visual marks of political affiliation. The reigning Qing emperors, of Manchu origin, had mandated that men wear the queue, a hairstyle which featured a shaven forehead and a long braid, to show their loyalty to the dynasty. Taiping men cut their queues as a sign of rebellion. Rebel women could be identified by their unbound feet, another form of protest against the traditional Chinese social order that would resurface in later revolutionary movements.

The Taiping Heavenly Kingdom, the regime established by the rebels, was centered in southeastern China, but eventually occupied parts of fourteen of the sixteen Chinese provinces. The rebels took over the city of Nanjing as their capital in 1853. In some regions, local elites frustrated by government incompetence supported the rebels; in others, they opposed them in fear of social disorder. After years of warfare, the Taipings were ultimately put down by local militias, rather than by the Chinese imperial army, whose weaknesses the rebellion laid bare. The relative strengthening of these local governments accelerated the decentralization of imperial authority in China. Thus, even though the Taiping Rebellion was a "failed revolution," it had the long-term consequence of weakening Imperial rule and contributing to the eventual overthrow of the dynasty. The Taipings also provided a precedent for a social and political critique of Imperial China and of gender roles and the Chinese family as elements of their revolutionary vision. Sun Yat-sen, who was to be an important leader in the overthrow of the dynasty in 1911, was an admirer of the Taipings.

Revolts of the mid-nineteenth century: India

The Indian Rebellion, which began in 1857 as a small protest in the Bengal army, soon engulfed much of north central India in revolt against British colonial rule. The rebellion originated in widespread opposition to British intervention into Indian life. The British East India Company—a trading company holding a concession from the British Crown—had controlled much of the Indian subcontinent since 1757. It had undertaken a reorganization of agricultural production, including moving peasant households toward opium production, to suit metropolitan interests. Moreover, in many areas under Company control, including the territory of Awadh which had come under Company control in 1856, traditional landowning elites were displaced by new landowning classes whose power derived from the role they played in collecting taxes for the East India Company. Additionally, both Hindus and Muslims feared that a growing British presence would expand the process of converting Indians to Christianity.

East India Company control of India was enforced by an army composed of soldiers from Britain along with about 280,000 Indian troops. In the mid-nineteenth century, tensions arose within the army over conditions of employment: wages were not keeping up with the cost of living; native officers were not compensated as well as officers from Great Britain; nor were they well respected by their British counterparts. The rebellion was provoked late in 1856 by rumors and resentment about a new kind of rifle cartridges. The cartridges were wrapped in stiff paper lubricated with pork and beef fat. The pork was offensive to Muslim soldiers and the beef to Hindus.[26] In May 1857, when eighty-five soldiers at Meerut (in Bengal) were imprisoned for refusal to use the cartridges, the entire regiment mutinied, killing their commanders. Later that same month, mutinous soldiers marched on the capital of Delhi and established Badhur Shah, the elderly Mughal emperor whose position had been usurped by the British, as their leader.

Anti-British rebellion soon spread through northern India and expanded to include peasants and landowners who had been dispossessed by the British. Mutineering soldiers killed their commanders, captured ammunition storehouses, burned buildings, and abandoned their posts. Word of the rebellion was spread in a number of ways. People were called to rebellion by bells, drums, and horns, sounds which in other contexts called them to work or to the hunt, but which in this context called them to attack seats of British power.[27] Ranajit Guha suggests that the use of musical instruments emphasized "the family likeness between fighting and other forms of communal labor."[28] Civilian rebels broke open jails, attacked police stations, and burned account books of money-lenders and magistrates. Europeans (and their property) were a main target of the rebels, but so were Bengali middle men seen as complicit with the colonial enterprise.[29]

The circulation of rumors fed the rebellion—for example, stories that the British had put ground bones into flour and sugar, and that cows and pigs had been thrown into wells to pollute drinking water.[30] But the rebels also relied on newspapers (until they were shut down) and printing presses as a way of distributing proclamations that articulated their concerns. One such proclamation, probably written by Firoz Shah, the grandson of Bahadur Shah, was published in the *Delhi Gazette* in September 1857. The proclamation begins with an appeal to the wealthy, especially those with connections to the princely Mughal past, to join the rebellion, calling for a cross-class coalition. The proclamation underscores the disruptive economic impact of the British presence: "It is evident that the Europeans, by the introduction of English articles into India, have thrown the weavers, the cotton-dressers, the carpenters, the blacksmiths, and the shoemakers, &c., out of employ . . . every description of native artisan has been reduced to beggary." The proclamation promises that once the British are expelled, the native artisans would be employed by "the kings, the rajahs and the rich; and this will no doubt ensure their prosperity."[31] British forces defeated the rebels by June of 1858. The rebellion, though it met with defeat, forced a reorganization of colonial rule: the British government took direct control of the colony away from the East India Company.

The Taiping Rebellion and the India Rebellion were embedded in global processes—trade relations, imperialism, and missionary activity. Like the 1848 revolts in Europe, they began with broad coalitions among groups sharing hostilities to existing regimes while not adhering to a common agenda. Nevertheless, they seem to have had little direct connection at the grassroots level, in terms of the ideas or repertoires, with the revolutionary movements of Europe around the same time. The European rebellions were continent-wide in scope and their repertoires traveled rapidly from one insurrection to the next within Europe. But the dominant political framework of 1848 was one of emergent European nationalisms; ironically, though the idiom was migratory, the attachment to political communities often defined in terms of nation was at odds with a readily exportable language of universalism, such as was generated during the early phases of the French revolution. Conversely, the explicitly anti-colonial orientation of the Asian insurrections no doubt discouraged messages to which rebellious Europeans might have been receptive, at least in the short run. Immediate reverberations in Europe were dominated by elite expressions of sympathy and concern for European victims of the rebellions.

Global revolutions in the era of World War I

Sympathy within Europe for anti-colonial revolts of the mid-nineteenth century did feed into emergent transnational revolutionary political organizations that increasingly linked grassroots rebels across the globe. By the end of the nineteenth century, new revolutionary ideas and organizations would be making direct theoretical and practical connections between forms of oppression in Europe and in its colonies. The major revolutions of the decades surrounding World War I were all arguably anti-imperialist. But they were not all anti-imperialist in the same way.

Global revolutions in the era of World War I: Anti-colonial revolt in East Africa

Some—such as the Maji Maji uprising in German East Africa in 1905–7—were rebellions directed against European overseas empires. Provoked by European imperialism, they were nevertheless rooted in local and regional conflicts, coalitions, and identities; the tactics reflected this local rootedness as they had in India in 1857. The Maji Maji rebellion drew on grievances related to economic policies pursued in German East Africa: the introduction of market crops including cotton, environmental degradation, and the subversion of local peasant household economies.

In the 1880s the German East Africa Company had set up cotton plantations using slave labor. As slave labor became harder to defend politically, the slave system was replaced by a new forced-labor system designed to produce cotton on government-run farms (*shambas*). Men were conscripted to work for two days a month at an extremely low wage. In areas where there were many cotton *shambas*, women and children had to increase their labor on subsistence plots to make up for absent male labor. As the forced cotton regime spread through German East Africa, the workload increased as food production decreased. The system was open to abuse; for example, the local village headmen who worked with colonial authorities for a share of the profits could benefit by pressuring more workers into the fields for longer hours. Peasant families were pitted against the complicit headmen from their villages, who sometimes even tried to push women and children to cultivate cotton if men refused.[32]

The insurrection started in July 1905 when some headmen in the area of the Rufiji River resisted demands by district colonial authorities for caravan labor.[33] Then, in the nearby Kilwa district, men refused to perform cotton labor service and instead uprooted cotton and attacked the homes of the local officials working with colonial authorities; a German plantation owner was killed. Local authorities quelled these initial outbreaks, but the rebellion quickly spread, following a pattern described by John Iliffe: "The men of a locality ... congregate into a 'band,' leaders and spokesmen emerge, the property of notable local enemies is destroyed ... The band may coalesce with another and march jointly on a more prominent provincial centre."[34]

Similar to other resistance movements in the region, the broadening of the rebellion was facilitated by a millenarian movement that linked otherwise disparate local communities. According to a local official, the rebellious actions were preceded by the provision of water (*maji*) by the prophet Kinjikitile, water imbued with the power to bestow invulnerability: "They receive water which, as they pass through the land, they sprinkle ... to make them immune to any mishap and to European weapons."[35] Kinjikitile was executed by colonial authorities in 1905, but other spirit mediums who provided *maji* became important nodes in the spread of the movement. German reinforcements were sent in to suppress the rebellion and they did so very brutally, in some regions in alliance with local leaders. German armed forces burned the villages of rebels to the ground and destroyed crops. Planting was also disrupted by warfare. It was crop destruction more than anything else that defeated the rebellion, since people in rebel areas were starving by the spring of 1906. At least 75,000 people died as a result of the Maji Maji rebellion and its suppression.

The rebels were defeated, but their revolt did have global-historical consequences. This rebellion, along with one in German Southwest Africa, made manifest the abuses of German colonial rule. Opponents of colonialism in the German metropole made colonial administration a major issue in the 1907 election campaign. Subsequent reform policies ended forced labor. In terms of African political development, the impact has been much debated. Some leaders of subsequent anti-colonial movements, such as Julius Nyerere, would later evoke Maji Maji as an early form of African nationalism. But while anti-colonial sentiment, and opposition to forced cotton production in particular, clearly fed into the movement, it did not produce a broad unity among the colonized. Local political divisions remained clear.

Global revolutions in the era of World War I: Transnational revolutionary networks

Other revolutions of this era—such as the Russian, the German, the Chinese, and the Mexican—were global in a different way: they demonstrated the growing influence of the transnational grassroots networks associated with anarchism and socialism, new types of protest movements that embodied political visions that were explicitly internationalist. Transnational activism was also encouraged by unprecedented levels of global migration—both transcontinental and trans-oceanic. Swelling streams of international migrants in these decades were fed mostly by laborers, for example the Chinese and Italian migrants who moved to factory, mine, and railroad jobs in the United States, Mexico, and France. But they were joined by a growing number of young people who crossed national boundaries and global regions for university studies, for example Russian and North American women seeking medical education in Switzerland, or Chinese students in Japan. Along with these worker and student migrants, a small but influential number of political exiles formed key nodes around which global revolutionary networks were built. (For a discussion of the migrations of people and ideas that played a role in the Mexican Revolution, see Chapter 3.)

From the late nineteenth century onward, anarchists and socialists disseminated revolutionary ideas and tactics throughout the world. Ironically, sending radicals into exile in the wake of repressions—for example, the diaspora that followed the defeat of the Communards of France in 1871—did much to encourage the globalization of radical organizing. Some anarchist and socialist Communards, many of whom had been attracted to Paris from elsewhere in the first place, ended up in the French prison colony of New Caledonia; others regrouped in Switzerland, Italy, Latin America, or the US. Exiled Spanish anarchists played a role in radical movements in Cuba and Latin America; Filipino anti-imperialist activists drew on both anarcho-syndicalist and socialist ideas.

Anarchists became notorious for their "propaganda of the deed" tactics of bombings and assassinations. For example, in 1906 Tatiana Leontieva, a Russian woman studying medicine in Zurich, assassinated an Alsatian businessman vacationing in the Swiss resort town of Interlaken, mistaking him for the former Russian Minister of the Interior. Leontieva had apparently become radicalized the year before when she witnessed the repression of a strike in Russia; in Switzerland she was likely affiliated with anarchist and feminist circles influenced by the teachings of Mikhail Bakunin and Emma Goldman.[36] Switzerland was an ideological training ground for anarchists and socialists, many of whom played roles in later years in revolutionary movements in Russia, Germany, and Latin America.

Such individual actions of protest drew media attention, but the quieter activities of grassroots network building were of far greater consequence for the spread of the revolutionary ideas and tactics—such as mass demonstrations and strikes—that began to play an increasingly prominent role in revolutionary movements throughout the world. Andrew Hoyt's investigation of the network around the Italian anarchist newspaper *Cronaca Sovversiva*, published in Barre, Vermont and Lynn, Massachusetts from 1903 to 1920, provides a concrete example. The journal was a node in a global radical network; between 1907 and 1915, the anarchist community that included the journal's publishers attracted speakers such as Emma Goldman, Big Bill Haywood, Eugene Debs, and Mother Jones.[37]

Luigi Galleani, the primary editor of the *Cronaca*, was born in Italy and became an anarchist while studying law in the late 1870s. He was arrested multiple times in Italy, France, and Switzerland. His second arrest in Italy in 1894 led to "internal exile" on a Mediterranean island along with many other anarchist and socialist radicals. Galleani's escape from Italy was followed by time in Tunisia, Malta, Alexandria, and Cairo in 1900. Eventually Galleani and his family made their way to the US, where they would join a vibrant community of Italian-speaking anarchists.

Global revolutions in the era of World War I: Russian revolutions

Transnational networks of anarchist and socialist activists seized opportunities opened in the era of World War I to develop new tactics of protest. They played a critical role in the Russian Revolution, which began with the February Revolution of 1917 in Petrograd, Russia's capital, and eventually established the world's first socialist state. The Russian Empire had long been politically fragile, given the resistance of the autocratic tsars in the face of ongoing calls for political and social reform. Disgruntled reformist and revolutionary intellectuals had been operating in Russia and in exile throughout the late nineteenth century, and they built underground organizations of populists, anarchists, and socialists. At the grassroots, the relatively small but concentrated factory workforce was drawn into these networks, in part because of the government's refusal to allow legal union organizing. Moreover, many factory workers retained ties to peasant villages from which they had only recently been recruited, which created connections between rural villages and international radical networks.

These widespread networks help to explain the dramatic protests of 1905 that emerged in the context of the Russo-Japanese War (1904–5). Japan had embarked upon an ambitious program of political and economic modernization after the Meiji Restoration of 1868. Japan's ambitions

brought it in conflict with Russia in Manchuria and Korea. Early support
for the war in Russia dissipated as the Japanese won battle after battle. It
seemed to an increasing number of people, both inside and outside of Russia,
that the Japanese success demonstrated that Russia was "inferior, stagnant,
and unsuited to conditions of technical progress."[38] Anti-war sentiment fed
into the pre-existing networks of anti-government organizing. Demonstrators
in the Russian town of Mariupol in September 1904 carried signs that read
"Down with Autocracy" and "Down with War."[39]

In January 1905, a group of factory workers affiliated with a workers'
welfare organization led by the priest Georgy Gapon organized a march to
carry a petition to the tsar. Identifying themselves in the petition as "workers
and inhabitants of the city of St. Petersburg, members of various *sosloviia*
(estates of the realm), our wives, children, and helpless old parents" they
appealed to the tsar for help against their employers and the bureaucrats
who denied them their rights. The list of specific demands clearly echoed the
discourse of international workers' organizations: "freedom for producer-
consumer cooperatives and workers' trade unions," "an eight-hour working
day and regulation of overtime work," and "freedom for labor to struggle
with capital."[40] Instead of the fatherly support the demonstrators had
sought, troops fired on the marchers killing or wounding hundreds.
Demonstrations quickly broke out across the country, going beyond
workers' circles to include students, middle-class liberals calling for reform,
and military and naval mutinies. The 1905 insurrection was brought to an
end through a combination of political concession and further repression,
but the underlying issues did not go away. A tactical innovation of the 1905
revolt—the establishment of *soviets*, or local councils of workers and
soldiers as the form of revolutionary government—would survive in the
collective political repertoire to resurface later in Russia and elsewhere.

The First World War brought about circumstances that rekindled the
revolutionary situation. Military defeats and unprecedented casualties laid
bare the weakness of the Russian Imperial state and economy. Shortages of
food and fuel on the home front further undermined morale. A wave of
strikes between 1912 and 1914 abated only temporarily at the war's
outbreak, and then gathered new momentum beginning in 1915.

The collapse of political authority came about between late February and
early March of 1917 as the result of grassroots actions. On February 23 a
group of women workers left their Petrograd textile factories on International
Women's Day—a workers' holiday established in 1911 at the instigation of
international women's socialist and union organizations—to protest against
food shortages. As the women marched past metalworking plants they called
on the men working there to join them (Figure 1.7). By the end of the day,
over 100,000 workers had walked off the job and joined mass demonstrations
converging toward the center of the city. Similar marches, issuing demands
for bread and peace, would eventually result in a mutiny by army troops
unwilling to attack their own people, the establishment of two competing

FIGURE 1.7 *March by striking workers, Petrograd, Russia, 1917. The protest march initiated by women to mark the new socialist holiday—International Women's Day—sparked the February Revolution. The banners read: "Feed the children of the defenders of the motherland!" and "Increase rations for soldiers' families – defenders of freedom and world peace!" Credit: Heritage Images.*

political authorities and finally, the abdication of the tsar on March 3. Leadership of the subsequent revolutionary state would involve leaders holding divergent visions—many returning from years of exile abroad.

The transnational movement of individuals, tactics, and political agendas all played a role in the overthrow of the Tsarist regime in 1917. In the fall of 1918, a similar combination of strikes, socialist-led anti-war marches, demonstrations of housewives over food shortages, and mutinies would come together in Berlin and other German cities to overthrow the German Empire. The abdication of Kaiser Wilhelm in November 1918 also led to competing claims to rule. In many localities workers and soldiers set up local governments in the form of councils that echoed the Russian *soviets* in form and vision.

Global revolutions in the era of World War I: Chinese revolutions

Although it would take a different form and follow a different pattern of political development, the revolutionary movement that brought an end to the Chinese Empire combined elements of nationalist critique and local popular mobilization with a selective adoption of ideas and tactics learned elsewhere. One of the earliest calls for revolution in China came from Zou Rong, a revolutionary thinker who had as a student in Japan admired Japanese political and economic institutions. In 1903 he published a tract called "The Revolutionary Army," which began: "Sweep away millennia of despotism in all its forms, throw off millennia of slavishness, annihilate the five million and more of the furry and horned Manchu race."[41] The tract was published in the French concession of Shanghai where Zou lived, an area off-limits to the Chinese authorities. His target was both "despotism in all its forms" and the Manchu rulers in particular, perceived as foreigners against which a Han Chinese nationalism might rally.

The tract was produced in a transnational space (the French concession in Shanghai) and had a transnational circulation. China's transnational connections had intensified in the nineteenth century with substantial migration of Chinese students, workers, and political activists to Europe, the Americas, Australia, Japan, and Southeast Asia. Overseas Chinese workers kept in touch with local communities through a network of newspapers and letters.[42] Revolutionaries saw overseas Chinese communities as sources of intellectual and financial support; revolutionaries like Sun Yat-sen made regular trips to North America and Southeast Asia to promote revolution and raise funds among "petty shopkeepers, laundrymen, gardeners, and other laborers."[43] When the 1911 uprising that brought an end to the Chinese Empire began, Sun was actually on a train in Colorado.[44]

Beginning in the late nineteenth century, Chinese students, both male and female, went in increasing numbers to Europe, North America, and Japan for education.[45] Some studied alternative economic and military models; others studied socialist and anarchist critiques. Not all of the students who went abroad were members of the elite. Li Shizeng, the son of a prominent Qing dynasty official, established a bean curd factory outside of Paris in 1909; he imported soybeans and 30 Chinese workers, including at least two women, to work in the factory. He also established a prototype work-study program that allowed some of these workers to get an education. While in Paris, Li also founded an anarchist journal which was a center of revolutionary thought and activity.[46]

Fueled by ongoing critiques and anti-government organizations, numerous unsuccessful attempts were made at the beginning of the twentieth century to overthrow the Chinese government. In October of 1911, after an uprising in the large inland city of Wuhan, the Imperial army defected to the rebels, leaving the dynasty without defense. By February 1912, the emperor had abdicated and the Imperial state had fallen. It would take four decades of civil war to establish a stable new state; in the interim ongoing global flows of individuals and ideas would continue to feed into the Chinese revolutionary process.

World War I intensified the movement of people, civilians as well as soldiers. Around 140,000 Chinese went to Europe as laborers, most of them to France, but some to England. Chinese intellectuals studying in Europe organized classes for the workers: they taught them basic literacy skills and also introduced them to new political ideas.[47] Chinese intellectuals in France formed cross-class alliances with workers more readily than they would have at home. Workers and students played important political roles once they returned home. In 1919, workers who had returned from France formed a labor union in Shanghai, called the Returned Laborers Union, one of the first labor unions in China.[48] Chen Duxiu, one of the founders of the Chinese Communist party and himself formerly a student in France, recalled that: "After Chinese students [who had returned from France] began to lecture the masses on principles of citizenship and equality ... workers gradually came to realize that they had obvious rights."[49] Women students who studied abroad also came home with new ideas about the roles that women could play in the development of new China.[50]

Alliances between students and workers created in national and transnational spaces played an important role in the May Fourth Movement. The movement began in 1919 in Tiananmen Square in Beijing with students at Peking University protesting against the conditions of the Treaty of Versailles, which granted concessions formerly held by Germany to Japan (Figure 1.8). The students occupied the square, outside the old palace complex of the Forbidden City, thus claiming a potent symbolic space.[51] The conditions imposed on China by the Treaty of Versailles made it clear to the students that the Chinese revolution was unfinished business, and that it was their task as members of a new generation to chart the future of China.

FIGURE 1.8 *Students' march during the May Fourth Movement, Beijing, China, 1919. The banners identify the students as being from Peking University. The flag is a Peking University flag, modeled after the French tricolor, with the colors red, yellow, and blue standing for freedom, equality, and fraternity. Credit: Sovfoto.*

The movement spread to other cities, especially Shanghai. City streets were filled with demonstrators; shops were shut down. Even while critical of aspects of Chinese tradition, workers and students expressed anti-imperialist sentiments. Marchers carried banners, written in Chinese, English, and French, with slogans like "Refuse to Sign the Peace Treaty" and "Down with the Traitors." In this case, global modes of protest took a decidedly nationalist turn, although transnational communist networks and visions would play a deciding role as the revolution continued in the 1920s and after.

Toward global 1989

Connections between the communist parties of China and the Soviet Union and elsewhere remained important throughout most of the twentieth century. These networks took on new significance after World War II, with the beginning of the Cold War and the triumph of the Chinese Communists in 1949. The Cold War division of the globe into two embattled blocs—one affiliated with the US and its "Free World" allies, and the other with the USSR—had some "de-globalizing" consequences. Contact among grassroots political movements in the opposing blocs was made very difficult, as travel and communications across the borders was curtailed and heavily policed.

Some states refused to become fully aligned with either bloc. It was in the so-called Third World, in fact, that some of the most notable revolutionary movements of the postwar era were launched; these included a new wave of anti-colonial revolutions. Heather Streets-Salter's discussion of anti-colonial movements in Chapter 2 offers an extended discussion of international communism as a global framework for anti-colonial rebellions in the Cold War era.

Still, despite Cold War obstacles to global grassroots organizing, international connections among protesters across the political divide never really disappeared even during the tensest confrontations of the era. In fact, it was precisely because of those tensions—and the fears of nuclear annihilation that they evoked—that a transnational peace movement evolved. The peace movement would eventually contribute to the demise of many Soviet bloc regimes beginning in 1989.

Toward global 1989: The East German revolution

It is appropriate that the opening of the Berlin Wall in November 1989 became the iconic moment of collapse of the Soviet bloc. Since 1961, the Wall had symbolized Cold War efforts to stop the flow of people and goods and ideas between East and West. The underlying Cold War division of Germany into two states—one aligned with the West and one with the Soviet Union—ironically set up the region as a site of both Cold War confrontations and creative protests in the name of alternative visions.

The fall of the Wall, and of the state that had built it, had roots in a decades-long tradition of grassroots protest, especially the international peace and anti-nuclear movements. These movements had begun in the 1950s in the wake of the horrific demonstration of the destructiveness of nuclear weapons in Japan at the end of World War II. Anti-war sentiments grew in response to nuclear proliferation in the context of Cold War re-armament and again in the era of the Vietnam War. By 1980 peace movement activists were developing new tactics of protests on both sides of the "Iron Curtain" at a moment when both NATO and the USSR were simultaneously increasing their nuclear arsenals in Europe.[52] In the US, some activists who had first gained experience in the anti-Vietnam War movement of the 1960s were turning to tactics that focused on the symbolic destruction of nuclear weapons and the penetration of sites that produced or deployed them. This so-called Plowshares Movement, affiliated with Christian pacifism, was based on the Scriptural admonition to turn "swords into plowshares."[53]

A similar spirit soon motivated peace movement activists in Europe, especially in the Netherlands and West Germany. Stanley Hoffmann, writing in 1981, had this to say about the spread of the anti-nuclear movement:

> It is a mass movement of continental dimension, which mobilizes and moves people across borders ... It entails the active participation of women and of a large number of religious movements and churches. . . . It is particularly strong in the country that has been, until now, the most reliable partner of the United States on the continent and the linchpin of NATO strategy: the Federal Republic of Germany. While it ... is often led by well-known priests, intellectuals or politicians, the movement is largely a gathering of young people, a generational protest.[54]

Connections among pacifists within the Evangelical Church encouraged similar actions in Communist East Germany. In 1981, the East German church leadership chose "Swords into Plowshares" as the slogan of its peace initiative, purportedly inspired by a statue with that name donated by the USSR to the United Nations after World War II. (Some would claim the name was meant to embarrass the regime, but reference to the Soviet statue also provided political cover.)

Other tactics of peace protest also crossed the Iron Curtain. In December 1982, some 30,000 women peace activists held hands to surround a US Air Force base on Greenham Common in the UK. Shortly thereafter, in September 1983, East and West German women advocating peace tried to form a chain connecting the US and Soviet embassies in Berlin. East German state police broke up the demonstration, but the women had made a stance both for peace and for ending the Cold War divisions (Figure 1.9).

In East Germany such anti-government actions took on new energy with growing economic problems of the late 1980s and Soviet moves toward

FIGURE 1.9 *Peace demonstration, West Berlin, West Germany, 1982. Protesters against NATO nuclear arms installments carry banners with the words "Schwerter zu Pflugscharen" (Swords into Plowshares). The slogan and design had been adopted by the East German peace movement, based in the Evangelical Church, in 1980, and quickly became a peace movement symbol on both sides of the Iron Curtain. Credit: Ullstein Bild.*

rapprochement with the West, especially since the rigid East German government continued to hold the line against reform. By 1989 political challenges to Communist rule in Eastern Europe had multiplied. The Solidarity movement in Poland, which had begun when dock workers went on strike in Gdansk in 1980, had grown into an actual opposition party. In June 1989, in the first freely contested elections in the Soviet bloc, Solidarity won 99 of 100 seats in the Polish Senate.

In the same month but halfway around the world, the Tiananmen Square protest against the Chinese Communist regime, a peaceful protest that had begun in April 1989, was brutally repressed by the state on June 3–4, resulting in hundreds of deaths (Figure 1.10). This failed protest movement and its brutal suppression had direct and immediate repercussions not only in China but elsewhere as well. In East Germany the June 5, 1989 issue of the official Party newspaper *Neues Deutschland* commented on the bloodshed in Tiananmen Square, calling it a necessary response to a counter-revolutionary threat. On June 8, the GDR People's Congress officially declared the bloodbath in Beijing "a defeat for counter-

FIGURE 1.10 *Students march in Tiananmen Square, Beijing, China, 1989. The Chinese language banners identify the students' schools—a high school in Yangzhou and the foreign language department at Peking University. The English-language slogan originated in the American Black Panther and antiwar movements of the 1960s. Credit: Catherine Henriette.*

revolutionary forces." The Chinese rulers thanked the rulers of East Germany for their support.[55]

The hard line shared in Beijing and Berlin only intensified protest in East Germany, where protest took two very different forms: flight to the West, and growing anti-government demonstrations on the part of those determined to stay and change the system. In addition to the church-affiliated protest groups, the New Forum was founded in September of 1989 by protesters who proclaimed that "they did not want to go West, they did not want German reunification, they did not want capitalism. They wanted to create a political platform for the 'restructuring of the German Democratic Republic,' for a democratic socialism."[56] Some of the leaders of the new group, such as the radical pastor Sebastien Pflugbeil, who were veterans of the peace movement, could hardly believe how rapidly the mass protest mushroomed in the fall of 1989. "Things are moving much faster than we ever thought," Pflugbeil told *New York Times* reporter Serge Schmemann in October. "Now even in small cities and in small factories people are joining New Forum. But you shouldn't overestimate what we are doing. You shouldn't compare us to Solidarity. This is only the beginning, on a very small scale."[57] The scale did not stay small for long. In Leipzig, regular Monday night Peace Prayer Meetings in the Nikolai church grew from 8,000 protesters in late September to 300,000 by late October. The head of state Erich Honecker publicly threatened reprisals, based on the "fundamental lesson to be learned from the counterrevolutionary unrest in Beijing and the present [anti-government] campaign" in East Germany.[58] But his Politburo backed off and attempted to save the state by sacrificing the hardliner; Honecker was forced out of office on October 18, 1989. This overture to the protesters only served to embolden them and extend the protest. The Leipzig model had soon spread to Berlin, where huge crowds primarily of young people met in churches to demand reform. Under the slogan "We are the People!" protesters demanded free elections, political rights, the demolition of the Wall, and an end to one-party rule. On November 4, a million people gathered in the Alexanderplatz in the center of Berlin, the largest demonstration in German history. On November 9 crowds on both sides of the Wall opened it to symbolize and celebrate a new regime.

After that, events moved too quickly for any one protest group to command; the leaders of reform in East Germany saw their movement taken out of their hands as experienced West German politicians came in with new promises of support for reform and for a new agenda: reunification. In contrast with the Chinese protest movement of the same year, the East German protest did bring about regime change. However, as was true with other revolutionary situations, the outcomes were not what many protesters anticipated or hoped for. Still, this revolt was emblematic, at the end of the twentieth century, of the ongoing evolution of forms of grassroots protest, flows of agendas and repertoires across the globe, and new styles of making a revolution.

Timothy Garton Ash has argued that the type of revolution made in East Germany was an example of a type he refers to as "velvet revolutions." The term itself had first been used earlier, to describe the failed Czech protest of 1968, but, Ash suggests, it has come to signify a whole range of similar revolutionary events:

> tagged with variants of adjective + revolution. Thus we have read about singing (Baltic states), peaceful, negotiated (South Africa, Chile), rose (Georgia), orange (Ukraine), color (widely used, post-orange), cedar (Lebanon), tulip (Kyrgyzstan), electoral (generic), saffron (Burma), and most recently, in Iran, green revolution. Often, as in the original Czechoslovak case, the catchy labeling has been popularized through the interplay of foreign journalists and political activists in the countries concerned.[59]

In contrast with archetypical "1789 ideal type" revolutions—"violent, utopian, and class based"—these new revolutions have been based on broad coalitions and often result in compromises with rather than sudden and violent overthrows of regimes.[60]

FIGURE 1.11 *Protesters at barricades, Hong Kong, 2014. In the so-called "Umbrella Revolution," students and other citizens of Hong Kong occupied parts of the city, protesting restrictions on their political rights by the PRC government. The umbrellas, used as a defense against pepper spray, have been added to the repertoire of urban protest along with the more familiar barricades. Credit: Xaume Olleros.*

The revolutionary movements of the early twenty-first century suggest that we are entering a new era of the history of revolutions. Revolutionary forms and repertoires in many ways depart from familiar models of challenging and seizing power, although some tactics evoke the classics: mass demonstrations, posters, occupations. And as examples from the Arab Spring, or the Occupy movement, or the environmental movement suggest, networks and repertoires of protest are more global than ever. Transnational protest movements focus on bringing down powerful global corporations, rather than just aiming at the overthrow of national political regimes. Some new tactics even call attention to global flows and networks as part of their arsenal of protest: Occupy movements reveal global flows of capital; environmental activists track and "out" sources of global pollutants and track networks of polluters. New technologies of communication have brought the capacity to link grassroots movements with one another across huge distances and almost instantaneously (Figures 1.11 and 1.12).[61] A global framework is increasingly taken for granted, even as the many of the tactics of protest remain rooted in local spaces.

FIGURE 1.12 *Holographic protest, Madrid, Spain, 2015. In a new turn on an old form of protest, holographic images of protesters were projected in front of the Spanish Parliament on April 10, 2015 by the movement calling itself "No somos delito" (We are not a crime) to protest against the new laws punishing unauthorized protests. Credit: Pablo Blazquez Dominguez.*

Suggestions for further reading

Armitage, David and Sanjay Subrahmanyam, eds. *The Age of Revolutions in Global Context, c. 1760—1840.* New York: Palgrave Macmillan, 2010.

Hobsbawm, E. J. *The Age of Revolution: 1789–1848.* New York: New American Library, 1962.

Iliffe, John. "The Organization of the Maji Maji Rebellion," *The Journal of African History* 8:3 (1967), 495–512.

Lanza, Fabio. *Behind the Gate: Inventing Students in Beijing.* New York: Columbia University Press, 2010.

Liberty, Equality, Fraternity: Exploring the French Revolution. http://chnm.gmu.edu/revolution/chap8a.html.

Osterhammel, Jürgen. *The Transformation of the World: A Global History of the Nineteenth Century.* Princeton, NJ: Princeton University Press, 2014.

Spence, Jonathan. *God's Chinese Son: The Taiping Heavenly Kingdom of Hong Xiuchuan.* New York: W.W. Norton, 1996.

Streets-Salter, Heather. "The Rebellion of 1857: Origins, Consequences and Themes," *Teaching South Asia: An Internet Journal of Pedagogy* 1:1 (winter 2001), http://www.mssu.edu/projectsouthasia/tsa/VIN1/Streets.htm.

Tilly, Charles. *European Revolutions: 1492–1992.* New York: Wiley Blackwell, 1996.

Wade, Rex. *The Russian Revolution, 1917,* 2nd edn. Cambridge: Cambridge University Press, 2005.

Notes

1 The authors would like to thank colleagues and students who offered feedback and suggestions. These include the Workshop for the Comparative History of Women, Gender, and Sexuality at the University of Minnesota (November 2014), the "World Histories from Below: Dissent and Disruption, 1750–present" workshop at the University of Illinois (February 2015), Ron Aminzade, Andrew Hoyt, Lynn Hunt, Manu Berduc, and Andrei Stolarchuk.

2 Quoted in Robert R. Palmer, *The Age of the Democratic Revolution: A Political History of Europe and America, 1760–1800*, Vol. 1 (Princeton, NJ: Princeton University Press, 1959–64), 2. http://quod.lib.umich.edu/cgi/t/text/text-idx?c=ac ls;idno=heb00740.

3 Palmer, *The Age of the Democratic Revolution: A Political History of Europe and America, 1760–1800*, Vol. 2 (Princeton, NJ: Princeton University Press, 1959–64), 6–7. http://quod.lib.umich.edu/cgi/t/text/text-idx?c=acls;idno=heb00740.

4 E. J. Hobsbawm, *The Age of Revolution: 1789–1848* (New York: New American Library, 1962); David Armitage and Sanjay Subrahmanyam, "Introduction: The Age of Revolutions, c. 1760–1840—Global Causation, Connection, Comparison," in *The Age of Revolutions in Global Context, c. 1760–1840,* ed. David Armitage and Sanjay Subramanyan (New York: Palgrave Macmillan, 2010), xviii, xxxii.

5 For a discussion of the problem of historicizing and translating the word "revolution," see Armitage and Subrahmanyam, "Introduction: Age of Revolutions," xii–xvi.

6 Charles Tilly published a huge corpus of theoretical and historical works on European and global forms of contentious politics. For our definitions here, we draw on *European Revolutions: 1492–1992* (New York: Wiley Blackwell, 1996), 5–16.

7 The notion of "repertoires" of collective action is also drawn from Charles Tilly, here *Contentious Performances* (New York: Cambridge University Press, 2008), 15. For a fuller discussion and application of the notion in a specific historical case, see Charles Tilly, "Contentious Repertoires in Great Britain, 1758–1834," in *Repertoires and Cycles of Collective Action,* ed. Mark Traugott (Durham, NC: Duke University Press, 1995), 15–42.

8 See, for example, Gary B. Nash, "Sparks from the Altar of '76: International Repercussions and Reconsiderations of the American Revolution," in *The Age of Revolutions,* ed. Armitage and Subramanyan, 1–19.

9 "Draft of Declaration of the Rights of Man" from *Thomas Jefferson: A Revolutionary World*. Library of Congress Exhibition. http://www.loc.gov/exhibits/jefferson/jeffworld.html.

10 Peter Linebaugh and Marcus Rediker, *The Many-Headed Hydra: Sailors, Slaves, Commoners, and the Hidden History of the Revolutionary Atlantic* (Boston: Beacon Press, 2000). See also Clare Anderson et al, eds, *Mutiny and Maritime Radicalism in the Age of Revolution: A Global Survey* (New York: Cambridge University Press, 2014) and Jane Landers, *Atlantic Creoles in the Age of Revolutions* (Cambridge, MA: Harvard University Press, 2011), 15–16.

11 Jürgen Osterhammel, *The Transformation of the World: A Global History of the Nineteenth Century* (Princeton, NJ: Princeton University Press, 2014), 531.

12 "Slavery and the Haitian Revolution," *Liberty, Equality, Fraternity: Exploring the French Revolution.* http://chnm.gmu.edu/revolution/chap8a.html.

13 Osterhammel, *Transformation*, 530.

14 Elizabeth Colwill, "Freedwomen's Familial Politics: Marriage, War and Rites of Registry in Post-Emancipation Saint-Domingue," in *Gender, War and Politics: Transatlantic Perspectives, 1775–1830*, ed. Karen Hagemann et al. (New York: Palgrave Macmillan, 2010), 72.

15 Ibid. See also David Geggis, "The Caribbean in the Age of Revolution," in *The Age of Revolutions,* ed. Armitage and Subrahmanyam, 83–101.

16 Deborah Gray White, *Ar'n't I A Woman? Female Slaves in the Plantation South* (New York: W.W. Norton, 1999), 67 ff.

17 Peter Carey, "Revolutionary Europe and the Destruction of Java's Old Order, 1808–1830," in *The Age of Revolutions*, ed. Armitage and Subrahmanyam, 167–188.

18 Carey, "Java's Old Order."

19 Mark Traugott, *The Insurgent Barricade* (Berkeley: University of California Press, 2010).

20 On Germany, see Theodore S. Hamerow, *Restoration, Revolution, Reaction* (Princeton, NJ: Princeton University Press, 1958) and Jonathan Sperber, *Rhineland Radicals: The Democratic Movement and the Revolution of 1848* (Princeton, NJ: Princeton University Press, 1991).

21 Anne-Claire Ignace, "French Volunteers in Italy, 1848–49: A Collective Incarnation of the Fraternity of the Peoples and of the Tradition of French Military Engagement in Italy and Europe," *Journal of Modern Italian Studies* 14 (December 2009): 445–460.

22 Quoted in Clara Zetkin, *Zur Geschichte der proletarischen Frauenbewegung Deutschlands* (Frankfurt: Verlag Roter Stern, 1971). http://gutenberg.spiegel. de/buch/zur-geschichte-der-proletarischen-frauenbewegung-deutschlands-6278/2.

23 David Ludden, *India and South Asia: A Short History* (London: Oneworld, 2002), 152.

24 Robert Gardella, *Harvesting Mountains: Fujian and the China Tea Trade, 1757–1937* (Berkeley: University of California Press, 1994).

25 Rudolf Wagner, "Operating in the Chinese Public Sphere: Theology and Technique of Taiping Propaganda," in *Norms and the State in China*, ed. Huang Chun-chieh (Leiden: E.J. Brill, 1993), 125–126.

26 Heather Streets-Salter, "The Rebellion of 1857: Origins, Consequences and Themes," *Teaching South Asia: An Internet Journal of Pedagogy* 1:1 (winter 2001), 89. http://www.mssu.edu/projectsouthasia/tsa/VIN1/Streets.htm.

27 Ranajit Guha, *Elementary Aspects of Peasant Insurgency* (Delhi: Oxford University Press, 1983), 227.

28 Guha, *Aspects*, 228.

29 Priti Joshi, "1857; or, Can the Indian 'Mutiny' Be Fixed?" in *BRANCH: Britain, Representation and Nineteenth-Century History.* http://www.branchcollective. org/?ps_articles=priti-joshi-1857-or-can-the-indian-mutiny-be-fixed.

30 Guha, *Aspects,* 267.

31 Crispin Bates et al, *Mutiny at the Margins.* http://www.csas.ed.ac.uk/mutiny/ Texts-Part2.html.

32 John Iliffe, "The Organization of the Maji Maji Rebellion," *The Journal of African History* 8:3 (1967), 495–512. See also Thaddeus Sunseri, *Labor Migration and Rural Change in Early Colonial Tanzania* (Portsmouth, NH: Heinemann, 2002).

33 Sunseri, *Labor Migration and Rural Change,* 97.

34 Iliffe, "The Organization of the Maji Maji Rebellion," 500.

35 Iliffe, "The Organization of the Maji Maji Rebellion," 502.

36 Dominique Grisard, "A Case of Mistaken Identity: Female Russian Social-Revolutionaries in early 20th Century Europe," in *What's Queer about Europe?* ed. Mireille Rosello and Sudip Dasgupta (New York: Fordham University Press, 2014), 48–68.

37 Andrew Hoyt, "Active Centers, Creative Elements and Bridging Nodes: Applying the Vocabulary of Network Theory to Radical History," *Journal for the Study of Radicalism* 9:1 (Spring 2015).

38 Tsuchiya Yoshifuru, "Unsuccessful National Unity: The Russian Home Front in 1904," in *The Russo-Japanese War in Global Perspective*, Vol. 2, ed. David Wolff et al (Leiden: E.J. Brill, 2001), 332.

39 Tsuchiya Yoshifuru, "Unsuccessful National Unity," 341.

40 *Documents in Russian History.* http://academic.shu.edu/russianhistory/ index.php/Workers%27_Petition,_January_9th,_1905_%28Bloody_ Sunday%29.

41 *China Since 1644.* http://chinasince1644.cheng-tsui.com/sites/default/files/ upload/7-11.pdf.

42 Madeline Hsu, "Migration and Native Place: Qiaokan and the Imagined Community of Taishan County, Guangdong, 1893–1993," *Journal of Asian Studies* 59:2 (May 2000), 307–31; Madeline Hsu, *Dreaming of Gold, Dreaming of Home: Transnationalism and Migration between the United States and South China, 1882–1942* (Stanford, CA: Stanford University Press, 2000).

43 Lynn Sharman, *Sun Yat-sen: His Life and its Meaning: A Critical Biography* (Stanford, CA: Stanford University Press: 1934), 83.

44 Jianli Huang, "Umbilical Ties: The Framing of the Overseas Chinese as the Mother of the Revolution," *Frontiers of History in China* 6:2 (2011).

45 See Gotelind Muller, "Chinese Women Between Education and Money: Ideal and Reality of Female Worker-students in the Early Years of the Republic" (University of Heidelberg, 2013). Translated in collaboration with Subei Wu. http://nbn-resolving.de/urn/resolver.pl?urn=urn:nbn:de:bsz:16-heidok-154163.

46 He Yan, "Overseas Chinese in France and in the World Society: Culture, Business, State and Transnational Connections, 1906–1949," in *State, Society*

and Governance in Republican China, ed. Mechtild Leutner and Izabella Goikhman (Berlin: LIT, 2014), 53.

47 Xu Guoqi, *Strangers on the Western Front: Chinese Workers in the Great War* (Cambridge, MA: Harvard University Press, 2011), 233. See also Paul Bailey, "'An Army of Workers': Chinese Indentured Labour in First World War France," in *Race, Empire, and First World War Writing,* ed. Santanu Das (Cambridge: Cambridge University Press, 2011), 44–45.

48 Xu, *Strangers,* 224.

49 Jean Chesneaux, *The Chinese Labor Movement, 1919–1949* (Stanford, CA: Stanford University Press, 1968), 140–41.

50 See for example, Joan Judge, *The Precious Raft of History: The Past, the West and the Woman Question in China* (Stanford, CA: Stanford University Press, 2008).

51 Fabio Lanza, *Behind the Gate: Inventing Students in Beijing* (New York: Columbia University Press, 2010). Tsung-yi Pan, "Constructing Tiananmen Square as a Realm of Memory: National Salvation, Revolutionary Tradition, and Political Modernity in Twentieth-century China" (PhD thesis, University of Minnesota, 2011).

52 See "The Race against Death," special issue of *Mother Jones,* September/October 1982.

53 Sharon Erickson Nepstad, *Religion and War Resistance in the Plowshares Movement* (New York: Cambridge University Press, 2008).

54 Stanley Hoffmann, "Nuclear Weapons in the 1980s: NATO and Nuclear Weapons: Reasons and Unreason," *Foreign Affairs* (Winter 1981/82).

55 "Volksbefreiungsarmee Chinas schlug konterrevolutionären Aufruhr nieder," *Neues Deutschland,* June 6, 1989; Diana Fong, "China's pro-democracy protests struck hope and fear in East Germany," *DW* (*Deutsche Welle*), March 6, 2009. http://www.dw.com/en/chinas-pro-democracy-protests-struck-hope-and-fear-in-east-germany/a-4298731.

56 Joel Edelstein, "Non-Violence and the 1989 Revolution in Eastern Europe," in *Justice without Violence,* ed. Paul Ernest Wehr and Heidi Burgess (London: Lynn Rienner, 1994), 99–124.

57 Serge Schmemann, "East German Movement Overtaken by Followers," *The New York Times,* October 16, 1989.

58 Serge Schmemann, "East Germans Let Largest Protest Proceed in Peace," *The New York Times,* October 10, 1989.

59 Timothy Garton Ash, "Velvet Revolution: The Prospects," *New York Review of Books,* December 3, 2009. http://www.nybooks.com/articles/archives/2009/dec/03/velvet-revolution-the-prospects/.

60 Ash, "Velvet Revolution."

61 On characteristics of early twenty-first-century global protest movements, see, for example: Donatella Della Porta and Sidney Tarrow, eds, *Transnational Protest & Global Activism* (Lanham, MD: Rowman & Littlefield, 2005) and Kurt Schock, *Unarmed Insurrections: People Power Movements in Nondemocracies* (Minneapolis: University of Minnesota Press, 2005).

2

International and Global Anti-colonial Movements

Heather Streets-Salter

Although anti-colonial movements took many forms in the period between 1750 and 1970, this chapter takes as its focus those movements that drew upon global networks or ideologies for inspiration and action. Some of these movements also imagined a postcolonial world whose boundaries did not fit neatly within those set by the former colonial power, and indeed went beyond the nation-state altogether.

The purpose in focusing on global and international anti-colonial movements is not to diminish the importance of other types of anti-colonial movements—particularly the constitutional nationalist movements that have heretofore received the lion's share of historical attention. Rather, it is to de-naturalize the idea that nation-states were always waiting to emerge from the colonial boundaries set by the colonizing powers. Instead, what comes to the fore are alternative visions that imagined political boundaries in terms of more global religious or class identities rather than those set by colonial powers, as well as anti-colonial activity that moved between—not merely within—colonial borders. Just as important, many of these international and global movements sought not only to disrupt colonial rule in one colony, but to attack colonialism everywhere as a systemic, worldwide problem in need of eradication.

Because so many histories of anti-colonial movements have focused on constitutional nationalist movements, they are usually set within an imperial framework and are told as a set of specific national-colonial stories about the transition from empires to nations. This chapter, however, explores anti-colonial movements within a world historical context, as part of a recognition by a wide variety of anti-colonial activists that the problem of empire was not specific to single nations but was instead a global problem requiring global resources and solutions. It is worth remembering that by the last decade of the nineteenth century, nearly all of Africa and the Pacific were ruled by European, American, or Japanese colonial powers, as was South Asia and most of Southeast Asia. In addition, both China and the Ottoman Empire, while technically independent, were managed under systems of informal control that appeared to most inhabitants to be strikingly similar to colonial rule. What this meant was that the condition of being a colonial subject—or at least considering oneself a colonial subject—was one of the most common experiences in the world until the mid-twentieth century.

Furthermore, thanks to steamship travel, railways, the proliferation of print culture, and mobile labor networks, individuals in colonized areas had far greater ability to learn about the experiences of other colonized people from the late nineteenth century onward than ever before. As Clare Anderson demonstrates in Chapter 6, millions of colonized subjects migrated as laborers to locations in the Indian and Atlantic Oceans and the South China Sea. Tens of thousands more moved along pilgrimage pathways to Mecca, while others traveled as students or professionals both between colonies and their metropoles as well as between neighboring colonies. Still others migrated outside the colonial world altogether to places like North America or Australia.

Besides serving as human connections between the various colonized populations around the world, workers and migrants traveling between, among, and outside colonies often brought print materials with them. Some also established newspapers and publishing houses in their new locations, and then sent printed material back to their locations of origin. All this movement and communication allowed colonized subjects around the world unprecedented access to information about conditions in other colonies. And this access, in turn, allowed at least some colonized subjects to recognize both broad similarities as well as important differences between colonial rulers in many parts of the world. Just as important, colonized people in any given location could now champion causes in other colonial locations in demonstrations of solidarity and support, such as when Muslim colonial subjects in India and the Dutch East Indies expressed support for the embattled Ottoman Empire in its struggles against Russia in the late nineteenth century. Alternatively, colonial subjects who had migrated to non-colonial states like the United States or Canada could now make use of their greater liberties in such locations to incite anti-colonial activities in their colonies of origin. What all this means is that the massive global acceleration in transportation and communication technologies that characterized the period following the late nineteenth century (discussed in Chapter 7 as well) also made it possible for anti-colonial activists to imagine colonialism not simply as a local issue but as a worldwide problem requiring international and global solutions.

Although there were a variety of international and globally oriented anti-colonial movements in this period, this chapter will focus on three in particular: revolutionary Indian nationalism in the early twentieth century, the phenomenon of pan-Islam during the late nineteenth and early twentieth centuries, and international communism. The chapter begins with a revolutionary Indian nationalist movement called Ghadar, which was a globally oriented movement that specifically advocated violence in order to achieve its goals. The chapter then focuses on pan-Islam from the late nineteenth century to the interwar period, arguing that this movement imagined a postcolonial world whose boundaries extended well beyond the nation-state. Finally, the chapter explores anti-colonial movements based on international communism via two examples: one centered on East and Southeast Asia, and the other centered on sub-Saharan Africa. These communist movements had a very different vision of the struggle for independence than many of the nationalist movements, for while they certainly imagined independence from colonial rule, they also imagined a close, ongoing, and mutually beneficial relationship not only with the Soviet Union but with those who struggled against exploitive capitalism everywhere. Through these examples, this chapter demonstrates just a few of the alternate political alliances and geographies with which anti-colonial activists imagined the postcolonial world.

Revolutionary Indian nationalism

India offers a rich variety of examples through which to explore anti-colonial movements. Although the Indian National Congress and its activities are the best known (at least outside India), many other groups organized to fight against colonialism in the nineteenth and twentieth centuries. These movements took different shapes and were driven by a variety of ideologies, from the small and regional to the large and diffuse, from secret societies to registered parties, and from those based on a belief in democratic reform to those based on revolution. Many of these movements were nationalist in orientation, in that they sought independence and self-determination for an Indian state that would occupy the boundaries of the colonial state. But as we will see below, the means by which they sought to attain these ends varied widely. In what follows, we will explore a revolutionary movement called Ghadar whose existence overlapped with the Indian National Congress in the early twentieth century but could hardly have been more different. Whereas the Congress sought power-sharing and constitutional change through mass protests and formal political agitation, Ghadar imagined immediate change through violent revolution. Whereas the Congress sought to make its actions public, Ghadar tried to keep its activities and its members secret. And while the birth of the Congress was certainly tied to an awareness of events outside India, it was nevertheless founded in India and slowly developed the machinery of a mass-based political movement within the colonial state. Ghadar, on the other hand, was founded by Indians living in the United States, became deeply reliant on non-Indian sources of funding, and was brought back to India with the express purpose of stirring up local discontent and inciting revolution. It was thus fundamentally indebted to the modern means of travel and communication—especially steamship and railroad locomotion and mass-produced print—that characterized the early twentieth century. A brief exploration of Ghadar's history reminds us that powerful visions of nationalism did not always arise from within the borders of the imagined nation, and that many anti-colonial movements sought violent rather than constitutional change.[1] It also demonstrates the ways in which even radical and violent attempts to disrupt colonial rule were often based on shared patriarchal values between both colonized and colonizers.

The Ghadar party was founded in 1913 not in India, but in San Francisco among Indian expatriates who had migrated to California. Many of its original members were Sikh peasants from the Punjab, who had migrated to the west coast of North America in the early years of the twentieth century in order to escape conditions of poverty and land hunger at home.[2] Most were farmers who sought to earn a living in the same trade once in North America, working small plots of land and doing agricultural labor on the fertile west coast. Once in the United States and Canada, however, Indians experienced increasingly hostile discrimination, not only at the state level but also from surrounding white communities. In fact, "Asians" of any nationality faced harsh discrimination on the Pacific coast of North America at this time, and were subject to laws that sought to limit immigration and property accumulation as well as violence and race riots. Explicit among the limitations that white communities sought to impose was to restrict Indian women from immigrating with their husbands and families. As a result, until 1912 the Indian immigrant population was composed entirely of men, which was a source of bitter complaint among them. The restriction on Indian women was intended to prevent Indians from establishing settled, self-propagating, racially distinct communities. By preventing female immigration, whites hoped the Indian population would be temporary sojourners for the purposes of work rather than permanent migrants.[3] Indians, for their part, argued that they possessed the same male rights to establish families and to head households as any white North American, and explicitly challenged these laws by attempting to gain entry for their wives.

Indians undergoing such hostile pressures sought diplomatic help from British consular authorities, only to discover that the authorities did not want to press for Indian liberties in North America, not least because they feared doing so would create similar expectations in India. Frustrated by British unresponsiveness, and taking it both as an indication of British misrule over Indians everywhere and as a deliberate attempt to deny migrant Indians their rights as men, expatriate Indians in California determined that the solution to the problem was to form a movement to overthrow British rule in India via armed rebellion. In 1914, one of the movement's leaders deplored the situation in which "our men, who valiantly shed their blood . . . can not have the privilege of bringing their wives and children in the lands of the British colonies." The response, he argued, must be "to remedy this situation, and acquire our inalienable rights."[4] They named the movement Ghadar, which means "mutiny." It was chosen deliberately to recall the Indian Rebellion of 1857, when a significant portion of the Bengal army and peasants in north-central India rose up against British power.

At its outset, then, the vision of the Ghadar party leaders was at once global, nationalist, and deeply gendered. The idea was to use the relative freedom of speech and organization in places like the United States to connect with individuals and organizations sympathetic to Indian revolution, and to produce materials designed to convince Indian men around the world to identify with the cause. The ultimate goal, however, was always to bring the revolution—backed with money, weapons, and soldiers—back to India, where the battle for an independent state would be waged.

Ghadar's first step after organizing was to publish, in November 1913, a newspaper devoted to the cause of Indian revolution. The newspaper—also called *Ghadar*—was published in San Francisco and then distributed in the United States, Canada, and India, as well as in other areas with significant Indian populations or garrisons, including South and East Africa, Hong Kong, Burma, Malaya, and Singapore. The first issue was unambiguous about the party's intentions, declaring that "the people can no longer bear the oppression and tyranny practiced under British rule and are ready to fight and die for freedom."[5] But the party was not just about propaganda: its leaders also created a militant action wing whose purpose was to plan an actual revolution in India. In pursuing this goal, they took inspiration not only from India's revolutionary past, but also from Sun Yat-Sen's 1911 revolution in China and Zapatista revolutionaries in Mexico.[6]

Although Ghadar's leadership was made up mostly of literate Hindus (one of its founding members, Har Dayal, was a lecturer in Indian philosophy and Sanskrit), its rank and file was made up primarily of Sikh agricultural workers—many of whom were relatively uneducated men from farming families in the Punjab. In the first several years of its existence, Ghadar was particularly successful in recruiting these men, who had come to the western United States and Canada for a better life, only to experience anti-Asian discrimination first-hand. The Ghadar party also made early efforts to target Indian Muslims, particularly those who served in the massive Indian army.

British authorities in India were aware of Ghadar party actions almost from their beginning, and tried without success to convince the United States authorities to shut down its press. They were more successful in convincing United States authorities to target individuals, and in February 1914 British officials convinced them to arrest and deport Har Dayal on charges of spreading anarchist literature. Before Dayal could be deported, however, he fled first to Switzerland and then, by invitation of the German government, to Germany.[7] Yet even without Har Dayal, the publication and global distribution of *Ghadar* continued in the United States unabated. And thanks in part to global steamship routes, by March 1914 a British Foreign

Office memorandum noted that copies had been found in Singapore, Hong Kong, and British concessions in China as well as in India itself. Indian merchant networks also facilitated the spread of *Ghadar*. Merchants from the province of Sind were especially important in this regard, as these individuals counted many Sikhs among them and also maintained extensive diasporic communities around the globe through which news and information could easily travel.[8] In all locations where *Ghadar* appeared, Sikh Gurdwaras (temples) became centers of dissemination where worshippers read poems from the paper aloud and discussed politics after prayers. In areas with large Indian Muslim populations, mosques served the same purpose.

The entry of Great Britain into the conflict that became the First World War provided a unique opportunity for Ghadar, because it aligned the party's interests with those of Germany, Britain's most powerful enemy. Even before the war the German government had taken an interest in Har Dayal and the activities of Ghadar, and had already invited him to Berlin. After Britain entered the war on August 4, Dayal was joined by two other Ghadar activists, Vivendranath Chattopadhyaya and Bhupendranath Datta. The Germans formalized the relationship by creating the state-financed Committee for Indian Independence, a department whose task it was to create anti-British propaganda for British colonial subjects and to coordinate the shipment of arms into India.[9] For Dayal and Ghadar more generally, the alliance with the Germans was an opportunity to attain financial, logistical, and technical support for furthering its own ends—the complete disruption of British rule in India through violent revolution. For the Germans, it was a means of securing its explicit war aim of encouraging the collapse of India—Britain's most important colonial possession—by arming its colonized population. As the *Ghadar* put it on July 21, 1914, "All intelligent people know that Germany is an enemy of Great Britain. We also are the mortal enemy of the British Government and an enemy of my enemy is my friend."[10]

Once the war began, Ghadar activists began to send more than just propaganda around the world. With German money, they also sent people and munitions. The goal was to send fighters and weapons directly to India, where they would be used to start a revolution. To facilitate these transfers and to round up additional recruits, Ghadarites also sent party activists from North America to the Far East. They specifically targeted Hong Kong, the Malay States, Rangoon, and Singapore—each of which had Indian army garrisons that Ghadarites were eager to penetrate and recruit for their cause. Indian soldiers, Ghadar leaders believed, would be particularly useful to win over because of their military training, their access to weapons, and their claims to a hyper-masculine ideal with which they could challenge British claims to masculine superiority.[11]

Ghadar activists traveled to East and Southeast Asia during the fall and winter of 1914 and 1915. In places like Hong Kong, Burma, and Singapore, they sought to infiltrate Indian army regiments, to distribute Ghadar propaganda, and to encourage discontent among Indian populations more generally. In officially neutral places like Canton, Manila (both until 1917), and Batavia, they sought to establish contacts with German agents who would provide the means to funnel weapons and money to India from North America via the Strait of Malacca or the Sunda Strait. Over the course of 1915, Ghadar activists and German sponsors initiated several elaborate plans to accomplish this goal, of which the best known involved two ships called the *Maverick* and the *Annie Larsen*.

In early 1915, a German shipping firm commissioned the *Maverick*—an oil tanker—from an American-owned company. The ship's crew included five men posing as "Persian waiters" but who were in fact Ghadar revolutionaries from San Francisco. The *Maverick* set sail with its crew at the end of April 1915 from California, after which it was supposed to meet the American ship *Annie Larsen* in the remote Socorro islands. There, the *Annie Larsen* was to transfer its cargo of an estimated 30,000 rifles and revolvers to the *Maverick*, and the *Maverick* was to sail on to Java. In Java, the *Maverick* was to make contact with German agents, who would arrange for the munitions—and the Ghadar activists—to be moved on to India and met by Ghadar contacts already in place.[12] While neither the mission of the *Maverick* nor any of the other similar missions planned by Ghadar activists and German agents succeeded in transporting arms to India, they nevertheless revealed the complex networks that lay between Indian revolutionaries in North America and the object of their activities in India.

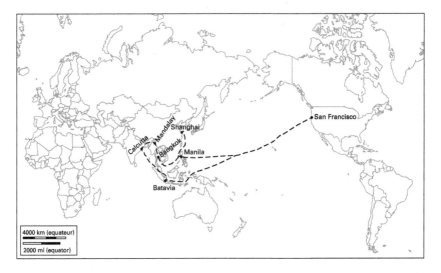

FIGURE 2.1 *Ghadar networks in the Pacific and Eastern Indian Ocean. Credit: Heather Streets-Salter.*

Ghadar activists also prepared the ground for revolution in India. At the same time as party members traveled to East and Southeast Asia, many more made the journey to India for the cause. Although the numbers are not exact, it seems clear that at least several thousand men returned to India from abroad between 1914 and 1915. Those who were not arrested and detained on arrival set out to make contacts and recruits in two main areas: the Punjab, from whence so many of the North American Ghadarites hailed, and Bengal, home of the revolutionary and vehemently anti-British Yugantar party, which had been active in the region for nearly a decade. In the Punjab, Ghadar activists set up their own printing press to produce revolutionary materials, raided local treasuries for funds, and infiltrated most of the regimental cantonments in the region.[13] Strong contingents of several regiments—including the Twenty-third Cavalry at Lahore and the Twenty-sixth Punjabis at Ferozepore—were willing to mutiny by early 1915. In Bengal, Ghadar activists successfully sought to incorporate Yugantar party activists into their plans for revolution. Some of these, including Narendra Nath Bhattacharya—better known in his later life as M. N. Roy—even accepted missions to travel to Shanghai and Batavia in order to make contact with German agents.

In spite of the fact that Ghadar activists in India never received their promised shipments of arms and money from North America, leaders in India set the date for the start of the revolution for February 21, 1915. However, their plans were betrayed by an informer, and British authorities were able to stop nearly all of the violence before it even began. Several trials in India ensued following the exposure of the Ghadar plot, which brought 175 people up on charges of conspiracy. Of these, 136 were convicted, and 42 were sentenced to death. Things continued to go badly for the Ghadar party, for when the United States entered the war on the side of the British, the United States government convicted Ghadar leaders for conspiring with an enemy power on its own soil. In the longest-running and most expensive trial to date in the United States, the Hindu German Conspiracy Trial brought 35 Indians and Germans to trial, all of whom were convicted.[14]

Not surprisingly, by the end of World War I the Ghadar party had lost a lot of its momentum: its tactics and contacts had been exposed, most of its leaders had been arrested, and its main source of funding—the German state—had been defeated by the British. Notwithstanding these problems, the party continued to exist until Indian independence, and was formally disbanded only in 1948. During the interwar period, Ghadar party members continued their activism in the fight against colonial rule in general, and against British rule in India in particular. In this period, however, Ghadar party members—like many other anti-colonial activists—were increasingly attracted to two ideologies that viewed national independence in the context of greater, more international ideologies: pan-Islam and international communism. But these ideologies were much bigger than Ghadar itself, and

FIGURE 2.2 *Image of Har Dayal as he awaited trial during the Hindu-German Conspiracy Trial in the United States. Credit: San Francisco Chronicle (public domain).*

for that reason we will leave the party behind and return to both pan-Islam and international communism in their larger context below.

At this point, let us conclude by returning to the original point of our focus on Ghadar: to provide a concrete example of an Indian nationalist movement wholly different from the Indian National Congress in terms of ideology, organization, and tactics. Ghadar was based on an ideology of total disruption through armed revolution, was organized in covert cells, and sought to achieve its goals through sabotage and violence. Moreover, the Ghadar party was not the violent exception that proved the constitutional rule: it is simply one example of many other anti-colonial movements whose members imagined revolutionary methods to achieve their goals, and who relied on an international network of support to try and bring them to fruition.[15] In the case of Ghadar (and many other anti-colonial movements), it is also worth remembering that one of the inspirations for the movement had been over conflicts about gender—particularly about the right of Indian colonial subjects to establish and maintain families in the same way as white British settlers.

Pan-Islam

Whereas the Ghadar movement was intensely nationalist in the early years of the twentieth century despite being internationalist in its methods, pan-Islam envisioned a different kind of political organization based on worldwide religious affinity. Pan-Islam was a movement that sought to unite Muslim believers around the world under the authority of the Caliph, or spiritual head of Islam. This movement began in the late nineteenth century, and continued to gain adherents in the first quarter of the twentieth.[16] While pan-Islam was not incompatible with the idea of nation-states—and indeed many pan-Islamists also fought for national independence as well—the ideology also called for a transnational community of believers under the loose authority of the Caliph. Pan-Islamists imagined a different kind of solidarity than nationalism, for whereas nationalism imagined unity within the boundaries of the state, pan-Islam imagined, in addition, unity that also included Muslims from all over the world, whether colonized or not. In essence, pan-Islamists imagined a disruption of state and colonial borders in order to include all believers within a single religious polity.

While pan-Islam was uniquely based on the unity of Islamic believers, it was not the only anti-colonial pan-movement of the nineteenth and twentieth centuries. Two of the most important of these, at least in terms of geographical range and scope, were pan-Africanism and pan-Asianism. Their rough coexistence with pan-Islam demonstrates, as Rebecca Karl has noted, "that there was a time when non-Western peoples' perceptions of shared experiences of oppression led them to construct for themselves global blocs that were independent of existing states and incipient national formations."[17] The timing was hardly coincidental. As we saw with the Ghadar movement, that so many of these pan-movements occurred at around the same time was due to a world historical moment in which transportation and communication technologies allowed peoples around the world to move and share their ideas more rapidly and more effectively than ever before. To understand the importance and appeal of pan-Islam, therefore, it must be viewed within the larger global context of these anti-colonial pan-movements, each of which sought alternatives or additions to nationalism.[18]

Pan-Africanism, for example, was a political movement that sought the liberation of peoples of African descent from racialized oppression all over the world, whether in the Americas, Europe, or Africa. As a political movement, pan-Africanism coalesced around the beginning of the twentieth century. Over the first half of the century, leaders of the movement organized a series of congresses in which Afro-European, African-American, and African anti-colonialists came into contact and strategized about how to achieve independence for colonized Africans and racial equality for African descendants everywhere.[19] The movement led to important physical and intellectual connections across continents and oceans, including the philosophy of *negritude* developed by Aimé Césaire of Martinique and Léopold Senghor of Senegal, which posited that blackness was a positive and beautiful quality rather than a negative one. In Africa itself, pan-African leaders sought to support one another across the continent by giving aid to ongoing African independence struggles.[20]

Pan-Asianism was a similarly powerful pan-movement that gained enormous popular support in the early twentieth century. Like pan-Africanism, pan-Asianism called for the solidarity of Asian peoples everywhere to counter the global dominance of the west. Although there were multiple versions of this philosophy, by the first decade of the twentieth century the most influential was led by Japanese intellectuals.[21] Meiji philosophers in the late nineteenth century had postulated that Japan could revitalize the oppressed and colonized regions of Asia because it had successfully transitioned to an industrial state without having lost its Asian identity. Once Japan defeated Russia in the Russo-Japanese war of 1904–1905, Japanese thinkers increasingly believed that only Japan could provide the necessary leadership to raise the rest of Asia from servitude and poverty. Yet the Japanese were not the only ones impressed by the magnitude of Japan's victory: many colonized Asians also came to believe that Japan held the key to overcoming colonial oppression. While the Russo-Japanese war was raging, for example, even non-literate people around Southeast Asia became interested in Japanese successes, and gathered around those who could read to listen to newspaper accounts about Japanese victories. After the war, anti-colonial activists from India, Indochina, the Dutch East Indies, and China traveled to Japan for education and training, with the idea of returning to their home countries to fight against colonial rule. While there, activists from many colonies met and learned from one another, sometimes forming groups like the 1907 Asian Solidarity Society—which was founded by Indians and Chinese but was intended to include activists from every Asian state.[22]

Yet Japanese-centered pan-Asianism was also fraught with tension after Japan's annexation of Korea in 1910, as many Asian anti-colonial activists decried the action as blatantly imperialist. When the Japanese army occupied the Chinese Shantung peninsula during World War I, the outrage—particularly among the Chinese and Chinese diaspora—was particularly acute.[23] Although pan-Asianism caused the colonial powers significant anxiety, especially in the Dutch East Indies and Indochina, the movement fell even further out of favor by the start of World War II, when Japan's brutal treatment of Asians disillusioned many former admirers of the ideology.

While both pan-Africanism and pan-Asianism were based around loosely conceived ideas of "racial" unity, pan-Islam cut across race by appealing to believers around the world—including both Asians and Africans. In fact, the ideal of a unified *dar-al-Islam* (dominion of Islam) under the Caliph was not new to Muslims in the nineteenth and twentieth centuries. When the Ottomans captured Istanbul in 1453, Mehmet II claimed authority as the spiritual head of Islam. As the Ottomans gained suzerainty over ever-larger Muslim territories, their claims as defenders of the holy cities of Mecca and Medina reinforced the credibility of their declaration of caliphal authority.

By the second half of the nineteenth century, these older ideas of an Ottoman Caliphate were in the process of merging into a more conscious ideology of Pan-Islam. Somewhat ironically, the original intent behind the ideology had been nationalist, and was developed by a dissident group called the Young Ottomans who sought to create a more Turkish, Muslim Ottoman state. Yet once the ideas of the Young Ottomans had been translated into Arabic, the specific Turkish nationalist meanings of Pan-Islam evolved into the more general idea "that all Muslim peoples should cooperate with each other in their individual efforts to gain independence from infidel rule."[24] Such ideas traveled quickly over the sea-lanes to places as distant as India and Southeast Asia, and were reflected in vernacular newspapers featuring stories sympathizing with Ottoman struggles against Europeans in the 1860s and 1870s.

The most aggressive anti-colonial phase of pan-Islam began with the reign of Sultan Abdulhamid II (r. 1876–1908). For Abdulhamid, pan-Islam was a political strategy designed to disguise the weakness of his government in relation to the European powers that dominated his economy and treasury. Rather than try to assert a military capacity he did not have, Abdulhamid II sought strength instead in reinvigorating the claim that the Ottoman Sultan was the rightful Caliph of Sunni Muslims worldwide. He then set about trying to counter European authority by initiating a campaign to assert his jurisdiction over those Muslims who were living under non-Ottoman, non-Muslim governments—particularly in areas where colonial powers ruled over large Muslim populations.[25]

While Abdulhamid II clearly had his own reasons for initiating such a campaign, it nevertheless resonated with many colonial subjects who sought an alternative method for imagining their status or addressing their grievances. This campaign had a marked effect on both the Dutch East Indies and British Malaya, whose colonial populations were overwhelmingly Muslim. As part of his invigorated program in support of Pan-Islam, Abdulhamid II reached out through the Ottoman consulates in Singapore (established 1864) and Batavia (established 1883) to encourage Muslims to regard the Sultan as their Caliph and protector. Ottoman consuls played the

FIGURE 2.3 *Sultan Abdulhamid II (1842–1918). Credit: W. and D. Downey.*

role of intermediary for the Sultan-Caliph, and reinvigorated links between the Indies and Istanbul by establishing scholarships for young men to study in the Ottoman capital.[26]

Yet Muslims in Southeast Asia did not only learn about pan-Islamic ideas from Ottoman officials posted in the colonies in which they lived. Rather, by the end of the nineteenth century thousands of Muslims from the East Indies and British Malaya were making the long pilgrimage to Mecca each year to participate in the Hajj. In 1898 alone, 13,325 Southeast Asian pilgrims made the trip. By 1911, this annual number had nearly doubled, which meant that pilgrims from Southeast Asia made up nearly a quarter of the world's total by that time.[27] Once in Mecca—which was closed to non-Muslims—ordinary Southeast Asians were able to discuss their colonial overlords with relative freedom, and often shared their own tales of colonial exploitation as well as cultural and religious insensitivity. They also came into contact with Muslims from many other parts of the world, including India and North and West Africa. These pilgrims often had their own experiences with colonialism, the details of which could be compared outside of colonial boundaries. And importantly, pilgrims to Mecca had access to a wide variety of printed materials in Arabic and other languages, which could then be shared orally among communities of believers. In fact, many Ottoman-produced pan-Islamic tracts were distributed to pilgrims in Mecca with the intention that they would be brought back to colonial territories like India and the Dutch East Indies and then shared among the general population. It is for these reasons that Sugata Bose has called the Hajj a crucial "vehicle for an anticolonial current that state boundaries could not contain."[28]

During the nineteenth and early twentieth centuries, the pilgrimage was, in fact, one of the main sources of outside information and ideas for Southeast Asian Muslims. And of course, when Hajjis returned to their homes, they brought these ideas back with them. Some of these ideas were related to the meanings of Islam and its proper practice, which meant that some returning pilgrims tried to insist on a more rigorous practice of Islam. Other ideas were related to pan-Islamic anti-colonialism, based on a new sense of Islamic community discovered at Mecca. Indeed, some pilgrims returning to Java in the late nineteenth century reported returning home with the sense of having become more than just Javanese, or even of having lost their Javanese-ness in favor of a new sense of having become Islamic global citizens.[29]

Ottoman-sponsored pan-Islam entered its most blatantly political phase during World War I. Abdulhamid's reign had come to an end in 1909, when he was deposed by the nationalist Young Turk Revolution and replaced by Mehmed V. In the five years between the Revolution and the start of the war, the new Ottoman state had desperately sought to conclude an alliance with one of the Great Powers in order to protect itself in the event of a general war. In the end, with the enthusiastic support of the German Kaiser but only lukewarm support from many of his officials, Germany and the Ottoman Empire concluded a secret alliance on August 2, 1914. With the Muslim Ottomans as an ally, one of the Kaiser's advisors convinced him that the Sultan-Caliph could contribute to Germany's campaign to foment revolution in the colonies of the Entente powers by declaring a jihad against them. On the Ottoman side, although the ruling party was not initially convinced about the advisability of such a strategy, it was difficult to ignore the potential power of Islam for attracting support from around the world. Thus when the Ottomans publicly entered the war on October 28, 1914, they declared the liberation of occupied Muslim lands as a specific war aim. Then on November 14, 1914, the highest religious authority in the empire declared a jihad on behalf of the Sultan-Caliph, demanding that "the Moslem subjects of Russia, of France, of England and of all the countries that side with them in their land and sea attacks dealt against the Caliphate for the purpose of annihilating Islam" must "take part in the holy War against the respective governments from which they depend."[30]

From this point forward, the Germans, Ottomans, and their allies sought to capitalize on the Sultan's claim to be Caliph. These allies, as we already know, included the Ghadar revolutionaries who worked on the Committee for Indian Independence financed by the German state. The Committee helped to spread propaganda, in *Ghadar* and other publications, indicating that Kaiser Wilhelm had converted to Islam, and that large segments of the German population had converted as well. Muslim soldiers continued to be of particular interest to the Committee. In order to reach as many Muslim soldiers as possible, the editors of *Ghadar* published special pamphlets in languages like Pushtu (spoken in Afghanistan and parts of Northwest India). One example, from August 1915, represented an attempt to reach soldiers fighting for the British on the Northwest Frontier. This particular pamphlet claimed:

> The wicked English and their allies are now attacking Islam, but the German Emperor and the Sultan of Turkey have sworn to liberate Asia from the tyranny. Now is the time to rise ... Only your strength and religious zeal are required.[31]

Although the principal targets of the Central Powers were Muslims living under British colonial rule in India, Southeast Asia, and Egypt, they also spread jihadist and pan-Islamic propaganda in French colonial territories in Africa as well as in Muslim areas in Central Asia under the dominion of the Russian Empire. In other words, elite and well-traveled Indians sought, with their German and Ottoman allies, to create massive disruptions in the colonial empires of their rivals by appealing to ordinary Muslim soldiers and laborers. These efforts deeply alarmed all of the Entente powers with significant Muslim populations, and prompted increased surveillance of Muslim populations as well as counter-propaganda efforts emphasizing their friendliness to Islam. In general, however, the panicked response of the Entente powers was disproportionate to the success of the jihadist strategy and its expensive propaganda campaign.[32] Almost everywhere, Muslim soldiers and civilians in the British, French, and Russian Empires remained loyal in spite of pan-Islamic propaganda, whether or not they sympathized with it. Specific efforts to incite mutiny among French Muslim soldiers were mostly unsuccessful, as were similar efforts among Muslim soldiers in the massive British Indian army.

Despite the widespread appeal of pan-Islam in various places around the world since the late nineteenth century, it is perhaps not surprising that a call to jihad on behalf of the Ottoman Sultan was unsuccessful. Among ordinary Muslims who harbored grievances with their colonial rulers, pan-Islam had offered an attractive alternative to working within the boundaries of the colonial state. It is difficult to know, however, how many Muslims outside of the Ottoman Empire fully accepted the idea that the Sultan was the rightful Caliph and, even if they did, what kind of loyalty he should inspire. It was one thing to ask for Ottoman intervention or to promote pan-Islamic ideas when they meshed with the interests and agendas of anti-colonial activists, but it was another thing altogether to obey a command of jihad from a distant ruler who had not demonstrated his ability to successfully intervene in colonial affairs. To do so would have carried the highest personal risk, and as Richard Fogarty has observed with respect to French Muslim soldiers, most individuals were able to see through the propaganda of both sides to realize they were being manipulated, and then acted in the way that suited their own interests.[33] In any case, with the defeat of the Central Powers in 1918, the political project of Ottoman-sponsored pan-Islam lost most of the power it once had.

Yet what interests us here is not the lack of success of the Ottoman-sponsored pan-Islamic movement. Rather, it is the fact that many ordinary Muslims living under colonial rule were deeply attracted by the idea of an Islamic alternative to European rule, and sought to encourage it. It is also the ways in which some Muslims saw themselves as part of vast transnational and trans-colonial networks knit together both by religious conviction and by opposition to European rule. Pan-Islamists envisioned the community of Islam as one that transcended colonial rule, class, and race, and that united believers in a spiritual kingdom that also had earthly potential. Indeed, the pan-Islam that existed in the late nineteenth and early twentieth centuries demonstrated that not all movements seeking independent space within colonial borders imagined that space to be limited within those borders.

International communism

Although Ottoman-sponsored pan-Islam offered an anti-colonial ideology that expressly cut across existing and incipient national borders, its imagined postcolonial structure remained vague. In contrast to pan-Islam—and indeed to other contemporary pan-movements—international communism had a clear vision for a global alternative to nationalism and also for the global structure of the movement. And unlike nationalist movements and pan-movements, international communism did not exclude on the basis of the boundaries within which people lived or on the basis of race or religion. What mattered to communists, at least in theory, was that its adherents share an antipathy to global capitalism and a commitment to the well-being of workers and peasants. Yet international communism was not incompatible with national independence. On the contrary, the ideology encouraged independence for colonial states, and many colonists who were members of local communist parties also fought for national independence. At the same time, international communism imagined a super-structure that would include all states led by communists in a global union of support—with firm financial and logistical backing from the communist leadership in the Soviet Union. And unlike many other anti-colonial movements—national or otherwise—international communism imagined a world in which gender equality was the norm, and in which women would serve in the cause alongside men. Although this vision was usually followed only imperfectly, it was nevertheless quite different from movements like Ghadar that sought the same patriarchal rights as British men, or like pan-Islamist movements that did not question the subservient role of women in public life. In this section, we highlight two anti-colonial movements based on international communism: one from East Asia during the interwar period, and one from sub-Saharan Africa in the last half of the twentieth century. Although separated in time, circumstances, and space, both highlight the intersections between local and regional anti-colonial movements and the global interests that characterized international communism.

For the first few years after the Bolshevik Revolution in October 1917, communists in the Soviet Union were preoccupied with winning a civil war, consolidating power, and exporting the communist revolution to Europe. To achieve this last goal the Soviet leadership established, in 1919, an institution called the Communist International—better known as the Comintern. Its primary purpose was to offer support for the defeat of the international bourgeoisie through revolution and to replace it with an international Soviet republic. Soviet communists assumed that the worldwide communist revolution would have to be led by industrialized proletariat classes, and thus that the industrialized states of Europe were the logical targets for the Comintern. In 1920, however, the Comintern broadened its focus to the colonized areas of the world, and shifted to an explicitly anti-colonial program. At its second annual meeting, Lenin himself argued—in his *Theses on National and Colonial Questions*—that communists in the West should partner with communists in the colonies in order to damage the economic foundations of the capitalist powers.[34] To bring about this end, communist parties in the colonies would henceforth be formally incorporated into the

Comintern, and would thus be eligible for aid in return for being subject to Comintern supervision and direction.

Given the increase in anti-colonial activity across much of the colonial world in the first two decades of the twentieth century, even rhetorical solidarity with colonial activists would have been enough to provoke anxiety among European colonial authorities. But the solidarity and support offered by Lenin's *Theses* took on a far more threatening guise when colonial subjects began almost immediately to form communist parties of their own. The first to form were the Parti Komunis Indonesia (PKI) and the Algerian Communist Party (PCA) in 1920. Thereafter, in spite of efforts by the various colonial powers to outlaw communist parties or to harass and arrest their members, their number only grew. The PKI and PCA were followed by the establishment of the Chinese Communist Party (CCP) and the South African Communist Party (SACP) in 1921, the Lebanese Communist Party (LCP) in 1924, and the Communist Party of India (CPI), the Communist Party of Korea, and the South Seas Communist Party in 1925. By 1930, communists had formed the Indochinese Communist Party (ICP), the Malayan Communist Party (MCP), and the Filipino Communist Party (PKP). To colonial authorities, this activity meant that many of the most important colonies were now host to vehemently anti-colonial, revolutionary political parties that were in a position to receive aid and advice from a well-organized and powerful foreign source. To make matters more threatening, colonial communist parties frequently established ties with their corresponding metropolitan communist parties, which opened up the possibility that metropolitan citizens were actively involved in undermining colonial rule in their own national colonies. For all of these reasons, colonial authorities in nearly every colony made communist party membership illegal, and sought to punish members they did apprehend. During the 1920s and 1930s, colonial authorities also learned to collaborate with authorities in neighboring colonies to trade information on suspects who crossed colonial boundaries.[35]

Given the dangers associated with communist party membership, why might colonized subjects have felt drawn to the movement? The answer to this question varied by individual, of course, but several factors appear to have motivated many of the anti-colonial activists who embraced communism. Some activists had grown disillusioned with constitutional methods for change, arguing that they were too slow or too easily deflected by colonial authorities. In contrast to constitutional measures, communism advocated violent revolution that promised more immediate—and more fundamental—change. Moreover, since the Russian Revolution had been successful, activists could point to a positive model demonstrating that such violent revolution was possible. Additionally, from a practical standpoint the formation of colonial communist parties could mean significant financial and material support from the Soviet Union and its satellites, including funds for purchasing weapons and sustaining party members as well as personnel to train colonial activists. This outside support and training made it possible for relatively small parties to maintain their existence even in the face of harsh repression. There were philosophical attractions to communism as well. For one thing, communism often appealed to poor peasants and urban workers because it promised an ultimate relief from poverty and the creation of a class-less state. Equally important, and unlike colonialism, communist ideology did not blame colonial subjects for their own subjugation by claiming they represented inferior races. Instead, communist ideology placed the blame for the oppression of the colonized squarely on the shoulders of the capitalist imperialists and the global capitalist system.[36] Finally, for some the promise of gender equality under communism was attractive, although women who wished to take part in communist anti-colonial movements in East and Southeast Asia often found it necessary either to maintain their traditional roles as helpers for men, or to commit themselves to strict asexuality and celibacy in order to be taken seriously by male comrades.[37]

During the 1920s and 1930s, communists in the colonies embarked—in conjunction with Comintern operatives—on active campaigns to undermine or overthrow colonial rule in locations around the world. Their goal was clear: complete disruption of colonial rule by violent revolution. In each location, communist colonial subjects served in both leadership roles and as the foot-soldiers in campaigns that drew upon people and resources that crossed national and colonial boundaries. One example of these campaigns was the work of the Far Eastern Bureau (FEB), a Comintern-funded organization, which began its operations in Shanghai in 1928. The FEB was a covert organization established in the wake of severe repression of the communist party by the Chinese nationalist Guomindang party. Its purpose was to serve as a critical node of communication and finance for an organized communist network that spanned an enormous area in East and Southeast Asia, including not only China but also Japan, Korea, Formosa (Taiwan), the Philippines, Malaya (including Indonesia), and Indochina. Since communist activity now had to be conducted covertly, the FEB was established under the cover of a legal German firm called the Metropolitan Trading Company—a ruse that would allow the transfer of large sums of money, the extended use of the mail, and regular meetings with a wide variety of "clients." The FEB was headed by European Comintern agents, but paid the salaries of a wide variety of Chinese and Southeast Asian agents and informers. While the FEB was active, its agents communicated with Moscow via Berlin using a series of post boxes in Shanghai and a constantly shifting set of residences in Berlin as well as complex, multi-part, enciphered telegrams. From Shanghai, the FEB communicated with the various communist parties in East and Southeast Asia via couriers, whose main routes ran from Shanghai to Japan; from Shanghai to Hong Kong, Saigon, Bangkok, Singapore, and Rangoon; and from Shanghai to Hong Kong, Formosa, and Manila. Subsidiary routes also extended from Saigon to Haiphong and Yunnan, and from Singapore to Batavia. The whole operation was funded by the Comintern with gold dollars, Reichsmarks, Yen, and Mexican dollars to the tune of approximately £120,00–150,000 per year.[38] The goal of the FEB had been to strengthen the communist party in China for an eventual contest with the Guomindang party, and also to revitalize communist parties around Southeast Asia and to bring them more closely into line with Comintern directives. The FEB functioned fairly well until 1931, but in that year British authorities in Shanghai uncovered the network's headquarters, seized all of its top-secret files, and turned the Comintern leaders over to the Chinese authorities. This bust disrupted communist networks in the region so badly that they did not fully recover until World War II. What its existence had demonstrated, however, was an active network with an international vision, whose goal was to facilitate violent, anti-colonial communist revolution.

Although the Comintern ceased to exist during the crisis of the Second World War, anti-colonial movements based on international communism did not. After the war, however, these movements were complicated by the global politics of the Cold War, which pitted the Soviet Union against the United States (and their respective allies) in a contest for the hearts and minds of the millions of people who achieved political independence after 1945. During the Cold War, anti-colonial activists who chose to align themselves with international communism could be virtually certain of local interference by the United States or one of its anti-communist allies. What this meant was that international communism after 1945 continued to be marked by trans-regional alliances and both covert and overt international aid as the two superpowers fought for global dominance using local proxies. This was true no matter where these struggles took place, whether in Korea, Cuba, Indochina, Indonesia, Egypt, or Mozambique, to name only a few. Here, we use the example of Angola to demonstrate the ways a local communist anti-colonial movement could become enmeshed in a complex web of international aid and interference during the Cold War. In addition, Angola is instructive for demonstrating that in the context of the Cold War, local struggles between communism and anti-communism sometimes extended well past independence.

Portuguese involvement in Angola went back as far as the sixteenth century, but it was only in 1891 that the boundaries of the colony were delineated and recognized by the European powers. Nearly four decades later, in 1930, the resource-poor state of Portugal passed the Colonial Act that made all of the Portuguese colonies—including Angola—provinces integral to the Portuguese state. However, Angola itself only really became profitable to Portugal in the years just after World War II, when it became clear the colony was rich in diamonds, iron, and copper, and that its soil and climate were good for growing cash crops like cotton and coffee. It was at this point that large numbers of Portuguese settlers began to move to Angola to seek their fortunes, with the result that the colony soon became the second largest settler colony in Africa after South Africa. Yet the influx of settlers after 1945 also increased tensions between the Portuguese and the Africans and mixed-race peoples already living there, particularly because the new settlers fostered a culture of increased racism against non-Europeans.[39]

Tensions came to a head by 1960 for several reasons. For one thing, given the importance of Angola to the Portuguese economy, the Portuguese government had made it clear that it was in no way amenable to Angola moving toward independence. At the same time, other sub-Saharan African colonies claimed by Britain and France were in the process of decolonizing, making Portugal's reluctance to follow suit that much more frustrating to the growing number of anti-colonial activists who advocated independence. Moreover, anti-colonial activists already chafing under a regime that sponsored increased racism reacted with outrage to the Sharpeville massacre (March 21, 1960) against unarmed African protesters in neighboring South Africa, pointing to the killings as yet another example of colonial brutality against Africans.[40]

In 1961, these tensions resulted in widespread rebellion against Portuguese rule, igniting a colonial war that lasted thirteen years. Once the war broke out, however, it quickly became clear that Angolans fighting for independence were not united. Rather, the anti-colonial struggle coalesced into three separate, and competing, movements: the Movimento Popular de Libertação de Angola (MPLA), the União Nacional para a Independência Total de Angola (UNITA), and the Frente Nacional de Libertação de Angola (FNLA). While each of these groups supported armed guerrilla forces and shared an authoritarian style of leadership, the ideology of the MPLA leadership was the most radical and internationalist of the three. Most of its support initially came from *mesticos* (mixed-race peoples) and *assimilados* (Africans who had adopted Portuguese language and culture) who lived in the urban areas in and around the Angolan capital of Luanda.[41] Early members of the MPLA had been inspired by the pan-African movement that developed in the early twentieth century, and aligned themselves with men like Leopold Senghor who saw beauty and power in black African culture. By 1960, the MPLA leadership also identified with the tenets of Marxism, and because of this had strong links to both the Portuguese Communist Party and, through it, to the Soviet Communist Party. As a result of these alignments, the MPLA professed itself to be not only for independence in Angola, but to be against imperialism and capitalism everywhere. Moreover, it declared its policies to be anti-racist, anti-tribalist, and in favor of gender equality.[42]

Because of its connections to communism, the MPLA became a target for the Portuguese secret police in Angola, and many of its members were either arrested or killed during the period of the colonial war. But also because of its connections to communism, the MPLA drew sympathy from the Soviet Union and other communist states. Conscious of the possibility of being used as pawns in the global Cold War, however, during the 1960s the MPLA tried to maintain distance between itself and the Soviet Union, and chose instead to pursue the friendliest relations with minor communist states like

Yugoslavia and Cuba. As part of these friendly relations, Cuba's Che Guevara traveled to Angola in the mid-1960s to train MPLA guerilla troops, and Castro's government-sponsored Angolan students to travel to Cuba to receive education and military training. Perhaps not surprisingly, the MPLA's friendly relations with communist states made both UNITA and the FNLA targets for outside assistance by the enemies of communism, which in this case included especially the United States and South Africa.

After thirteen years of brutal fighting, the colonial war came to an abrupt and sudden end in 1974. In that year, Portugal's authoritarian government was overthrown in a bloodless coup known as the Carnation Revolution, and was replaced by a democratic government that sought an immediate end to its colonial wars. Three months after coming to power, the new Portuguese government signed a cease-fire in Angola that stipulated a temporary power-sharing arrangement between all three rival groups, which would remain in place until official Angolan independence was declared in November, 1975. But the power-sharing agreement did not last: instead, it dissolved into civil war in the spring of 1975 as the MPLA, UNITA, and the FNLA each sought to gain sole control of the country.[43]

It was at this point that the MPLA's links to communism drew the most concentrated attention from the international community, as each "side" in the Cold War saw an opportunity to determine the ideological allegiance of the new Angolan state. In the summer of 1975, both the United States and the South African government sent weapons and advisors to support UNITA and the FNLA against the MPLA for precisely this reason. For the United States, victory for UNITA and the FNLA would mean a defeat for the Soviet Union, which it believed was the main support behind the MPLA. For South Africa, the desire to crush the MPLA stemmed from its communist-inspired anti-racism, which had made it an outspoken opponent of South Africa's apartheid regime. Faced with US and South African support for its rivals, the MPLA responded by asking Cuba, its long-time supporter during the colonial war, for help: Fidel Castro answered by sending Cuban military advisors to the MPLA in July 1975. In response, the United States government urged the South African government to take direct military action to defeat the MPLA once and for all. Accordingly, in October 1975 South African troops invaded Angola and set off toward capturing the MPLA's strongholds around the capital at Luanda.[44]

The invasion by South African troops would likely have resulted in the defeat of the MPLA if Castro had not decided—against the wishes of Leonid Brezhnev in the Soviet Union—to send Cuban troops to the area. Between November 1975 and April 1976, 36,000 Cuban troops arrived in Angola to fight alongside the MPLA. The result, by mid-1976, was the defeat of South African forces and the assumption of control by the MPLA leadership—a feat that had only been possible with Cuba's support.[45]

Yet even once the MPLA had assumed control of the government in a now-independent Angola, the global context of the Cold War meant that the local politics of the new state were still matters of international concern. Thus, even after the decisive defeat of South African troops in Angola in 1976, the South African government's antipathy to the MPLA led it to continue to provide weapons and training to UNITA until 2002—which in turn allowed the civil war to continue unchecked. The ongoing threat from UNITA and South Africa also kept both the Cubans and the Soviets engaged in Angola as well: by 1991, when Cuban forces withdrew from Angola once and for all, more than 400,000 Cuban soldiers and 50,000 Cuban civilians had served in the country to help keep the MPLA in power. Not only that, although the Soviet Union had initially been reluctant to provide aid to the MPLA in 1975, Castro eventually succeeded in convincing the Soviet leadership to provide the financial aid and materials necessary for maintaining such a large presence in Angola.[46]

The point of exploring the Angolan example is that—like the other anti-colonial movements discussed above—it was clearly and from the outset based on the premise that national independence was compatible with strong commitments to, and massive support from, the international communist community. In the context of the Cold War, however, Angola also illustrates the extremely high cost of such an international vision—since involving

FIGURE 2.4 *Some young people stand on voting day at the Boa Vista slum, in the outskirts of Luanda, on August 31, 2012. At issue in this election was the promise of the ruling Popular Movement for the Liberation of Angola party (MPLA), which has been in power since independence 37 years ago, to rebuild the country after the destruction that accompanied the civil war that ended in 2002. AFP Photo / Stephane de Sakutin.*

communist states guaranteed interference by the United States and its anti-communist allies. By the 1990s, the civil war had resulted in massive destruction to the land and infrastructure in Angola, and a half million dead.[47]

Moreover, in the midst of the constant violence of the civil war, the internationalist, anti-racist, and anti-tribalist vision of the MPLA's original leadership did not stop its armed forces from committing brutalities against its perceived enemies. Finally, as in East Asia, the MPLA's commitment to gender equality did not eliminate or solve longstanding patriarchal traditions that saw household labor as the female domain, making it difficult for the MPLA leadership to fully accept women's roles as equals in the struggle for independence. Indeed, despite the fact that the MPLA set up the Organization for African Women in 1962 specifically in order to facilitate women's liberation, MPLA leadership continued to emphasize the importance of women in the armed struggle either as supporters of fighting men or as victims of brutality.[48] Thanks to the politics of the Cold War, the vision that MPLA leaders once had of an international community of communist solidarity and aid, had ended instead in the virtual destruction of the country.

Conclusion

Taken together, the examples of Ghadar, pan-Islam, and international communism demonstrate that anti-colonial movements took many forms beyond the constitutional nationalist movements routinely featured in histories of imperialism and decolonization. Although some of the activists involved in all three movements certainly sought national independence, they did so within a framework that explicitly relied on global networks or trans-regional ideologies to effect that independence. In addition, many of these activists imagined independence not simply within the borders outlined for them by the colonial state, but as a set of relationships defined by religious belief or by commitment to class solidarity. Their commitment to these trans-colonial, even global relationships—not to mention their mobility and contact with people from distant areas—also allowed them to envision colonialism as a worldwide problem that needed to be wiped out everywhere. In other words, the disruption they sought was intended not only for one single colony, but for the oppressed and colonized around the world.

Suggestions for further reading

Aydin, Cemil. *The Politics of Anti-Westernism in Asia: Visions of World Order in Pan-Islamic and Pan-Asian Thought*. New York: Columbia University Press, 2007.

Bose, Sugata. *A Hundred Horizons the Indian Ocean in the Age of Global Empire*. Cambridge, MA: Harvard University Press, 2006.

Gleijeses, Piero. *Visions of Freedom: Havana, Washington, Pretoria, and the Struggle for Southern Africa, 1976–1991*. Chapel Hill, NC: University of North Carolina Press, 2013.

Hanioğlu, M. Şükrü. *A Brief History of the Late Ottoman Empire*. Princeton, NJ: Princeton University Press, 2008.

Hatsky, Christine and Mair Edmunds-Harrington, *Cubans in Angola: South-South Cooperation and Transfer of Knowledge, 1976–1991*. Madison: University of Wisconsin Press, 2015.

McDermott, Kevin. *The Comintern: A History of International Communism from Lenin to Stalin*. New York: St. Martin's Press, 1997.

Ramnath, Maia. *Haj to Utopia: How the Ghadar Movement Charted Global Radicalism and Attempted to Overthrow the British Empire*. Berkeley: University of California Press, 2011.

Reynolds, Jonathan. *Sovereignty and Struggle: Africa and Africans in the Era of the Cold War, 1945–1994*. New York: Oxford University Press, 2015.

Sareen, T. R. *Select Documents on the Ghadr Party*. New Delhi: Mounto Publishing House, 1994.

Tagliacozzo, Eric. *The Longest Journey: Southeast Asians and the Pilgrimage to Mecca*. Oxford: Oxford University Press, 2013.

Notes

1 This is the subject of Henrik Chetan Aspengren's "Indian Revolutionaries Abroad: Revisiting Their Silent Moments," *Journal of Colonialism and Colonial History* 15:3 (Winter 2014).

2 Harish K. Puri, *Ghadar Movement: Ideology, Organization, and Strategy*, 2nd edition (Amritsar: Guru Nanak Dev University, 1993), 15.

3 Enakshi Dua discusses this is the context of Canada in "Racialising Imperial Canada: Indian Women and the Making of Ethnic Communities," in *Gender, Sexuality, and Colonial Modernities*, ed. Antoinette Burton (London and New York: Routledge, 1999), 123.

4 Taraknath Das, *The Hindustanee*, April 1, 1914. Quoted in Enakshi Dua, "Racialising Imperial Canada," 127.

5 T. R. Sareen, *Select Documents on the Ghadar Party* (New Delhi: Mounto Publishing House, 1994), 84.

6 Maia Ramnath, *Haj to Utopia: How the Ghadar Movement Charted Global Radicalism and Attempted to Overthrow the British Empire* (Berkeley: University of California Press, 2011), 46.

7 Richard Popplewell, "The Surveillance of Indian 'Seditionists' in North America, 1905–1915," in *Intelligence And International Relations, 1900–1945*, ed. Richard Popplewell, Christopher Andrew, and Jeremy Noakes (Liverpool: Liverpool University Press, 1987), 62, 65, 69.

8 Claude Markovits, *The Global World of Indian Merchants, 1750–1947: Traders of Sind from Bukhara to Panama* (Cambridge: Cambridge University Press, 2000), 224–225.

9   Kris Manjapra, "The Illusions of Encounter: Muslim 'Minds' and Hindu Revolutionaries in First World War Germany and After," *Journal of Global History* 1 (2006), 372; Ramnath, *Haj to Utopia*, 73.

10 T. R. Sareen, *Select Documents on the Ghadr Party* (New Delhi: Mounto Publishing House, 1994), 85.

11 Ramnath, *Haj to Utopia*, 55.

12 Kees Van Dijk, *The Netherlands Indies and the Great War, 1914–1918* (Leiden: KITLV Press, 2007), 334; Earl E. Sperry and Willis M. West, *German Plots and Intrigues in the United States During the Period of Our Neutrality* (Kessinger Publishing, 2010, originally published 1918).

13 Ramnath, *Haj to Utopia*, 51–52, 56.

14 Seema Sohi, *Echoes of Mutiny: Race, Surveillance, and Indian Anticolonialism in North America* (Oxford: Oxford University Press, 2014), 178, 195; Ramnath, *Haj to Utopia*, 60.

15 For this kind of Indian international anti-colonialism prior to 1914, see Harald Fischer-Tiné, "Indian Nationalism and the 'world Forces': Transnational and Diasporic Dimensions of the Indian Freedom Movement on the Eve of the First World War," *Journal of Global History* 2:3 (2007).

16 Chiara Formichi, "Pan-Islam and Religious Nationalism: The Case of Kartosuwiryo and Negara Islam Indonesia," *Indonesia* no. 90 (October 2010), 125.

17 Rebecca E. Karl, "Creating Asia: China in the World at the Beginning of the Twentieth Century," *American Historical Review* 103:4 (October 1998), 1114.

18 For a good overview of pan-movements and their relationship to nationalism, see Cemil Aydin, "Pan-Nationalism of Pan-Islamic, Pan-Asian, and Pan-African Thought," in *The Oxford Handbook of the History of Nationalism*, ed. John Breuilly (Oxford: Oxford University Press, 2013).

19 Minkah Makalani explores radical Pan-Africanism in the United States in the early twentieth century in chapter 2 of *In the Cause of Freedom: Radical Black Internationalism from Harlem to London, 1917–1939* (Chapel Hill: University of North Carolina Press, 2011).

20 For more on pan-Africanism, see Toyin Falola and Kwame Essien, eds, *Pan-Africanism and the Politics of African Citizenship and Identity* (London: Routledge, 2013).

21 For versions of pan-Asianism not only dominated by the Japanese vision, see Prasenjit Duara, "The Discourse of Civilization and Pan-Asianism," *Journal of World History* 12:1 (2001); Carolien Stolte and Harald Fischer-Tiné, "Imagining Asia in India: Nationalism and Internationalism (ca. 1905–1940)," *Comparative Studies in Social History* 54:1 (January 2012); and Rebecca Karl, "Creating Asia: China in the World at the Beginning of the Twentieth Century," *American Historical Review* 104:3 (October 1998); Cemil Aydin, *The Politics of Anti-Westernism in Asia: Visions of World Order in Pan-Islamic and Pan-Asian Thought* (New York: Columbia University Press, 2007).

22 Michael Francis Laffan, *Islamic Nationhood and Colonial Indonesia*, 162; Rebecca Karl, "Creating Asia," 1111.

23 Guoqi Xu, *China and the Great War: China's Pursuit of a New National Identity and Internationalization* (New York: Cambridge University Press, 2005), 97.

24 Formichi, "Pan-Islam and Religious Nationalism," 129. The ideology of Pan-Islam offered the possibility, but not the necessity, of a common political and spiritual leadership.

25 M. Şükrü Hanioğlu, *A Brief History of the Late Ottoman Empire* (Princeton, NJ: Princeton University Press, 2008), 130; Anthony Reid, "Nineteenth Century Pan-Islam in Indonesia and Malaysia," *The Journal of Asian Studies* 26:2 (n.d.), 279.

26 Michael Laffan, "'Another Andalusia': Images of Colonial Southeast Asia in Arabic Newspapers," *The Journal of Asian Studies* 66:3 (2007), 703.

27 Fritz Schulze and Holger Warnk, *Insular Southeast Asia: Linguistic and Cultural Studies in Honour of Bernd Nothofer* (Wiesbaden: Harrassowitz, 2006), 141; Eric Tagliacozzo, *The Longest Journey: Southeast Asians and the Pilgrimage to Mecca* (Oxford: Oxford University Press, 2013),181.

28 Christopher Low, "Empire and the Hajj: Pilgrims, Plagues, and Pan-Islam Under British Surveillance, 1865–1908," *International Journal of Middle East Studies* 40:2 (2008), 279; Sugata Bose, *A Hundred Horizons the Indian Ocean in the Age of Global Empire* (Cambridge, MA: Cambridge, Mass: Harvard University Press, 2006), 195.

29 M. C. Ricklefs, "The Middle East Connection and Reform and Revival Movements Among the Putihan in 19th Century Java," in *Southeast Asia and the Middle East: Islam, Movement, and the Longue Duree*, ed. Eric Tagliacozzo (Stanford: Stanford University Press, 2009), 125.

30 Cemil Aydin, *The Politics of Anti-Westernism in Asia*, 94, 110. Text of the fatwa taken from *Source Records of the Great War, Vol. III*, ed. Charles F. Horne, *National Alumni 1923*. http://www.firstworldwar.com/source/ottoman_fetva.htm.

31 Puri, *Ghadar Movement: Ideology, Organisation, and Strategy* (Amritsar: Guru Nanak Dev University Press, 1993), 110.

32 Richard Standish Fogarty, *Race and War in France: Colonial Subjects in the French Army, 1914–1918* (Baltimore: Johns Hopkins University Press, 2013), 170.

33 Fogarty, *Race and War in France*, 199.

34 Sophie Quinn-Judge, *Ho Chi Minh: The Missing Years, 1919–1941* (Berkeley, CA: University of California Press, 2002), 45, 47–48.

35 Heather Streets-Salter, "The Noulens Affair in East and Southeast Asia: International Communism in the Interwar Period," *Journal of American-East Asian Relations* 21:4 (2014), 394–414.

36 Joachim C. Häberlen, "Between Global Aspirations and Local Realities: The Global Dimensions of Interwar Communism," *Journal of Global History* 7:3 (2012), 433.

37 Sophie Quinn-Judge has done some important work on women in communist networks: see her "Women in the Early Vietnamese Communist Movement: Sex, Lies, and Liberation," *Southeast Asia Research* 9:3 (2001).

38 The Noulens Case uncensored report, FO 1093/92. The National Archives, Kew, 1932, 16, 17, 5.

39 Christine Hatsky and Mair Edmunds-Harrington, *Cubans in Angola: South-South Cooperation and Transfer of Knowledge, 1976–1991* (Madison: University of Wisconsin Press, 2015), 35–36.

40 Hatsky and Edmunds-Harrington, *Cubans in Angola,* 37.

41 Jonathan Reynolds, *Sovereignty and Struggle: Africa and Africans in the Era of the Cold War, 1945–1994* (New York and Oxford: Oxford University Press, 2015), 71.

42 Hatsky and Edmunds-Harrington, *Cubans in Angola,* 42–43.

43 Piero Gleijeses, *Visions of Freedom: Havana, Washington, Pretoria, and the Struggle for Southern Africa, 1976–1991* (Chapel Hill, NC: University of North Carolina Press, 2013), 28.

44 Gleijeses, *Havana, Washington, Pretoria, and the Struggle for Southern Africa,* 29.

45 Gleijeses, *Havana, Washington, Pretoria, and the Struggle for Southern Africa,* 9.

46 Hatsky and Edmunds-Harrington, *Cubans in Angola,* 49, 52, 4.

47 Reynolds, *Sovereignty and Struggle,* 72.

48 Catherine V. Scott, "'Men in Our Country Behave Like Chiefs': Women in the Angolan Revolution," in *Women and Revolution in Africa, Asia, and the New World,* ed. Mary Ann Tetrault (Columbia: University of South Carolina Press, 1994), 105; Horace G. Campbell, "Militarism, Warfare, and the Search for Peace in Angola," in *The Uncertain Promise of Southern Africa,* ed. York Bradshaw and Stephen N. Ndegwa (Bloomington: Indiana University Press, 2000), 174.

3

Insurgent Citizenships:

Armed Rebellions and Everyday Acts of Resistance in the Global South

Eileen M. Ford

History is a kind of listening for traces of other lives beneath the frequencies of the present, for the past is not just an absence; it is below us, the grounding of the now. The past reaches up from below the waves of history, telling us something again and again, if only we can hear it. But often the volume is turned too low, and those who are living are too loud. Beneath the dominant citizenship regimes of liberalism and republicanism and the noisy politics of the public sphere are hints of an alternative...[1]

For some, citizenship may seem like a straightforward concept at first glance. One thinks perhaps about the rights and obligations of those individuals defined as citizens within a particular geopolitical boundary. Yet, if we move back in time and take a global view, we see that the meanings of citizenship were never static, never fully formed but rather always in the process of being negotiated and redefined. We can consider a citizen to be someone legally recognized by a particular government and guaranteed to have certain agreed-upon rights and obligations. But who decides who is legally recognized? How have those in power used legal and extralegal tactics to deny aspects of citizenship to certain social groups and individuals? This chapter investigates the ways in which organized rebellion and informal acts of resistance represent the continuity of insurgent citizenship in world history. Viewed in this way, dissent and disruption rise to the surface in the historical narrative as the norm rather than the exceptional moments in history. We only need to find new ways of "listening for the traces of other lives beneath the frequencies of the present."

In the second half of the eighteenth century, philosophers and other intellectuals increasingly contemplated how individuals related to governing bodies and challenged ideas regarding inherited rights to rule. The American Revolution (1776), the French Revolution (1789), and the Haitian Revolution (1791), brought radical ideological challenges to hierarchical systems of authority. While an individual's claim to citizenship—predicated on political, civil and socioeconomic equality—failed to materialize in any meaningful way this early on, the conflicts inherent over access to all aspects of citizenship clearly rose to the surface in many parts of the globe, usually within the context of colonial regimes beginning in the late eighteenth and early nineteenth centuries. The ways in which colonized peoples of all sorts, indigenous groups within colonial and national regimes, and individuals from assorted social groups were deprived of full inclusion into the body politic differed tremendously. Ideas brought forth from the Enlightenment influenced many to challenge authority, but it is equally important to consider the organic beginnings of rebellion and resistance. As C. L. R. James said in his classic 1938 study of the Haitian Revolution, *The Black Jacobins*: "In a revolution, when the ceaseless slow accumulation of centuries bursts into volcanic eruption, the meteoric flares and flights above are meaningless chaos and lend themselves to infinite caprice and romanticism unless the observer sees them always as projections of the sub-soil from which they came."[2] The subsoil is constantly shifting and creating new circumstances in which resistance is sown.

Because insurgent citizenship repeatedly sprang forth in new incarnations within the same geographic locations, this chapter is principally organized in a geographic way. This way continuity over time, and to a lesser extent change, is highlighted as we witness dissent from colonized people—for example in New Spain or colonial Mexico—continue in new forms under new political regimes, in say contemporary Mexico. Thus, the major sections considered in this chapter are Latin America and the Caribbean, Asia, and Africa, a part of the world that historians sometimes refer to as the Global South. Within each section, selected specific locations follow a chronological thread wherever possible. While many of these insurgent citizenships have common ideological bases, they were oftentimes more locally or nationally contained before the twentieth century, albeit never far removed from the imprint left by colonial structures and hierarchies. As such, the last section deals with the global interconnectedness of rebellions and resistance in the twentieth century as people took advantage of the increasing flow of ideas and peoples that accompanied innovations in technology and communication to demand inclusion.

While historical narratives traditionally stress the triumph or continuity of imperial projects or of dominant groups holding power over subjugated populations, this is largely a product of how history is written by some historians rather than the actual lived historical reality experienced by individuals in the past. Partly, the dilemma lies in how rebellion is defined and by whom. What constitutes a rebellion? How is it different from a revolution? How is its success or failure measured? If we conceive of rebellion as organized armed resistance from below to authority situated above *and* individual acts of resistance and sabotage in all their varied forms, then we see that continuity of insurgent citizenship characterizes the historical narrative in the modern era. As such, rebellion is never complete, always changing shape, and ever present in everyday actions: they exist alongside organized armed insurrections more readily identifiable as threatening to those in the dominant position of power. Throughout the period under consideration, from the mid-eighteenth century to the present, rebellions and acts of resistance characterized the lives of people in the Global South and beyond. Although the form that resistance took varied, the intention was the same: to exert control over their own lives and to challenge economic, social, or political oppression. Rebellion involved taking up arms and violent protests as well as less obvious forms of resistance like sabotage, foot-dragging or using the written word or peaceful protest as a means of contestation. While it may be more difficult to find the archival evidence of these less dramatic acts to flesh out their meanings, it is the job of the professional historian to locate the everyday voices of protest. From these multifaceted acts of rebellion and resistance to oppression the student of history can locate commonalities. Ultimately, these acts of rebellion constituted ways of laying claim to modern citizenship.

Scholars studying oppressed groups have often invoked the work of Haitian American anthropologist Michel-Rolph Trouillot and his discussion of how voices are silenced in the historical narrative.[3] According to Trouillot:

> any historical narrative is a particular bundle of silences. . . . Silences enter the process of historical production at four crucial moments: the moment of fact creation (the making of sources); the moment of fact assembly (the making of archives); the moment of fact retrieval (the making of narratives); and the moment of retrospective significance (the making of history in the final instance).[4]

In addition to these acts of silencing at work in the archive and written historical narratives, individuals experienced degrees of dependency within a complex web of unequal relations of power, oftentimes compounding the difficulties they faced in rebelling or laying claim to their rights.

The definition of citizenship and the ways in which rights associated with it are denied have historically been inscribed on the physical body of the globe's inhabitants. In her study of post-emancipation Jamaica and Haiti, Mimi Sheller argues: "When slavery ended, techniques and practices of sexual domination and biopolitical power remained entrenched. Violence against the body continued to be exercised in corporeal forms of private and public embodiment that reproduced racial, gender, sexual, and class hierarchies."[5] Perhaps it should come as no surprise that the legacies of slavery and oppression continued after emancipation. Yet, it is important to note that individuals continued to exist within a framework that limited their choices and made them define themselves in opposition to others more subjugated than they. Indeed, she argues "to act and make claims as a free citizen, political subjects must first position themselves as raced, gendered, national, and sexual subjects of particular kinds (i.e., as free men, or heads of patriarchal families, or good mothers, or British subjects, or loyal soldiers) in discursive performances that always rest on the exclusion or repulsion of others."[6] Forged in the crucible of slavery and emancipation, the process of claiming modern citizenship often meant denying that very right to others.

If we look at citizenship in the context of many locales around the world, we see that the meanings of the word on the ground look quite different from the idealized notion. For example, in her study of 1990s Ethiopia, where ethnic and linguistic divisions and gender inequality prevail, Lahra Smith uses the term "meaningful citizenship" as "recognition, participation, and, centrally, equality of lived experience."[7] That "equality of lived experience" has proven most elusive in the context of world history across time and space. This chapter considers not just the desires of individuals to have full political recognition and rights, but also the collective desire articulated by social movements for the right to live with access to basic human needs like food and shelter: the right to live like a human being, in short.

Just as a precise definition of insurgent citizenship matters, so too does the identification of its location across the globe. The chapter design purposefully privileges the examination of insurgent citizenships in areas outside of Europe and the United States. To be sure, contestation and resistance abound in the historical record for these regions. We could consider, for example, struggles over citizenship in the United States during the early Republic or in France in the wake of its much studied 1789 Revolution. But what if we focus instead on events that transpired in the same period, the "Age of Revolutions" in the Caribbean island of Saint Dominique? How does the location under examination change the way we conceive of citizenship? Similarly, we could analyze acts of rebellion like the well-known 1831 Nat Turner Slave Revolt in Southampton County, Virginia, where slaves killed approximately 60 whites and Turner eluded capture for months. We would find that Southern whites lived in fear of slave insurrections and that enslaved persons often fled the horrific conditions of plantation life. Indeed, between 1790 and 1860, white masters published approximately 8,400 newspaper advertisements seeking the return of runaway slaves in five southern US states, frequently offering hefty sums for their return. Upon further investigation, we might discover how one former slave, Joseph Taper, escaped to Canada and in 1840 reported that he was "in the land of liberty" and "enjoyed more pleasure with one month here than in all my life in the land of bondage."[8] Students of history will find ample evidence of resistance and rebellion in Europe and the United States in their recent textbooks. They are less likely to be familiar with, for example, the 1835 Bahian Slave Revolt in Brazil, which is covered in depth later in this chapter. Instead of examining the notorious 1886 Hay Market Riot in Chicago and its legacy for the international labor movement, what if we examine protests and efforts to gain control over one's labor in non-Western cities and rural areas? Looking at student protest movements like the New Culture Movement in China (1915–21) or the Kinshasa Student Circle in Congo-Zaire (1969–71) rather than say, the well-documented Berkeley or Paris student demonstrations in 1968, similarly challenges longstanding associations of "modern" citizenship with US or European models. Because the writing of history often locates insurgent citizenship in the context of the West, this chapter takes a view from the Global South in an effort to disrupt this notion.

Latin America and the Caribbean: Slaves revolt, prostitutes rally, and mothers rebel

It always amuses me that the biggest praise for my work comes for the imagination, while the truth is that there's not a single line in all my work that does not have a basis in reality. The problem is that Caribbean reality resembles the wildest imagination.

GABRIEL GARCÍA MÁRQUEZ

Colombian-born, Nobel Prize-winning author Gabriel García Márquez (1927–2014) was perhaps the most famous Latin American writer of the twentieth century. His 1967 masterpiece *One Hundred Years of Solitude* presents the reader with a poetic and devastating portrait of the continuity of violence and exploitation the region has faced since the time of the Spanish conquest. In this section, cycles of violence and oppression recur while indigenous people, enslaved persons, women, and later dispossessed urban dwellers form the focus of our actors contesting their exclusion from political participation and "meaningful citizenship" in Latin America and the Caribbean, a region that suffered at the hands of many imperial powers and modern day exploiters. We turn now to one of the most important revolutions in the modern era, the Haitian Revolution of 1791.

The events that transpired in the French colony of Saint Dominique during the 1790s through the first years of the nineteenth century can be analyzed within nested layers of developments. The 1791 Caribbean slave uprising and subsequent movement for an independent nation of Haiti separated from the French metropole represented a complex interplay between local conditions and sweeping changes in ideologies regarding the rights of man and the types of political organization and governance. Envisioning this historical moment through the metaphor of today's Google Earth Satellite Map feature—or different size lenses on a camera—to view the historical problem at hand allows for a glimpse into these nested layers of developments. We first hone in on a small location and then gradually zoom out, stopping to view from increasingly broader perspectives until we finally are able to see the transatlantic connections and reverberations across the Western Hemisphere of the 1791 slave insurrection.

The first images would be of a specific sugar plantation in Saint Dominique where the observer would see its enormous and brutal slave plantation system. Here humans from Africa or creole slaves born in the Americas were literally worked to death harvesting and processing sugarcane for exportation to the mother country of France. We would see and consider, and be puzzled by, the complex race relations in a system of slavery where overseers negotiated the "in between position" with whites or free people of color and then their enslaved charges of African descent. The problem was not simply black versus white or enslaved versus free but a more complex one. Next, we might zoom out from the plantation itself to see economic and political relations, exemplified by the local and absentee planter class, wealthy Frenchmen making their fortunes in an imperial system designed to extract wealth, as all colonial projects were designed to do. The third time we would zoom out further still to witness the relations of Empire: the metropole of France and its complex system of colonial holdings, Saint Dominique being but one, albeit the most lucrative one. On the eve of the revolution, the island produced the most sugar and coffee in the world and was "the centerpiece of the Atlantic slave system."[9] Lastly, we would pull the perspective out as far as possible, hovering over the Atlantic world and its system of exchange between colonial powers (mostly the Spanish, the French, the British, the Dutch, and the Portuguese), colonies, and diverse regions of Africa. Products, ideas, and, of course, people moving about, back and forth across the Atlantic for consumption and exploitation. An estimated 850,000 to 1 million slaves were forcibly brought to the island of Saint Dominique, accounting for roughly 10 percent of the total Atlantic world slave trade. The complex layers of economic and political systems of oppression continued to influence the lives of inhabitants even after legal conditions changed. At the end of the eighteenth and beginning of the nineteenth centuries, colonial powers in Latin America and the Caribbean lost their hold over their territorial possessions, sometimes explosively, sometimes gradually. In some cases, indigenous groups rebelled continuously.

In what is now northwest Mexico, indigenous groups frequently rebelled against Spanish colonial authorities and later, against the Mexican nation, which had formed officially in 1821 after three centuries of colonial rule. Prominent among these groups were the Yaqui. Segregated into Jesuit missions in the early colonial period, the Yaqui ironically developed a strengthened identity and autonomy under this system of attempted religious conversion and economic exploitation. While *mestizaje,* or racial mixing, was prevalent in New Spain over the colonial period, some indigenous groups like the Yaqui remained more isolated and maintained a strong ethnic identity. Having first rebelled against the Spanish in 1740, they waged a serious campaign against the Mexican federal government between 1826 and 1833, which historian Evelyn Hu-DeHart called "just the beginning of a century-long Yaqui struggle against loss of land and autonomy." State and federal governments struggled to control the Yaqui rebellion, repeatedly offering amnesty for Yaqui rebels in hopes of ending it. Indeed the government forces had their hands full with the Yaqui and the Apache raids in the north of the current day state of Sonora. The captain general of the Yaqui, Banderas, was captured in December 1832 and sentenced to death the following month, along with a rebel leader from the Opata group named Dolores Gutiérrez. The Mexican government sought to differentiate non-rebels from rebels by issuing passports to Yaqui laborers, a tactic that failed miserably as laborers and rebels frequently changed roles. Colonial and national governments often set limits on freedom by restricting and/or monitoring the physical mobility of their subjects.[10]

From the 1830s to the 1870s, the Yaqui were able to wield political power in their home state and negotiate their own terms. In 1875, the Yaqui nation declared itself independent from Mexico. A new, armed crisis erupted in 1881. An embarrassing defeat of government forces led to the federal troops exiling Governor Ortiz to the United States. By 1885, after a failed assassination attempt of the Yaqui leader, Cajemé, tensions rose. President Porfirio Díaz authorized a formal campaign against them on March 31, 1885.[11] After suffering a crushing military defeat and capture and execution of their leader Cajemé, the Yaqui switched tactics and began a long campaign of guerilla warfare.

For enslaved persons in the Global South, citizenship remained an impossibility due to their status as property, yet their resistance often bore the mark of incipient claims to citizenship. As such, the earliest acts of rebellion for Afro-Brazilians were slave rebellions. For example, between 1807 and 1835, there were multiple slave uprisings in Bahia, a sugar-producing region of colonial Brazil with a large slave population. In 1824, population estimates for Bahia reveal that the vast majority of inhabitants were slaves or free blacks: over 60 percent slaves, about 15 percent mulattoes and free blacks, and 22 percent whites. Most slaves in Bahia by the 1830s were African-born and many were from the same ethnic group; most were Muslims. Most African-Brazilians and Afro-Brazilians were male, which prevented the development of a slave family and, according to historian João José Reis, increased the possibility of revolts as many would have been unwilling to risk retribution on their families if they had them. On January 24, 1835, a *malê* or Muslim revolt erupted in Salvador do Bahia. The rebels intended to begin the revolt at dawn on January 25, but a freed Nago woman informed officials of their plot the day before. When soldiers searched the suspected house, about 60 rebels fled, shooting at them as they shouted "kill the soldiers" and later in the streets of Salvador "Long live the Nago." Participants in the revolt were Muslim slaves and freedmen; many had Muslim charms around their necks and carried books or notes written in Arabic. As with many oppressed groups, particularly slave populations, religion and shared culture provided fertile ground for rebellions. Five rebels met their death in front of the firing squad and many received harsh punishments of 600 lashes.[12] Even the most oppressed groups contested their exclusion by those above them in the social hierarchy.

The rebellion of 1835 should have come as little surprise to the free population in the region. Evidence points to the Portuguese colonists' longstanding fears of an uprising and, perhaps more importantly, to the interconnectedness of revolts in the Atlantic world. In 1814, local merchants and citizens from Bahia sent a petition to the prince regent Dom João communicating the fears they had about the behavior of black slaves and organized uprisings. They reported:

> Gatherings of blacks can be seen at night in the streets as before, conversing in their language and saying whatever they like, and with constant whistling and other signals. They are so impertinent that even in our language [Portuguese] they blurt out their reasons for putting off the day of their planned revolt. They know about and discuss the disastrous occurrences that took place on the Island of Saint Dominique, and one hears mutinous claims that by St. John's Day there will not be one white or mulatto alive.[13]

Slaves in the northeast of Brazil possessed intimate knowledge of the 1791 revolt in Saint Dominique and used it to their advantage in intimidating whites in the area.[14]

Slaves also ran away to form separatist communities, known as *quilombos* or *mocambos*, where they lived away from the horrors of slavery, often aided by the rugged terrain's ability to make their discovery extremely difficult. Throughout the nineteenth century but especially in the 1850s, 1860s, and 1870s, numerous campaigns were launched in Maranhão, Brazil to track down and destroy *mocambos* and arrest their inhabitants, known as *quilombolas* or *mocambeiros*. As Flávio dos Santos Gomes has shown, these were "genuine peasant communities—some with more than 600 inhabitants—and a developed commercial network combining the production and commercialization of manioc flour and gold extraction."[15]

One of the most interesting facets of these communities is that they relied upon extensive social and economic networks with local merchants, slaves, indigenous groups and, at times, slave plantation owners. That is, their existence lays bare the cooperation and negotiation with individuals inherently threatened by their very presence. Even when authorities successfully destroyed and burned some *mocambos*, individuals often eluded capture and found refuge in neighboring slave quarters only to redouble their efforts and form new, or join established, maroon communities. On April 7, 1843, the Maranhão police chief José Mariani wrote:

> In the agricultural plantations the disgrace is greater. The slaves steal cotton from the planters and go sell it either to the peddlers or neighboring landowners. Generally landowners buy the stolen cotton from the slaves of their neighbors, pretending that it came from the provision grounds of the sellers or that they had purchased it. Also, it is almost general that they give shelter to one another's fugitive slaves, enjoying the benefits of the service they give in exchange for food and the promise of purchase or protection.[16]

Mocambeiros sometimes forced reluctant plantation owners into cooperating with their communities economically by conducting raids as retaliation for prior refusals to trade with or assist them. One official complained in 1862 that *mocambeiros* could sometimes be seen in broad daylight moving freely between plantations without reprisal. The importance of these former runaway slave communities continues to cause political debates in Brazil, as article 68 of the 1988 Federal Constitution guaranteed the right to these lands for descendants of the *quilombos*.[17] Nevertheless, many in Brazil still fight for basic citizenship rights.

In the twentieth century, the urban poor in the Brazilian megacity Rio de Janeiro also experienced exclusion from full citizenship rights. Historian Brodwyn Fischer examines citizenship during and after the rule of Getúlio Vargas and finds that while the era witnessed expansion of citizenship rights for workers,

> that citizenship mostly excluded rural people, and it extended only partially to the urban poor, thus also helping to create an urban underclass whose position in Brazilian society was often akin to that of undocumented immigrants: people for whom neither economic prosperity nor citizenship was fully attainable, who built their lives with a patchwork of scanty rights and hard-won tolerance, and whose access to theoretically public benefits and guarantees was scarce or nonexistent.[18]

The area where the urban poor most visibly fought for their citizenship rights and sometimes won was in carving out tiny pieces of land for their existence in the form of *favelas* or shantytowns. "Informal communities wrote letters to the full gamut of local and national politicians, courted the press, demonstrated publicly, and openly confronted police and judicial officials sent to enforce court decrees." Residents of *favelas* were quick to appeal to the press and journalists often reported their hardships in Rio de Janeiro's newspapers. For example, in 1948, an elderly rural migrant named Fernando Rosa de Silva complained to a reporter about mass evictions:

> They want to beautify the city at our expense. So our lives and work mean nothing. And the children that I gave the fatherland. And the right to live in peace? We helped to make this great city. We constructed the skyscrapers, the *palacetes*, and they don't even want to allow us to live in the wretched cardboard shacks we live in. But, Mr. Reporter, you can write in your paper: I will only leave my home dead. I couldn't continue living after being expelled from my own house, I wouldn't even have anyplace to go. I am 68 well-lived years old. I worked like a slave. I came from the countryside fed up with exploitation, and I am not going back there as an old man.[19]

Making reference to slavery was not at all uncommon in *favela* dwellers' complaints to officials and the press. An 88-year-old woman living in a different *favela* in the same city said of herself: "Josefa is not the one who is going to be anyone's slave in the fields. Josefa is poor, but she has shame and dignity, son."[20] Although legal protection was often denied these mid-century *favela* dwellers, most "remained in place, never enjoying real security, but at least anchored to the city by the combined weight of community resistance, populist politics, and scarcely viable alternatives."[21]

Women, politically disenfranchised in much of Latin America until the mid-twentieth century, often used creative tactics to demand justice or to exercise their rights as citizens. Yet they were never far from the political foray, and often incorporated contemporary political debates and rhetoric into their actions. While Mexico's 1910 Revolution has been studied and written about extensively, the effects of the social revolution that occurred in the 1920s and 1930s and its effects on women and later students have been less well documented until recently. Historian Andrew Grant Wood maintains: "countless women and men took an active role in reshaping Mexican political culture as they became emboldened by revolutionary rhetoric informing them of their newfound rights as citizens (articulated in the Constitution of 1917) as well as a variety of international events that were interpreted by many as a cause to work for social justice." His research on the port city of Veracruz, where poor living conditions in working-class tenements in combination with rising rents led a group of prostitutes to "launch a citywide rent boycott" in 1922, gives credence to this claim. The women attempted to start a large bonfire of furniture and other goods in the streets and with the assistance of the newly formed Sindicato Revolucionario de Inquilinos (Revolutionary Syndicate of Tenants), persuaded the city to boycott the squalid living conditions and high rents by refusing to pay their landlords. That over half of residents heeded this call and that it spread to other cities in Mexico is a testament to its success. The strike led to pitched battles in the street with the military, jail terms for some of the syndicate's leadership, and continued coverage in the press until the strike ended in 1927. That women, deprived of formal political participation in the electoral process, led this strike speaks to the importance of re-examining what constitutes claims to citizenship. As Wood phrases it: "The fundamental influence of gender identity combined with new ideas regarding citizen rights in a powerful way in many urban popular neighborhoods throughout Mexico during the social revolution."[22]

Similarly, Katherine Bliss's work on syphilitic prostitutes quarantined in the Hospital Morelos in Mexico City during the same decade reveals a parallel use of the revolutionary language of citizenship. Part of the postrevolutionary reform project of the 1920s involved the use of scientific approaches to cleansing and maintaining the body politic. Increasing state power translated into regulations aimed at punishing and rehabilitating those groups deemed dangerous by governing elite and social reformers alike. Prostitutes were one such group and they were held against their will and without their children in a special hospital. On September 8, 1926, a group of five women (collectively signed as "Women without a Home") wrote to the president of Mexico asking for assistance using their newfound politicized language and a strategy of maternalism. They wrote:

> To you, Citizen President, as an honorable and just man, we acclaim, asking you for justice, which we hope you will give to us, ordering immediately the attention which we ask for our children, in fulfillment of the attentions which are necessary for every innocent child; and we sincerely beg of you that you give us facilities necessary for the unfortunate women who by disgrace have fallen by the wayside without being able to care for our necessities. We make this complaint known to the Citizen President of the Superior Council of Health by sending him a copy, so that he may be informed of our petition, and consult with you. We ask for your attention for the most just and sincere reasons, due to an unbearable suffering, invoking at the same time the principles of the Revolution, and asking for respect for the liberties of the same.[23]

Despite being marginalized by reformers, politicians, doctors, and society more generally, sex workers used what power they had to protest their exclusion from the benefits of full citizenship. In the context of reform and public health initiatives, doctors often classified women, especially prostitutes, housed in La Castañeda mental institution in early twentieth-century Mexico City as "morally insane" because of their failure to uphold societal norms regarding appropriate femininity and sexual propriety. According to historian Cristina Rivera Garza, "Sexual practices deemed as deviant constituted by far the trademark of women suffering from moral insanity."[24] Even before the Mexican Revolution, prostitutes in Oaxaca City protested informally before the offices of a Catholic women's lay organization that had publicly attacked and shamed legal prostitutes in the local press, thus laying claim to their right to work unencumbered.[25] In twentieth-century Latin America, women often used their power as women to contest oppression from above in many contexts. As the century progressed, many countries in the region, including Brazil, Argentina, Chile, and several nations in the Caribbean and Central America, experienced dictatorships and here too women played an integral role in registering their dissent from below.

The military has historically held considerable power in Latin American countries as a product of struggles for independence whereby military officials stepped into government positions during periods of political vacuums. During the twentieth century, many countries experienced military coups and subsequent dictatorships whereby citizens' rights all but disintegrated. The military dictatorships were particularly brutal in that they often "disappeared" individuals thought to be subversive or for simply speaking out against a particular regime. As Marguerite Guzman Bouvard put it: "Under a semblance

FIGURE 3.1 *Mothers protest peacefully in the Plaza de Mayo in Buenos Aires, Argentina. Between 1976 and 1983, the Argentine government launched a "dirty war" against its own people where suspected radicals or opponents of the regime were tortured and disappeared. Beginning in 1977, mothers of disappeared youth gathered every Thursday to demand justice for their children. Credit: Christopher Pillitz.*

of normality, thousands of people were dragged from their homes, their places of work, from the streets by plainclothesmen in fleets of unmarked cars. Their families and friends were hurled into a limbo of terror and nightmare while the country continued to conduct its business as if nothing had happened." The Argentine example reveals the terror many felt at the hands of a military dictatorship but also the ability of some to rise above that terror and make their voices heard. In the wake of the 1976 coup, the military launched what became known as the "Dirty War" and countless individuals were disappeared, imprisoned, tortured and murdered in a campaign that lasted until 1983. While the state-sponsored violence against perceived leftists or opponents of the regime might indicate at first glance a defeat for protesting voices, the reaction of a group of women in the aftermath represents a triumph. Beginning in 1977, women whose children had been disappeared began gathering and protested in Buenos Aires' main plaza, the Plaza de Mayo. Despite meeting police repression (including tear gas and weapons), the Mothers met every Thursday donning white scarves and wrote to the president regarding their missing children. Their strategy was always peaceful; they marched with white masks or white cut-out silhouettes representing their missing children, and published their own newspaper which they sold in the plaza. In 1980, the Mothers traveled 36 hours via bus to try to persuade the Pope visiting in Brazil to meet with them. They succeeded and later found audiences with the Organization of American States and the United Nations.[26] According to Bouvard, these women

> not only transformed political action, but they also revolutionized the very concept of maternity as passive and in the service of the state into a public and socialized claim against the state. Their vision of maternity ultimately served as a springboard for demanding a political system that would reflect maternal values and assure human rights, universal participation, and social welfare: they proclaimed themselves revolutionary Mothers.[27]

Child labor, taxation, women's rights, and apartheid in Africa

The basic tenet of black consciousness is that the black man must reject all value systems that seek to make him a foreigner in the country of his birth and reduce his basic human dignity.

STEVE BIKO (1976)

Steve Biko's statement from the 1970s during the height of apartheid in South Africa resonates with the continuity of exploitation and accompanying resistance seen on the continent of Africa throughout much of the modern era. The Black Consciousness Movement (BCM) and its role in creating fault lines in the racist system of subjugation from above in apartheid will be considered shortly. In the meantime, let us turn to the nineteenth century and the contestations between imperial powers and native peoples. Groups rebelled against foreign colonial powers and within patriarchal structures of native rule. In what is present-day Zimbabwe, the Ndebele kingdom led by Lobengula (1836–94) first cooperated with the British South Africa Company (BSAC) by granting concessions in exchange for ammunition in 1888. Europeans had flooded the region after the discovery of gold near Bulawayo (named earlier by Lobengula, meaning "the place of killing" in reference to his prior military victories),[28] where there was a British altercation in 1893 that forced Lobengula into exile. The Ndebele rebelled again in 1896, in a movement that they called the *Chimurenga*.[29]

As political scientist Beverly Carolease Grier has shown for colonial Zimbabwe, child labor proliferated under the BSAC and while children often sought out paid labor to escape the patriarchal control they endured on rural homesteads, both children and parents contested unfair labor arrangements and educational policies. Working children known as *picaninnies* worked in mines, domestic service, agriculture, and the informal economy. These children were subjected to the British settlers' notion of childhood, which was predicated on class and racialized ideas bound up in the colonial project. From the early twentieth century to the 1950s, parents and students protested mission schools and later government schools that required manual labor, whereby children and youth were forced to construct schools, dormitories, and even build roads. Control over one's labor formed part of modern citizenship, and these young people lacked it. In addition, children often grew agricultural products and produced goods for sale to profit European missions, further evidence of the exploitative arrangement that existed. As such, children often fled, as was the case with the future political journalist Vambe, who left a mission school in Chishawasha at age 10. Grier characterizes these children as "assertive actors who were developing political consciousness that would prepare them for anticolonial political activism later in life." Around mid-century, officials concerned themselves with the increasingly difficult-to-control youth, especially in urban areas. According to Grier, "far from being hooligans or juvenile delinquents, troublesome and law-breaking young migrants and young town-born residents of the 1940s and 1950s were, in many respects, rebels." Many of these young people became vocal opponents of the colonial project and joined the guerrilla movement.[30] Contestations from below over labor and efforts to restrict physical mobility by those in power politicized young people.

Taxation was another issue that caused unrest in colonial Africa. Under British colonialism, African women located in the Oweri and Calabar region of present-day Nigeria revolted in 1929–30, in what became known as the Aba Women's Revolt. On November 18, 1929, when a census taker working for his local warrant chief Okugo asked a woman named Nawanyeruwa to report the number of people and livestock in her household, a rebellion protesting colonial taxation was born. Like many in the region, Nawanyeruwa farmed and also produced the cash crop palm oil—a commodity used to make soap and lubricant for industrial machinery—which had recently declined in value. She met with other women gathered in the town square and eventually over 10,000 women mobilized across several hundred square miles. These women protested the British system, demanded that they be exempted from paying taxes, and asked for the removal of warrant chiefs deemed offensive by the women. Moreover, ". . . the process of census taking violated many taboos. Throughout the region of West Africa and the Sahel, the counting of people, especially women, is considered abhorrent. Animals can be counted, but fruit-bearing trees and women cannot."[31] During the rebellion, women launched strikes, burned government buildings and destroyed European businesses. The colonial administration quelled the revolt with the use of British troops at the end of December, after fifty-five women had been killed. Eventually, the administration agreed to the women's demands and the offending warrant chief Okugo was tried and convicted. "The Aba Women's Revolt was a harbinger of the influence that rural Igbo women would exert on future political activities. As a consequence of the revolt the system of warrant chieftaincy was abolished, and women were appointed to the Native Court system, which was responsible for advising the colonial administration. These changes paved the way for the national political movements that led to Nigerian independence."[32] When concluding her testimony to the commission of inquiry on March 12, 1930, Nawanyeruwa stated: "That is my case. I told the District Officer that Okugo must be imprisoned and, if he were not imprisoned, we should not be satisfied. I am a poor woman to pay tax."[33]

Women sometimes communicated their voices of protest through the written word, whereby their means of resistance could be disguised in less openly combative ways. In Ghana, Mabel Dove-Danquah contested distasteful colonial legislation through satirical pieces published in her feature "Woman's Corner" in the *Times of West Africa* in the early 1930s. In a particularly ingenious piece, she published a letter written to the daughter of then-Governor Sir Shenton Whitelegge Thomas. Written to Miss Bridget Thomas, the letter took advantage of the "fine opportunity of telling you what we little African girls in the distant fields of the Gold Coast Colony and Ashanti, feel about your kind father's WATER and SEDITION BILLS." The letter writer continued and related a story in which she overheard her father weeping and then her father asked her, "'What fate would fall upon you and hundreds of thousands of girls like you, after these bills have been laws of the land is that which leads me and the country into lamentation and bitter sorrow.'" Dove-Danquah concluded by asking Miss Thomas to persuade her father governor to withdraw the bills, adding "Believe us as we believe you and your father that even in the distant Ashanti, our fathers have not the slightest idea of malice and war against the white race. Our fathers and mothers . . . as well as we and our brothers are perfectly loyal to your King in England and your noble father our Governor." Usually writing under a pseudonym, Dove-Danquah's forty-year journalism career included several different newspapers in the Gold Coast. Later in life she also contributed poems and plays to the British Broadcasting Corporation (BBC).[34]

In 1947, women led a revolt in Abeokuta in colonial Nigeria, where they demanded not only political and economic rights but also access to social services for themselves and their children. Mrs. Ransome-Kuti led the women's organization that headed the revolt. The Abeokuta Women's Union (AWU) represented a cross-class alliance of market women and women formerly part of the Abeokuta Ladies Club (ALC), though all women in the province were eligible to join. The ALC, the precursor to the AWU, introduced eight resolutions in March 1946. The women wanted: "improved public sanitation, public playgrounds for school children, government support for adult education, and no tax increase for women."[35] The AWU listed their objectives, which included: "To defend, protect, preserve, and promote the social, economic, cultural and political rights of the women in Egbaland. . . . To cooperate with all organizations seeking and fighting genuinely and selflessly for the economic and political freedom and independence of the people."[36] The ramifications of their demands were multifaceted; "The women's protests which unfolded over several months opened debate on specific issues around tax collection and fairness of tax structure, as well as a door to a much broader debate on the nature of colonial rule, gender relations, and the role of the state."[37] The women effectively claimed no taxation without representation and demanded inclusion in local political structures. These women also protested the physical manifestations of officials denying the rights of citizenship; women demanded an end to the practice of officials opening girls' blouses to see if they had developed breasts as a way to determine if they had reached the taxable adult age of fifteen. Thus, we see that insurgent citizenship also often manifested itself in contestations over women's bodies.

Insurgent citizenship in Asia: Rebellion, sabotage, and youth protests

You can chain me, you can torture me, you can even destroy this body, but you will never imprison my mind.

MAHATMA GANDHI

British interest in India originated with the East India Company in the mid-eighteenth century. Nearly a century later, a large-scale revolt occurred on May 10, 1857, when sepoys (Hindu and Muslim recruits) from the military station Meerut mutinied against the British forces. Within twenty-four hours "what began as merely the latest and ugliest of a long series of mutinous incidents in the Bengal army had swelled monstrously into full-scale political rebellion."[38] The armed rising spread terror throughout the British Empire, and the news swept across the globe. The rebellion so affected British culture and society in the nineteenth century that in addition to poems and various historical accounts, fifty to sixty novels were written dealing with the event.[39] The revolt occurred at the same time that popular novels proliferated making it a widely read about event, as were renditions of the Boxer Rebellion in China (1900) and the Anglo-Boer war (1899–1902). The 1857 revolt also garnered international attention from journalists, especially in Europe and the United States. Karl Marx wrote articles about the rebellion for the newspaper with the largest circulation at the time, the *New York Daily Tribune*. Significantly, Marx connected the rebellion in Dehli with larger discontent in Asia and said it was "intimately connected with the Persian and Chinese wars." Perhaps even more surprising, the revolt inspired Irish radicals in their home country and in America to view their struggles against the British in a similar vein.[40] But what caused this massive rebellion and how did contemporaries interpret it?

Popular notions begin with the story of religious objections by sepoys to the use of animal fat to grease their gun cartridges; rather than representing an accurate historical truth, that reductive explanation has only served British interests from the beginning of the rebellion. As historian Crispin Bates explains: "That they should take up arms over an issue as trivial and superstitious as the greasing of a cartridge, neatly diverted attention from other aspects of the Company's maladministration that provided more contingent and pressing causes for rebellion."[41] Indeed, insurgents had no qualms about using those very guns against the British when they rebelled. More convincing explanations reveal the long, ongoing history of insurgent citizenship in the region. Practices deemed unfair by locals—especially in regard to taxation, land rights, and other forms of economic oppression—caused them to rebel. For example, in 1852 the mere arrival of a British land survey team to assess for taxation in Khandesh provoked a riot. On the Malabar coast, "Muslim Mappila tenants were almost continuously in revolt against the Hindu landlords appointed by the British." In terms of land rights, the East India Company repeatedly seized kingdoms in the region under their 1850 policy announced by Viceroy Dalhousie whereby a dispute in succession provided justification for land seizure. Beginning in the mid-1850s, the British took control of several kingdoms including: Awadh, Nagpur (the largest), Jhansi, Satara, Udaipur, Balaghat, Sambalpur, Jaitpur, Carnatic, and Tanjore.

The right to earn a living was another grievance of local residents under British colonial rule. In the aftermath of the 1857 rebellion, the Azamgarh Proclamation highlighted the causes behind insurgent citizenship. Section II of that proclamation explained why merchants felt aggrieved: "It is plain that the infidel and treacherous British government have monopolised the trade of all fine and valuable merchandise, such as indigo, cloth, and other articles of shipping, leaving only the trade of trifles to the people. . . . It is therefore the duty of every merchant to take part in the war, and aid the Badshahi government with his men and money." Similarly, locals complained about the lack of equitable jobs as public servants in the colonial administration under Section III of that document: "It is not a secret thing, that under the British government, natives employed in the civil and military services, have little respect, low pay, and no manner of influence and all posts of dignity and emolument in both departments are exclusively bestowed upon Englishmen." While the British eventually suppressed the revolt, the legacy proved to be very influential in later years. As Bates stated: "the uprising helped create a mythology of resistance that became a powerful ideological weapon in the hands of the later Nationalists during the freedom struggle of the 1930s and 1940s."[42]

Conflicts in the fifty years after the defeat of the revolt were more easily resolved in favor of the British because of improved communications, the advent of the machine gun and disarming of Indian people, and expansion of military and police.[43] Nevertheless, rebellions continued. During British rule in India, official policy challenged traditional agricultural methods, and individuals and groups often employed protest and sabotage to register their discontent. In the early nineteenth century, forests in India proved particularly useful in supplying the British royal navy with teak wood for shipbuilding, and later in the century the need for lumber increased to meet railroad construction demands. The Indian Forest Act of 1878 "by one stroke of the executive pen attempted to obliterate centuries of customary use of the forest by rural populations all over India." Because over 20 percent of India's land was in control of the Forestry Department by 1900, the extraction of natural resources for profit affected a staggering number of people. The Rampa Rebellion of 1879–80, led by chieftain Tamman Dora, focused hostilities on police stations, several of which the rebels burned; ultimately, the rebels also executed a constable in ritualistic form. Despite the fact that police later shot and killed the revolt's leader, the uprising spread and took hundreds of police and ten army companies to quash it in November 1880. In many cases, acts of resistance included cutting telegraph wires, stacking wood on rail or roadways to block transport, and killing forest personnel.[44]

In a recent article, Franziska Roy and Benjamin Zachariah revisited the Meerut Conspiracy Case in India and connected the case to the rising youth movements in India of the 1920s. Traditionally, historians have located the dispute within the British Imperial context, relating it to the fear of international communism or socialism and the labor movements of the time. Yet as Roy and Zachariah have stated, the case "came to epitomize the arbitrariness of imperial authority" and "the staged trials ended up creating public sympathy for the prisoners and a legitimation of a broad language of civil liberties . . ." In the interwar years, youth movements swelled throughout the globe, partially a result of the horrors of the Great War and revolutions, like the 1917 October Revolution in Russia. After the initial arrest of 31 people for "depriving the King-Emperor of his sovereignty" according to the Indian Penal Code, one of the accused, future Indian leader Jawaharlal Nehru, characterized the arrests as directed at the youth movement. Furthermore "[m]embers of the nascent youth (league) movement also interpreted the Meerut arrests as a countermeasure to the political awakening and crystallizing unity of youth." A 1927 trade union publication of the time stated: "To-day youth is the prime factor in heralding the dawn of a new era, unfurling the standard of revolt against the old, breaking the barriers of custom, restrictions thereby raising the moral force of the world on a plane of ethereal effulgence. The history of the modern world is the history of and awakening of the Youth Movement." Oftentimes the connection between youth movements and socialism and labor movements was fuzzy, but one thing is clear: In 1927 youth organizations sprang up all over British India and in 1928 youth conferences proliferated. Increasingly, the authorities reacted with raids and arrests which "made the leagues more attractive as they became framed by the halo of anti-imperialism" and likely caused more youth leagues to spring forth throughout India.[45] Youth leagues often advocated independence from Britain but also challenged social customs that they deemed outdated, like child marriage and unequal gender relations.

In the 1929 Lahore Conspiracy Case, police charged twenty-five members of the Hindustan Socialist Republican Association with conspiracy. The charges against the revolutionary HSRA encapsulated several acts of violent rebellion over the previous few years including armed robbery, murder of the Assistant Superintendent of Police, and throwing a bomb in the Central Legislative Assembly. In the ensuing trial and its coverage in print media, Bhagat Singh and Jatindranath Das became famous as they and others launched hunger strikes from prison, demanding they be treated as political prisoners. The demand reflected the legal classification system used by the British to give special treatment to Europeans and uphold racialized power.[46]

In China, the May Fourth Movement of 1919 may have appeared to some as simply a spontaneous student demonstration in Beijing protesting the unfavorable terms for China of the Paris Peace Treaty that ended World War I. Yet the massive protest that occurred that day was the culmination of a mass movement of political and intellectual awakening of professors and students also known as the New Culture Movement (1915–21). Indeed antecedents have been located in the late nineteenth century through opposition to traditional cultural practices and political organization.

In Tiananmen Square on May 4, 1919, over three thousand students gathered representing thirteen colleges and universities, and were led by a group from Beida or the National Beijing University. They opposed the terms of the peace treaty, especially the notion of Japanese control of China's

Shandong peninsula. The students held placards that read "Give Us Back Qindao [the port city in Shandong]!" "Refuse to Sign the Peace Treaty!" "Oppose Power Politics!" and "China Belongs to the Chinese!" The students also circulated a manifesto as they marched that concluded "Our country is about to be annihilated! Up, brethren!" Frustrated after waiting for the government to respond, the students continued their protest by marching to the home of a government official, Cao Rulin. The students entered the house, destroyed furniture, and set the house ablaze. The police apprehended thirty-two of the protestors and had them jailed.[47]

The events of that day represented a much broader struggle within Chinese society. Historian Vera Schwarcz includes this event in part of a larger "Chinese Enlightenment." Part of the Confucian tradition in China included *lijiao* or "the cult of ritualized subordination" that

> had been perpetuated through the institution of the examination system and represented an adaptation of the ethic of filial piety to the needs of the imperial bureaucratic state. Using the most intimate emotions that prevail within the family, the cult of subordination was comprised of "three ropes and five bonds" (*sangang wuchang*)—all of which required that inferiors submit themselves to their superiors with a glad and open heart.[48]

Schwarcz compares and contrasts the Chinese Enlightenment to that of its European predecessor and finds that the fundamental difference is that, in the case of China, intellectuals were opposing not devotion to a heavenly God, "but rather the unquestioning obedience to patriarchal authority—be it that of emperor, father, or party chief . . ."[49]

In the few decades before the educational reformer Yan Fu (1854–1921) briefly held the post of superintendent of the Imperial University, he read and translated for his contemporaries the works of thinkers like Herbert Spencer, Adam Smith, John Stuart Mill, and Montesquieu. During his tenure, he changed the nature of the university by increasing the study of foreign languages and de-emphasizing the training for the bureaucratic examinations for government positions. Indeed, he changed the name in 1912 from Imperial University to Beijing University to reflect this transformation, making it known that it was "a modern institution of higher learning rather than a haven for old-fashioned office-seekers in the new republican era." It was in this dynamic environment that the May Fourth Movement intellectuals lived and became politicized.[50] Those individuals who were part of the New Culture Movement founded societies and spread their messages through student publications like *New Youth* and *New Tide*. A speech by Chen Duxiu (on May 1, 1920) to workers was published in *New Youth* as "The Awakening of Laborers": "Who are the most useful, the most important people in the world? People whose minds are confused would say that they are the emperors, or those who become officials or intellectuals. I say they are wrong, I say that only those who labor are the most useful and the most important."[51]

The highly visible New Culture Movement left its imprint on China and transformed the way politics were envisioned. Yet other scholars have pointed to social and political activism in the late nineteenth century as predecessors to the changes wrought by the New Culture Movement. In a recent essay, Xiong Yuezhi maintains that women's roles and political activities in Shanghai had drastically changed by the early twentieth century before the New Culture movement. He states: "women enthusiastically engaged in all kinds of social and political movements such as Shanghai's Resist Russia movement, the boycott of American goods, and the 1911 Revolution."[52] By that time, he locates approximately thirty-five women's groups organized by female intellectuals in China. In the late nineteenth and early twentieth centuries, many women and men spoke out against the practice of foot binding and some women organized groups designed to end the practice. Over time, the process of social change gradually erased the physical manifestations of women's inequality, their mangled feet. "In the evolving process of constructing a new Chinese womanhood, the late-Qing attention to women's rights to work, to freedom of choice in love and marriage, and to education set the stage for May Fourth men's and women's efforts to create new women."[53] Women's participation in the formation of modern citizenship rights in China included a call for rights associated with their domestic and social roles vis-à-vis men. Now, we turn our analysis to the twentieth century with an eye to how various movements intersected on the ground throughout the globe.

Interconnected global protests in the twentieth century

If we must die—let it not be like hogs
Hunted and penned in an inglorious spot,
While round us bark the mad and hungry dogs,
Making their mock at our accursed lot.
If we must die—oh, let us nobly die,
So that our precious blood may not be shed
In vain; then even the monsters we defy
Shall be constrained to honor us though dead!
Oh, Kinsmen! We must meet the common foe;
Though far outnumbered, let us show us brave,
And for their thousand blows deal one deathblow!
What though before us lies the open grave?
Like men we'll face the murderous, cowardly pack,
Pressed to the wall, dying, but fighting back!

CLAUDE MCKAY

When this poem appeared in 1919, race riots plagued the United States while at the same time international labor movements gathered tremendous momentum around the globe. Indeed, that year represented the height of the labor movement in the United States when over four million workers participated in strikes across a variety of occupations. Claude McKay (1889–1948), a Jamaican-born poet and novelist, contributed to black consciousness in the early twentieth century and was an integral part of the Harlem Renaissance in the 1920s. Like many exceptional individuals of his time, McKay's life demonstrates the interconnectedness of global struggles against oppression, especially racial discrimination and that of the working class. Perhaps it was no coincidence that his poem implored oppressed peoples not to "die like hogs;" socialist Upton Sinclair's novel The Jungle— an exposé of Chicago's meatpacking industry and the inhumane conditions it created for immigrant workers and animals alike—had garnered tremendous attention when it appeared in 1906. McKay briefly attended the African-American Tuskegee Institute before moving to New York City where he met fellow radical Max Eastman, co-founder of The Liberator, in which the poem was published. Both McKay and Eastman traveled to the Soviet Union in order to witness the aftermath of revolution and a style of governance they thought would bring about the triumph of the working class. The first decades of the twentieth century ushered in challenges to tyranny across the globe that upon closer inspection reveal the linkages to insurgent claims to citizenship.

In the case of the 1910 Mexican Revolution, some prominent individuals saw the connections between Mexico's revolution and larger forces seeking to resist or overthrow elite privilege in the global context. Long before John Reed (1887–1920), American journalist, radical, and revolution seeker, published his account of the 1917 October Bolshevik revolution, Ten Days that Shook the World (1919), he had been a correspondent in Mexico and traveled with Pancho Villa's forces for four months. Reed's 1914 Insurgent Mexico detailed the revolution up to that time as he lived and fought with Villa's forces. His admiration for Villa was clear: "His reckless and romantic bravery is the subject of countless poems. . . . In the time of famine he fed whole districts, and took care of entire villages evicted by the soldiers under Porfirio Díaz['s] outrageous land law. Everywhere he was known as The Friend of the Poor. He was the Mexican Robin Hood." Upon his return to the United States, John Reed found himself reporting on a case of striking workers and the repression they faced. The 1914 Ludlow Massacre in Colorado—a miners' strike that resulted in John D. Rockefeller, Jr. using the National Guard to attack the striking workers and their families—became his next assignment. Reed publicly opposed US intervention in the Mexican Revolution, but to no avail. He later traveled to Russia, where he witnessed first-hand the Bolshevik Revolution of October 1917. When he died in 1920, he was buried in the Kremlin. Reed was caught up in a variety of revolutionary movements, many of which were linked ideologically by what its participants

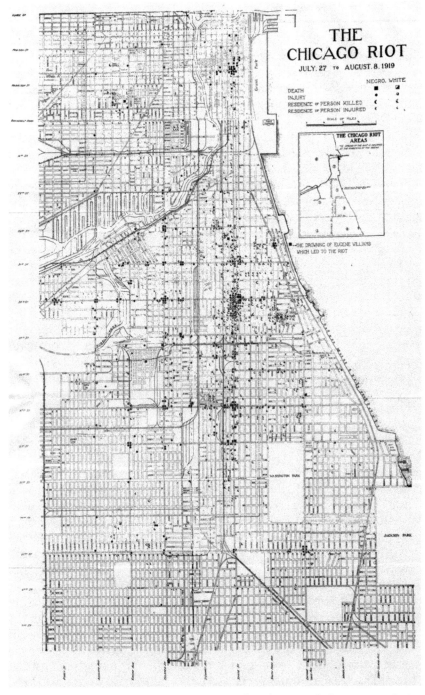

FIGURE 3.2 *Map indicating the extent of violence and destruction during Chicago's 1919 race riot. On July 27th, a riot broke out reflecting tensions between white ethnic groups and African-Americans on Chicago's Southside that lasted days, killed 53 people, and left over 500 injured. Credit: Chicago History Museum.*

viewed as the overthrow of the capitalist elite by the masses, mostly industrial workers and peasants. The revolutionary fervor found in Mexico during the early part of the twentieth century was not an isolated ideological fight against oppression; it occurred within a broader context of peasant and industrial workers protesting the onslaught of industrial capitalism and imperialism.

The revolution in Mexico attracted some Americans to Mexico, for a variety of reasons. The US heavyweight champion, an African-American named Jack Johnson, fled to Mexico after charges were brought against him in the United States for engaging in a consensual relationship with a white woman. In 1919, Johnson arrived in Mexico while race riots raged in the US and the Bolsheviks consolidated the revolution in Russia. Johnson, the son of former slaves, was fleeing the criminal charges but also the racial prejudice he experienced at home. The prizefighter briefly made Mexico City his home because he felt that racial prejudice did not exist in the country. His presence in revolutionary Mexico worried state department officials in the United States. One US official stated in 1919: "Jack Johnson, of pugilistic fame, has been spreading social equality propaganda among the Negroes in Mexico and has been endeavoring to incite colored element in this country." Johnson stayed in Mexico until his friend and protector, President Carranza, was assassinated in 1920. Upon his return to the US, he gave himself up to authorities and served a one-year prison term for the charge of white slavery under the 1912 Mann Act.[54]

Johnson's temporary relocation reveals a tale of one individual taking flight when meaningful citizenship was denied him. Others left their homeland and sought to cultivate international communism and anti-imperialist projects across national boundaries. Such was the case with Manabendra Nath (M. N.) Roy, a West Bengali-born anti-colonialist who lived in Mexico between 1917 and 1919, when he helped found the Mexican Communist Party (Partido Comunista Mexicano, PCM) and was elected its first Secretary-General with the support of Comintern envoy Mikhail Borodin. According to his memoir, Roy reportedly told a leftist Mexican newspaper editor: "We are in the same boat; my country is similarly stigmatised by the arrogant imperialism of the White race."[55] Nevertheless, it was Roy's commitment to working-class struggles and anti-imperialism that most attracted him to Mexico at this critical moment.

In the context of Cold War Mexico, students often led the vanguard of political protest as they actively contested their exclusion from the economic benefits wrought by the import substitution industrialization that characterized many Latin American countries in the post-World War II era. Students used peaceful protest and organized marches, took over buses, and spread leaflets of their demands, and the occasional Molotov cocktail to make their voices heard. They invoked the names and images of contemporaneous revolutionaries like Che Guevara. On October 2, 1968, a government-ordered massacre struck student protestors and civilians in the *Plaza de las tres culturas* in Tlatelolco, Mexico City, ending months of continuous student strikes and protests. An estimated 300 people lost their lives that day and many more were arrested. One killed in the melee was the brother of Mexican journalist Elena Poniatowska, prompting her to interview student protestors and publish a compilation of their testimonies in a book called *La noche de Tlatelolco: testimonios de historia oral* (1971, translated into English as *Massacre in Mexico*). The massacre represented the government's desperation as it struggled to contain students on the eve of Mexico's hosting of the Olympiad, the first ever held in an "underdeveloped" country. In an unrelated act of protest, African-American medal winners Tommie Smith and John Carlos raised their fists in a black power salute while the US national anthem played. The two athletes used the moment to make their exclusion from full participation in US society known to the international audience.

More recently, historian Jaime Pensado has documented the earlier advent of student radicals in Mexico City with a large-scale strike by students in 1956 marking the beginning of the "long sixties." His work demonstrates how members of the ruling party in Mexico, the *Partido Revolucionario Institucional* (the Institutionalized Revolutionary Party, or PRI, which had been in power since 1929 under the guise of a few different names) concerned themselves with student protestors beginning in the early 1950s. From 1958 to 1964, documentation produced by the Office of Federal Security and the General Directorate of Political and Social Investigations dramatically increased and became more detailed.[56] The result was increased surveillance of the students and other radicals by the PRI, but the growing voices of protest against Mexico's retreating revolutionary promises continued unabated. For the same decade, Robert Alegre has demonstrated how railroad workers resisted the ruling party's attempts to control their leadership of the country's unions. When they reached a stalemate, railway workers staged a massive strike in 1958 and the federal government sent troops to break up the strike.[57] Both scholars' research reveals that the student movement that erupted in 1968 added to a long legacy of dissent during a period of unequally distributed economic growth.

By the end of the 1960s, most but not all former colonial possessions in Africa had established independent nations. Nevertheless, rebellions did not subside as many rebelled against new authoritarian regimes and sought more inclusive citizenship rights. Unlike the youth movement in the United States, rebels in the Global South found little resonance in Timothy Leary's call to "turn on, tune in, drop out" of society. "The 1960s in the Third World was therefore a movement to drop *in* to society, a battle for inclusion and for representation."[58] In Catholic seminaries in Chishawasha (near Salisbury, Rhodesia) students rebelled between 1965 and 1979, sometimes forcing the closure of the school in an era before decolonization. According to Nicholas

FIGURE 3.3 *US athletes Tommie Smith (center) and John Carlos (right) after winning the gold and bronze medals respectively for the 200 meter race at the Olympics in Mexico City, Mexico in October 1968. The two men raised their fists in solidarity with the radical Black Power Movement.* Credit: Poperfoto.

Creary, the activism arose because of "the Jesuits' failure to break with the dominant white Rhodesian culture and its paternalistic mindset" and the students' "expressions of nationalism were part of a broader struggle to decolonize the Catholic Church." Seminarians fought to be treated as equal to their white instructors.[59]

The 1960s brought rampant protest throughout the continent. For example, between 1969 and 1971, students affiliated with Kinshasa Student Circle (CEK) in Congo-Zaire demonstrated and met with fierce resistance from the army, including a massacre of students on June 4, 1969. In the month before the demonstration and massacre, the CEK sent word to the repressive and authoritarian Mobutu government that they would defend themselves "by all means necessary, including revolutionary violence, with the same determination as our comrades from Africa, Latin America, Europe, and Asia." While student protestors in subsequent demonstrations were sometimes forcibly drafted into the army for short periods, the collective action resulted in Mobutu Sese Seko allowing for the formation of a new national university, no small feat considering his legacy as a ruthless dictator.[60] Five years later, Mobutu's country hosted the famous "Rumble in the Jungle" heavyweight fight between Muhammad Ali and George Foreman. Widely popular in Zaire for both his boxing and political stance against the Vietnam War, Ali won the fight and the hearts of the local people as showcased in the Academy Award-winning documentary *When We Were Kings* (1996). The extravaganza included a Pan-African musical celebration that joined some of the most influential African-American and African artists including James Brown, B. B. King, The Spinners, and Miriam Makeba of South Africa, who was also the wife of Stokely Carmichael.

In the context of late 1960s South Africa, several transnational phenomena point to the circulation of ideas and personas related to insurgent citizenship. While apartheid "the most extensive system of racial segregation ever devised anywhere" existed it was not without dissent from below.[61] The Black Consciousness Movement (BCM) in South Africa was at least tangentially informed by knowledge of US Civil Rights Movement and subsequently the more militant Black Power Movement. In 1968, Steve Biko (1946–77) founded the South African Students' Organization (SASO) for black students and was the most prominent leader of the BCM, which threatened apartheid throughout the 1970s. A compilation of his writings and speeches, *I Write What I Like*, details his work, writings, and speeches (he was banned from speaking in public in 1972). "The basic tenet of black consciousness is that the black man must reject all value systems that seek to make him a foreigner in the country of his birth and reduce his basic human dignity."[62] While police assassinated Biko in 1977, his legacy lived on in the anti-apartheid struggle. The book was so popular that people often stole or wrote extensive profound comments in the marginalia of copies from public and university libraries in South Africa.[63]

FIGURE 3.4 *April 29, 2014, Johannesburg, South Africa. South African man showing support for the socialist political party the Economic Freedom Fighters holding images of assassinated South African Black Consciousness Movement leader Steve Biko and slain Latin American revolutionary Ernesto "Che" Guevara. Protestors decried the exclusion of an EFF advertisement from the promised radio time during an election. Credit: Gianluigi Guercia (AFP).*

Global citizenship: Histories and counter-histories

The notion that the modern era ushered in the achievement of equal, uncontested citizenship in any part of the world, let alone across the globe, is patently false. From the mid-eighteenth century to the present, people in all regions of the world fought from below for citizenship rights under different circumstances, yet with the same resolve. The historical record confirms that access to citizenship rights differed across not only time and space but also by race, ethnicity, class, and gender. Individuals and groups rose up and challenged governments in order to lay claims to modern citizenship in all its varied forms. Demands far exceeded basic political recognition and participation in many cases as insurgent citizens demanded unrestricted physical mobility, basic housing rights, to freely enter into labor contracts, to not be harassed or discriminated against on the basis of race, gender or sexual orientation, as well as the right to choose their sexual and marriage partners. The tactics used to lay claim to modern citizenship throughout the world were as varied as the globe's inhabitants; ranging from acts of violence to peaceful protest to nearly invisible acts of resistance or sabotage, each allowed people to push back against exclusions or abuses wrought by national governments or colonial powers. Citizens throughout the modern era used dissent and disruption to define, contest, and remake the rights associated with citizenship.

Suggestions for further reading

Bates, Crispin. *Subalterns and Raj: South Asia Since 1600*. New York: Routledge, 2007.

Clark, Nancy L. and William H. Worger. *South Africa: The Rise and Fall of Apartheid*. New York: Routledge, 2011.

Cohen, Paul. *History in Three Keys: The Boxers as Event, Experience, and Myth*. New York: Columbia University Press, 1998.

Christiansen, Samantha and Zachary A. Scarlett, eds, *The Third World in the Global 1960s*. New York: Berghahn Books, 2013.

Ferrer, Ada. *Freedom's Mirror: Haiti and Cuba in the Age of Revolution*. Cambridge: Cambridge University Press, 2014.

Gilly, Aldofo. *The Mexican Revolution*. New York: The New Press, 2006.

James, C. L. R. *The Black Jacobins: Toussaint L'Ouverture and the San Domingo Revolution*. New York: Vintage, 1989.

Mitchell, Stephanie and Patience A. Schell, eds. *The Women's Revolution in Mexico, 1910–1953*. Lanham, MD: Rowman and Littlefield, 2007.

Trouillot, Michel-Rolph. *Silencing the Past: Power and the Production of History*. Boston, MA: Beacon Press, 1995.

Notes

1 Mimi Sheller, *Citizenship from Below: Erotic Agency and Caribbean Freedom* (Durham, NC: Duke University Press, 2012), 23.

2 C. L. R. James, *The Black Jacobins: Toussaint L'Ouverture and the San Domingo Revolution* (New York: Vintage, 1938), x.

3 See for example, Mimi Sheller, *Citizenship from Below*; Trevor R. Getz and Liz Clarke, *Abina and the Important Men: A Graphic History* (Oxford: Oxford University Press, 2012).

4 Michel-Rolph Trouillot, *Silencing the Past: Power and the Production of History* (Boston, MA: Beacon, 1995), 26.

5 Sheller, *Citizenship from Below*, 9.

6 Sheller, *Citizenship from Below*, 21.

7 Lahra Smith, *Making Citizens in Africa: Ethnicity, Gender, and National Identity in Ethopia* (Cambridge: Cambridge University Press, 2013), 6.

8   John Hope Franklin and Loren Schweninger, *Runaway Slaves: Rebels on the Plantation* (New York: Oxford University Press, 1999), 230; 324–325.

9   Laurent Dubois, *Avengers of the New World: The Story of the Haitian Revolution* (Cambridge, MA: Harvard University Press, 2004), 21; quotation from David Brion Davis, "Impact of the French and Haitian Revolutions," in *The Impact of the Haitian Revolution in the Atlantic World*, ed. David Geggus (Columbia: University of South Carolina Press), 4.

10 Evelyn Hu-DeHart, *Yaqui Resistance and Survival: The Struggle for Land and Autonomy 1821–1910* (Madison: The University of Wisconsin Press, 1984), 20, 47, 54.

11 Hu-DeHart, *Yaqui Resistance and Survival,* 102–106.

12 João José Reis, "Slave Resistance in Brazil, Bahia 1807–1835," *Luso-Brazilian Review* 25:1 (1988), 114, 119, 125, 129, 132.

13 Robert Edgar Conrad, *Children of God's Fire: A Documentary History of Black Slavery in Brazil* (University Park, PA: The Pennsylvania State University Press, 1997), 405.

14 Dale Torston Graden, *From Slavery to Freedom in Brazil: Bahia, 1835–1900* (Albuquerque: University of New Mexico Press, 2006).

15 Flávio dos Santos Gomes, "Peasants, Maroons, and the Frontiers of Liberation in Maranhão," *Review (Fernand Braudel Center)* 31:3, The Second Slavery: Mass Slavery, World-Economy, and Comparative Microhistories, Part III (2008), 374.

16 Flávio dos Santos Gomes, "Peasants, Maroons, and the Frontiers of Liberation in Maranhão," 385–386.

17 Flávio dos Santos Gomes, "Peasants, Maroons, and the Frontiers of Liberation in Maranhão," 388, 396.

18 Brodwyn Fischer, *A Poverty of Rights: Citizenship and Inequality in Twentieth-Century Rio de Janeiro* (Stanford, CA: Stanford University Press, 2008), 2.

19 Brodwyn Fischer, *A Poverty of Rights,* 270.

20 Brodwyn Fischer, *A Poverty of Rights,* 270

21 Brodwyn Fischer, *A Poverty of Rights,* 271.

22 Andrew Grant Wood, " 'The Proletarian Women Will Make the Social Revolution': Female Participation in the Veracruz Rent Strike, 1922–1927," in *The Women's Revolution in Mexico, 1910–1953*, ed. Stephanie Mitchell and Patience A. Schell (Lanham, MD: Rowman and Littlefield, 2007), 152–153, 160.

23 Katherine Elaine Bliss, "Theater of Operations: Reform Politics and the Battle for Prostitutes' Redemption at Revolutionary Mexico City's Syphilis Hospital," in *The Women's Revolution in Mexico,* 142.

24 Cristina Rivera-Garza, "She Neither Respected Nor Obeyed Anyone: Inmates and Psychiatrists Debate Gender and Class at the General Insane Asylum La Castañeda Mexico," *Hispanic American Historical Review* 81:3–4 (2001), 677.

25 Mark Overmyer-Velázquez, *Visions of the Emerald City: Modernity, Tradition, and the Formation of Porfirian Oaxaca, Mexico* (Durham, NC: Duke University Press, 2006), 130.

26 Marguerite Guzman Bouvard, *Revolutionizing Motherhood: The Mothers of the Plaza de Mayo* (Wilmington, DE: Scholarly Resources, 1994), 24, 69–76, 111–112.

27 Guzman Bouvard, *Revolutionizing Motherhood*, 62.

28 R. Hunt Davis, Jr., ed., *Encyclopedia of African History and Culture Volume IV The Colonial Era (1850 to 1960)*, (New York: The Learning Source, Ltd., 2005), 238.

29 Davis, *Encyclopedia of African History and Culture*, 295–296.

30 Beverly Carolease Grier, *Invisible Hands: Child Labor and the State in Colonial Zimbabwe* (Portsmouth, NH: Heinemann, 2006), 24, 16, 200–201.

31 Esi Sutherland-Addy and Aminata Diaw, eds, *Women Writing Africa: West Africa and the Sahel*, Vol. 2 (New York: The Feminist Press at the City University of New York, 2005), 170.

32 Davis, *Encyclopedia of African History and Culture*, 1–2; Sutherland-Addy and Diaw, *Women Writing Africa*, 169–174.

33 Sutherland-Addy and Diaw, *Women Writing Africa*, 174.

34 Sutherland-Addy and Diaw, *Women Writing Africa*, 174–176.

35 Judith Byfield, "Taxation, Women, and the Colonial State: Egba Women's Tax Revolt," *Meridians: Feminism, Race, Transnationalism* 3:2 (2003), 250–277. 266.

36 Byfield, "Taxation, Women, and the Colonial State," 267.

37 Byfield, "Taxation, Women, and the Colonial State," 269.

38 Eric Stokes, *The Peasant Armed: The Indian Revolt of 1857* (Oxford: Clarendon Press, 1986), 17.

39 Christopher Herbert, *War of No Pity: The Indian Mutiny and Victorian Trauma* (Princeton, NJ: Princeton University Press, 2008), 3.

40 Shaswati Mazumdar, *Insurgent Sepoys: Europe views the Revolt of 1857* (New Dehli: Routledge, 2011), 2–3, 6.

41 Crispin Bates, *Subalterns and Raj: South Asia Since 1600,* (New York: Routledge 2007), 66; 60–61; 66–67.

42 Bates, *Subalterns and Raj*, 69.

43 David Hardiman, *Peasant Resistance in India 1858–1914* (Delhi: Oxford University Press, 1992), 1.

44 Madhav Gadgil and Ramachandra Guha, "State Forestry and Social Conflict in British India," *Past and Present* 123:1 (1989), 141–177, 262, 264, 274–276.

45 Franziska Roy and Benjamin Zachariah, "Meerut and a Hanging: 'Young India,' Popular Socialism, and the Dynamic of Imperialism," *Comparative Studies of South Asia, Africa and the Middle East* 33:3 (2013), 360, 364, 369.

46 Taylor C. Sherman, *State Violence and Punishment in India* (London: Routledge, 2010), 93–95.

47 Vera Schwarcz, *The Chinese Enlightenment* (Berkeley: University of California Press, 1986), 14–15, 17.

48 Schwarcz, *The Chinese Enlightenment*, 3.

49 Schwarcz, *The Chinese Enlightenment*, 4.

50 Schwarcz, *The Chinese Enlightenment,* 41–43.

51 Edward X. Gu, "Who was Mr Democracy? The May Fourth Discourse of Populist Democracy and the Radicalization of Chinese Intellectuals (1915–1922)," *Modern Asian Studies* 35:3 (2001), 616.

52 Xiong Yuezhi, "The Theory and Practice of Women's Rights in Late-Qing Shanghai, 1843–1911," in *Beyond the May Fourth Paradigm: In Search of Chinese Modernity,* ed. Kai-Wing Chow, Tze-Ki Hon, Hung-Yok Ip, and Don C. Price (Lanham, MD: Lexington Books, 2008), 75.

53 Xiong Yuezhi, "The Theory and Practice of Women's Rights," 86.

54 Gerald Home, *Black and Brown: African Americans in the Mexican Revolution, 1910–1920* (New York: New York University Press, 2005), 32.

55 Michael Goebel, "Geopolitics, Transnational Solidarity, or Diaspora Nationalism? The Global Career of M.N. Roy, 1915–1930," *European Review of History: Revue européenne d'histoire* 21:4, 488, 491.

56 Jaime M. Pensado, *Rebel Mexico: Student Unrest and Authoritarian Political Culture During the Long Sixties* (Stanford, CA: Stanford University Press, 2013), 10–11.

57 Robert F. Alegre, *Railroad Radicals in Cold War Mexico: Gender, Class, and Memory in Cold War Mexico* (Lincoln: University of Nebraska Press, 2013), 2–5.

58 Samantha Christiansen and Zachary A. Scarlett, eds, *The Third World in the Global 1960s* (New York: Berghahn Books, 2013), 9.

59 Nicholas Creary, "Speaking the Language of Protest: African Student Rebellions at the Catholic Major Seminary in Colonial Zimbabwe, 1965–1979," in *The Third World in the Global 1960s,* ed. Christiansen and Scarlett, 117.

60 Pedro Monaville, "The Destruction of the University: Violence, Political Imagination, and the Student Movement in Congo-Zaire, 1969–1971," in *The Third World in the Global 1960s,* ed. Christiansen and Scarlett, 166.

61 Chris Saunders, "1968 and Apartheid: Race and Politics in South Africa," in *The Third World in the Global 1960s,* ed. Christiansen and Scarlett, 134.

62 From Steve Biko's evidence given at the SASO/BPC trial, 3 May 1976.

63 Isabel Hofmyer, "South Africa Remains: E.P. Thompson, Biko, and the Limits of the Making of the English Working Class," *Historical Reflections* 41:1 (Spring 2015).

4

Body Politics, Sexualities, and the "Modern Family" in Global History

Durba Ghosh

The family is often assumed to be an important unit of social organization, affecting who we become and how we relate to others. However "natural" we think it is to belong to a family, who we consider our kin and community— and how we feel toward our parents, siblings, conjugal partners, and children—shape and are shaped by history. Whether we identify as female, male, hermaphrodite, hijra, transsexual, or third gender, whether we love women, men, or both, the framework of the modern family has historically structured our access to social recognition and political rights. Beginning in the late eighteenth century and ending at the turn of the twenty-first, changing definitions of the modern family have been central to how we understand our bodies and sexualities in everyday life. This chapter focuses on five historical moments of transformation, in which particular ideas of family were produced to the exclusion of other possible social formations. Yet, as the chapter shows, the process of making the modern family has not been uniformly progressive. Over the course of history, definitions of family, bodies, and sexualities have continually been challenged by social practices, political debates, and cultural norms.

Using the optic of a world history from below, I show that there is no such thing as a "normal" family or normative sexuality. Throughout a range of historical and geographical contexts, a variety of familial formations and individuals have disrupted and challenged a singular or stable definition of family, sex, and gender. While many scholars argue that the modern nation-state is committed to making the labor of gendered bodies and capital productive for the purpose of economic and social progress, many women, men, and those who identify of neither gender have challenged dominant state-driven goals to demand that the state recognize different forms of social production and reproduction. Whether it is the polygamous family in which women share domestic and sexual labor, the matrilineal family in which children are not identified by their fathers' surnames, or joint families in which individual property matters very little to social and economic relations, these disruptions have put a great deal of pressure on whether we can ever have a settled definition of a "family." While sexual activity should not be understood as a dissenting activity or a defensive reaction to state policies, sexual and bodily politics in a world history from below—what we do in the privacy of our bedrooms—shows that a global historical struggle has long existed against a fixed or stable definition of the family.

We may imagine that our attachments to our loved ones are private concerns, but how each of us comes to belong to our communities and our nations has long been a question of public anxiety. At various moments, the state's or government's interest in making our bodily comportment and sexual behaviors productive have meant that we are subjected to laws, cultural norms, and social customs that dictate how we dress, how we carry ourselves, and even how we have sex. This chapter shows that familial norms are shaped by state, governmental, and civil practices that bring public goals about reproduction, sexual health, and social welfare into conversation with so-called private behaviors in the home and even the bedroom. Through an analysis of familial, bodily, and sexual practices and their connections to civil society, this chapter examines processes by which the state and civil institutions have been central to legitimating particular norms of bodily comportment and sexuality such as heterosexuality, monogamy, and reproductive kinship.

By addressing these questions from the eighteenth century to the present, this chapter argues that the historical development of the idea of family has been uneven, contradictory, and challenged by various actors and ideas. By rejecting the idea that families have progressed through various stages of development toward an agreed-upon definition of what it means to be "modern," I challenge the work of many social and political theorists who have argued that becoming a modern person is marked by adopting normative bodily and sexual behaviors such as heterosexuality, marital monogamy, and dressing in normatively gendered ways.[1] This chapter poses how we might think and rethink our assumptions that the "modern family" is made by heteronormativity, wherein a man and a woman cohabit with a number of dependents. In this framework, the man and woman are presumed to be monogamous, heterosexual, and the dependents are affiliated through some sort of emotional or affective attachment. Men and women are gendered so that men behave in one way and women behave in another; by urging that we historicize these assumptions, I show that family is closely linked to the construction of gender and sexuality.

This chapter also challenges a progressive modernization of the modern state. At some historical moments, such as the turn of the nineteenth century in Europe when women's property was transferred to her husband when she married, the state has been understood as a constraint on individual rights. At other moments and sites, such as modern-day India, where the census has recently listed transgender as a third category (in addition to male and female), the government has upheld laws that allow same-sex behaviors. By focusing on a genealogy of the family, this chapter will show how intimate relationships between men, women, children, and those who identify as neither gender have been transformed from the late eighteenth century to the present across the world, often in unpredictable ways.

In order to explain the historical present, I plot five historical moments as a way to show how ideas of the family were contested and challenged over the last two centuries by those who were neither exclusively heterosexual nor easily categorized into gendered forms of identification such as male or female.

The first section of the chapter explains the emergence of a putatively universal definition of the family in eighteenth-century Europe, which consisted of a nuclear family that contained a father who serves as the "head of the household," a mother who is often not his economic, political or social equal, and some number of children, servants, or slaves whose legal status is non-existent; this largely European form was an index of societies who were moving from "primitive" kinship models to more settled and modern forms of familial productivity and affect.

The second moment examines challenges to this ideal family form that came in various forms throughout nineteenth century. The emergence of colonial families in Asia, Africa, and Latin America—which often included multiple wives, mistresses, and concubines, mixed-race children, and a range of servants and slaves—undermined the claim that the nuclear family was the dominant modern form. Although homosexuality was criminalized by many governments in the nineteenth century, the widespread practice of men and women cohabiting in households as "sisters," "friends," or "mining wives," showed that not all women and men were living in heteronormative ways. Alongside these social challenges was an intellectual opposition from feminist scholars who noted that women had fewer rights when they married. Marriage was seen by some to constrain women's liberties, in terms of their legal rights to own property, to vote, and to divorce; it was also seen as a means to limit the sexuality of women by assuming that women could only be sexually active when they married.

The third historical moment that I examine occurs in the latter half of the nineteenth century. In addition to movements to pass legislation to grant women the same rights as men, the emergence of the figure or icon of the "new woman" and the "modern girl," in a range of sites across the globe, from the United States, Europe, Africa, and Asia, gave rise to new forms of gendering the behavior of those who identified as women. The "modern girl" was often described as resisting the pressures to conform to ideal family expectations and marry; instead, she worked outside the home, socialized in public places such as bars, cafes, hotels, and department stores. No longer subject to her father or a husband, who might have assumed the status of patriarch, the "modern girl" exemplified a new individualism for women and challenged social norms. Yet, the image of the "new woman" served a socially conservative nationalist agenda. Embraced by anti-colonial nationalists who characterized the new woman as a modern and patriotic figure, the "new woman" was often also a cast as a "good woman," whose middle-class comportment could serve her nation.

As the twentieth century unfolded, particularly after the two world wars, the definition of family was reconstituted yet again. Under centralized national governments, particularly in Britain, France, Germany, and the United States, national welfare programs turned to accommodating missing patriarchs, those who had died or been disabled in the war, in order to support families. Citizenship through membership in a family became an important way to gain legal recognition, thus providing state benefits and support for those who behaved in heteronormative ways.

The final historical moment of the chapter focuses on the end of the twentieth century, a movement for "marriage equality," or equal rights for all families, even those headed by two same-sex adults has become an important corrective to the notion that marriage and family should be limited by definitions of one's sexuality. Aided by the expansion of reproductive technologies, it is now possible to have children without having heterosexual intercourse, thus leading to a redefinition of heterosexual reproduction. Gaining recognition for same-sex marriage, surrogate motherhood, and transnational adoption have provided ways of expanding the definition of what might make the modern family in the United States and Europe; these expanded definitions have been met by challenges from formerly colonized states in Asia and Africa who would prefer to adhere to more "traditional" ideas about the family.

By using the idea of family as an organizing concept through these five historical moments, this chapter traces a genealogy of the idea of family, and by extension, gender, sexuality, and bodies to show that these ideas are produced out of particular historical contexts.

Bodies, sexualities, and families in transition in the eighteenth century

Changes in the definition of the premodern to modern family include the development of industrial economies, the emergence of nation-states, and the growing prominence of the individual as a subject and citizen with rights. Anthropologists have long argued that "modern" society has progressed through various stages of development so that a "civilized" society consisted of the "modern family" that could be formed into a national community and was productive for the nation-state.[2] This trajectory of progress has been challenged on a number of fronts by scholars, from Sigmund Freud to Michel Foucault, and more recently, Thomas Laqueur and Judith Butler. As they have shown, the transition from premodern to modern family life was marked by the repression of sexuality, rendering some sexual behaviors and desires, such as masturbation, homosexuality, and incest socially unacceptable. In Freud's psychoanalytic framework, transgressing sexual taboos such as incest or desire for a non-human subject (which Freud called a fetish) created a form of trauma as individuals transitioned from childhood to adulthood. His theories linked sexuality and family life so that the effective repression of desire is the hallmark of developing into a modern subject.[3] Repression of sexual desires have been differently configured by Michel Foucault, whose work on sexuality argued that sexualities were constrained by the advent of the modern family and government but that the possibilities of non-productive sexual desire were never completely repressed; indeed, in Foucault's formulation, repression could be productive (rather than traumatic, as Freud had claimed).[4] In the aftermath of Foucault, historians such as Thomas Laqueur have shown that not all sexual life could be understood through a conception of the male-centered pleasures of heterosexual intercourse. Instead, he has shown that many forms of non-reproductive sex were actively practiced and debated throughout the eighteenth and nineteenth centuries, rendering the idea of the male orgasm or heterosexual intercourse limited in understanding the range of sexual behaviors practiced by modern men and women.[5] Feminist scholars such as Judith Butler, Denise Riley, and Gayle Rubin have argued that heteronormativity understood as sex between a man and a woman might be a convenient biological explanation for sexual reproduction, but that it has rarely represented the full spectrum of gendered behavior and sexual norms that were expressed in any given society.[6]

In short, before circa 1750, the differences between men and women were not so stark. The seventeenth-century painting of Magdalena Ventura of Naples in what is now modern-day Italy shows a 52-year-old mother who is shown breastfeeding a child and also sporting a full beard (Figure 4.1).[7] While many of us might assume that mothers are women, and women do not grow beards, scholarship has shown that in the early modern period, depictions of the body were not gendered into conventionally male and female attributes. As a study on Iran before the nineteenth century argues, ideas of beauty were not distinct for men and women. Desire was openly expressed for youth, whose smooth complexions and slender bodies drew the erotic attention of others.[8] The absence of binary definitions of male and female meant that heterosexuality was not widely presumed, and premodern individuals engaged in a range of pleasurable activities that did not focus primarily on heterosexual intercourse.

By the late eighteenth century, the ideal of a nuclear family—with a male patriarch and a subordinate female matriarch and some number of children

FIGURE 4.1 *Magdalena Ventura with Her Husband and Son (José de Ribera, Naples, 1631). Credit: public domain.*

and other dependents—became the pre-eminent form of kinship, endowing men with civil rights that enabled them to be legally sovereign over the bodies and labor of those in their households.[9] The concomitant rise of nation-states supported the idea of the normative nuclear family in which heterosexual and monoracial marriages were legally and socially recognized by institutions such as the church in Europe and colonial governments in Latin America, Asia, and Africa.[10] Elite families, from royal families to those of the affluent merchant and landed classes were endowed with the possibility of owning slaves or availing themselves of the labor of servants, apprentices, and distant family members who needed familial support.[11] A family portrait of George Washington's family at the end of the eighteenth century shows what such a family, with an African-American slave in the background, might look like (Figure 4.2). Enshrined in the National Gallery of Art in Washington, DC, the globe and the map reflect a sense of American territorial expansion and mastery.

In India and in Jamaica, merchants and businessmen such as Richard Blechynden and Thomas Thistlewood had longstanding sexual relationships with female slaves that were structured by both physical coercion and economic dependence. Both Blechynden and Thistlewood left behind volumes of diaries that detailed secret activities with slaves in their households, and expressed how anxious they felt that these transgressive relationships across class and color lines would be revealed.[12]

FIGURE 4.2 *The Washington Family (1789–1796). Credit: Edward Savage.*

Legal changes supported the growth of nuclear families and consolidated a patriarch's hold over his household. During the eighteenth century, British legal scholars drew on the English common-law notion of "moderate correction," and adhered to Blackstone's eighteenth-century legal standard that a man had the right to "correct" the behavior of his wife by using the "rule of thumb," which stipulated he could use a stick no thicker than his thumb to physically chastise her.[13] When men went beyond their legal right to commit physical violence against their "wives," the courts stepped in and prosecuted them for domestic violence. By privileging the rights of men over the bodies of their wives, children, servants, and slaves, the ideal modern family became one with a (male) head of household whose legal rights to the family's property (which included a right to their labor) were recognized by the law as part of the social contract between male individuals and the state.[14]

Ironically, these classic social and political theories on the stages of family life and its relationship to being modern have overwhelmingly emerged from scholars based in Europe and the United States who have tended to argue that the "primitive tribes" lived in familial formations that were somehow uncivilized or backward. When anthropologists drew from research into kinship of indigenous populations in the Americas, Africa, Asia, and the Pacific Islands, they implied that non-Europeans "lagged behind" in their family formations because they practiced polygamy, polyandry, and matrilineal kinship.[15] By creating a hierarchy of the modern nuclear family over the so-called primitive family with multiple sexual partners and parents, scholars overlooked a large range of family forms that are practiced across the world. An examination of the scholarship shows that there is a great deal of contestation over whether the normative nuclear family ever existed, even in Europe.[16]

Among the most powerful criticisms of the nuclear family as a social unit that helped societies to progress was Frederick Engels. Working from notes made by Karl Marx, he argued that conjugal relationships between men and women were primarily based on an economic relationship that systematically diminished the importance of the labor of women. Engels viewed marriage as a form of economic inequality, understanding women's labor as a form of property. He asked why the work that women did in the home was uncompensated by wages. He showed that monogamous marriage entailed that the domestic labor of women was limited to unpaid labor in the home, thus keeping women tied to the home and in a subordinate position to men. As families and communities moved from a dependence on land to a dependence on wage labor, and as families moved from the agricultural or peasant classes to middle-class or bourgeois classes, women's labor was made less visible. A sign of the family's economic progress was that women did not work outside the home; inside their homes, their domestic labor was replaced by servants who took up the burdens of cleaning and household maintenance.[17] Thinking of the family as an economic unit assumed that it was a heterosexual unit, structured by a male breadwinner with women providing unpaid domestic labor in the home.[18]

In the modern period, families have been defined by a focus on individuality, particularly in defining the difference between men and women and their respective roles within the family unit. Familial obligations were increasingly structured by social expectations that a man and a woman entered into a lifetime contract to marry, have conjugal relations, and raise children. These children, would in turn, have more children, thus helping society to regenerate and progress from generation to generation. In the premodern era, laboring long hours on a farm to support one's family was considered a dominant expectation of all members of the family. As modernity unfolded through the nineteenth and twentieth centuries and the family's (and society's) fortunes improved, the development of each individual's goals became a priority and family members were no longer expected to work toward collective goals. The needs of children were particularly crucial, and cultivating young minds through education, and prohibitions on child labor became important signs of the progress of advanced capitalist societies.[19] An anonymous painting from mid-nineteenth-century Europe shows a woman sewing at her leisure, while the children play on the floor around her (Figure 4.3).

By the start of the nineteenth century, a more defined class system emerged in which middle-class homes were defined by women who could devote themselves full-time to homemaking and childcare, and did not need to earn wages for the household. In working-class households, however, the wages earned by women's labor were required to sustain the household economy. In order to maintain the respectability of the middle-class home, boundaries between those who were affluent and elite and those who had to labor were drawn. Increasingly, sexual transgressions and gendered behaviors became the site on which these disciplinary regimes occurred. From keeping children from masturbating or expecting that women limit their sexual appeal by wearing a chastity belt, the relationship between maintaining one's class position was sustained through familial and sexual behaviors.

The long-term relationship between Hannah Cullwick, who was a servant to Arthur Munby, in Victorian England is one such example. Munby, who was a British civil servant, carried out a decades-long relationship with his servant Hannah that culminated in a clandestine marriage. Through diaries, Munby documented his illicit desire and expressed fascination for Hannah's working-class body. Her work as a household servant rendered her hands dirty and brown (rather than soft and white), her skin dry, and her body substantially more muscled and brawny than if she had been a middle-class woman. Munby's desire for a body that was gendered more masculine than traditionally feminine was a form of transgression that he grappled with as he attempted to understand why he did not find women of his own class desirable.[20]

FIGURE 4.3 *Sewing Mother with Her Children (1854). Credit: Imagno.*

Even as legal recognition and economic demands for patriarchal rights emerged in the context of modern family life in the eighteenth century, thus according privileges to men to have sexual, economic, and legal access to the bodies of women, children, and slaves, many people in a range of societies did not live in strictly heteronormative ways. The nuclear family norm depended on a sense that the stages of civilizational development could be represented by the stages of family life, yet as historians of the global South have shown, this norm was generated by European colonial encounters. In particular, missionary activity pressed African, Asian, and

Latin American populations to accept monogamous companionate marriage as a normative civilizational form, even when this was not primarily the case in Europe.[21]

Challenges to the nuclear family form: Colonialism, homosociality, and women's rights

As the nineteenth century began, the nuclear family as the pinnacle of social development was complicated by the growing visibility of non-normative families and kinship networks. Institutions such as the church and emergent colonial states were particularly concerned about families produced out of mobility. As various types of subject bodies, slaves and convicts, as well as "free" travelers, such as colonial officials, settlers, and other emigrants moved from one part of the world to another, they settled into a relationship that threatened the normative European family. The growth of colonial families, often made up of European men and non-European women who had children classified as "natural," or "illegitimate," challenged the prevalent idea that families were made up of those who shared a common culture or racial background. Women and men who chose to live as "sisters," or "friends," further dissented from heteronormative assumptions about marriage and family and complicated the idea that familial attachments only existed between men and women. Figures such as Mary Wollstonecraft, John Stuart Mill, and others identified the institutions of marriage, family, and the law of coverture as a means to constrain women's liberties, particularly opportunities for economic and social advancement and recognition as citizens. The next sub-section sketches these three challenges as a way of examining how family arrangements of different kinds enabled the production of a variety of sexual and bodily behaviors.

As a range of Latin Americanists, Asianists, and Africanists have argued, definitions of the modern family varied during the colonial period, particularly when Europeans and non-Europeans met, married, or entered into consensual and coercive conjugal relationships. The existence of interracial colonial families produced anxieties for (white) colonizers, as they imagined their own sexualities were being transformed by intimate contact with indigenous (non-white) populations from the Indies in the east to the Indies in the west.[22] Concubinage, companionship, temporary marriages, and even marriages performed in church constituted the majority of heterosexual relationships; as well, same-sex relationships between those who identified as male, female, or transgender were crucial to the expansion of colonial territories.[23] Offspring were categorized in a range of ways, either as "natural" or "illegitimate" children, suggesting that these relationships existed outside respectable society. In some parts of the world, "Indian marriages" worked to bring a settler population into dialogue and collaboration with an indigenous population; in others, these interactions proved to be more conflict-ridden, giving rise to racial hierarchies between those considered "white," and those considered "black," "indio," "mixed-race," or "metis." As those working in colonial Latin America have shown, church and public approval mattered a great deal in how widely one could embrace one's indigenous wife and mixed-race children.[24] An important feature of territorial expansion involved European colonizers building new families and communities with indigenous women and men.

The project of "making empire respectable" created new mechanisms to limit the possibilities of what was called "unnatural vices," such as same-sex activity or interracial sex that threatened to undermine colonial and national identities. Colonial governments and institutions such as schools, orphanages, churches, and corporations became involved in managing racial and sexual relationships between Europeans and non-Europeans, particularly if these relationships involved people of different class or social status. Europeans sleeping with Asians, Africans, indigenous peoples in the Americas and the Pacific threatened to dilute colonizers' access to whiteness. The threat of "going native" diminished Europeans' claims to racial superiority. Thus, one of the key components of keeping European colonial empires intact throughout the nineteenth and early twentieth centuries was to ensure that men and women of different racial groups did not sleep together or desire one another, whether they were of the same gender or not.[25]

As scholars have shown, same-sex activity has existed across the world for much of history, but anxiety about it as a form of contagion that could contaminate the presumed heterosexuality of Europeans proliferated in the period of colonial expansion in the nineteenth and twentieth centuries.[26] In homosocial spaces where there were many more men than women—military cantonments, convict colonies, mining communities, and public schools—authorities were keen to ensure that white male workers remained heterosexual. The military was one of the most heavily male spaces, where the risk of men sleeping with one another provoked governments that hoped to link masculinity and soldierly behavior with heterosexuality to take action. Thus, regulating the sexual health of local female prostitutes became a key state prerogative. In the middle of the nineteenth century, when British officials discovered that more British soldiers were dying from venereal diseases than from combat injuries, schemes such as the Contagious Diseases Acts were enacted in Britain and its colonies in the Caribbean, India, South Africa, the Straits Settlement, Australia, and New Zealand.[27] Prostitutes were subjected to regular medical inspections to keep them available for sex work with British soldiers who were considered able-bodied and heterosexual.

As a global economy—dependent on plantation products such as tea, sugar, and rubber—proliferated in the nineteenth century, and in areas that required large populations of convict or indentured labor to work the land, economic productivity became closely linked to conjugal harmony. In the case of convict colonies and areas that depended on the import of indentured labor, women were seen to be simultaneously vulnerable to too much male sexual attention and prone to being enticed by multiple male partners, thus rendering them "unfaithful" or "immoral." For instance, in late nineteenth-century Trinidad, colonial officials and planters noticed a rise in "wife murders." A disproportionate number of women who had emigrated from India to Trinidad were being killed at the hands of their sexual partners, who were often also indentured laborers. Understood as a crisis in the provisioning of local labor, plantation and government officials undertook an investigation. The investigation showed that in most cases, men became jealous enough to kill their "reputed wives," which seemed a "natural" response to the problem of too few women. In order to resolve the moral and labor crisis of women laborers being killed and male laborers being hanged for murder, officials argued that more Indian women should be recruited into labor contracts into Trinidad so that families could be formed and indentured women could be induced to behave more monogamously. When this proved impractical, the British colonial government in Trinidad enacted marriage laws that gave men the right to seek intervention from the local magistrate, either to move the family to another plantation or to punish men who sought to entice women were already married. Similar projects of creating families in colonies of indentured and convict labor were attempted in northeastern Assam where women working on tea plantations were subjected to sexual aggression that rendered them unable to work, and in the Andamans, where the disruptions of jealousy threatened the expansion of the settlement.[28]

From mining towns in South Africa to farming and mining communities in the North American west, an economic boom in products such as gold, diamonds, wheat, and other agricultural products generated a growth in largely male communities of Asian and African migrants working alongside white men. In southern Africa, as the gold mining industry went through a boom in the early twentieth century, mining officials from European companies were keen to regulate same-sex relationships between white and African miners, believing that such "unnatural vices" were a practice that were being imported into the mines by East Africans and their tribal customs. In order to limit these interactions, British colonial and church officials in Witswatersrand ordered a "Confidential Enquiry" that investigated miners' sleeping arrangements and showed that "thigh sex," a form of non-penetrative sex, was more likely than what church officials feared, which was sodomy or anal sex. A marriage system of relationships between older and younger men—"mining wives"—structured the mines; this system did not preclude older men from remaining married to their wives at home or younger men from marrying women later. British missionaries viewed this custom as stemming from African practices that threatened British masculinity; highly educated British elites noted that the practice did not disturb the smooth functioning of the mines, and argued that it was coterminous with public school boys in Britain "fagging" one another in school. Mining officials kept the report secret and there was little public controversy about the practice. By comparison, the specter of white American miners sleeping with Chinese migrant laborers and Indian farmers in North America led to a proliferation of laws banning sex between men, and increasingly, sex between those of different races. Along the western coast of North America, local and state laws stipulated the differences between a range of sex acts such as sodomy, oral sex, and under-age copulation, making private acts into public crimes.[29]

As the modern nation-state grew in the late nineteenth century and turned toward protecting what was considered the "public interest," laws prohibiting sodomy, indecency, and same-sex activity were constructed and enforced in a range of global sites. In British India, the passage of sec. 377 of the Indian Penal Code made anal intercourse into an "unnatural offence," although in the process of enforcing the law, judges struggled over how to make sense of those who identified as eunuchs, hijras, or neither male or female.[30] In the United Kingdom, the famed novelist and playwright Oscar Wilde was charged with engaging in sodomy with a man. Sentenced to two years in prison, the Wilde trials were a spectacular indictment of same-sex activity. The global emergence of legislation at the end of the nineteenth century to ban homosexual activities showed how governments viewed same-sex practices as a significant challenge to the idea of the normative heterosexual family form; gays, lesbians, queers with a range of sexual attachments found their intimate lives criminalized by the state.

Yet, the visibility of gay men and lesbian women in public life demonstrated two contradictory historical developments. Urban centers in Europe and North America became the home of gays, lesbians, and third-gendered people that generated a sex-positive culture for same-sex relationships. Scholarship in sexology by Havelock Ellis, John Addington Symonds, Richard von Krafft-Ebing, and others recast homosexuality as a form of human sexuality that should not be repressed, as Freud suggested, or managed, as it was under labor regimes on plantations and convict colonies. In Berlin, New York, London, and elsewhere, gay culture thrived somewhat openly, often explicitly linking the efflorescence of cultural creativity with sexual experimentation.[31] In spite of laws and regulatory regimes to punish those with same-sex desires, historians have shown that the widely known practice of long-term companionship and cohabitation were structured by passionate sexual desires in the nineteenth- and twentieth-century relationships. These widespread examples of sexual partnerships disrupt the idea that homosexual practices were ever successfully suppressed by laws or social customs.[32]

A final challenge to the normative nuclear family form in the nineteenth century came from liberal feminist thinkers, many of whom had opposed slavery as representing the continued ownership of one person over another. Anticipating Engels' critique, they noted that marriage and laws of coverture constituted a form of constraining women's liberty and status. From the publication of Mary Wollstonecraft's *A Vindication of the Rights of Women* to John Stuart Mill's challenge of marriage, traditional (largely European) definitions of marriage between men and women were the subject of critique from the early nineteenth century onward.[33] As Mill noted in the opening pages of *The Subjection of Women* (which is often bound together with his treatise *On Liberty*), "That the principle which regulates the existing social relations between the two sexes—the legal subordination of one sex to the other—is wrong in itself and is now one of the chief hindrances to human improvement." The marital contract was seen to constrain women's personal liberties, limiting women's right to own property, become educated, and be treated as equal citizens who had the right to vote. The right for women to be recognized as legally equal to men was a demand that raised questions about why women's sexuality—or the right of women to enjoy sexual activity—was normatively constructed in the service of reproduction and motherhood. Although Victorian sexuality was conventionally understood as a time of repressing women's sexuality and non-normative sexual desires, a consideration of the rights of women opened the possibility that not all women had to be mothers and wives, nor did they have to be sequestered in the home and limited access to public life, nor were they required to be with gendered "female" in a conventional sense.

The "new" woman at the turn of the twentieth century

By the end of the nineteenth century, as women in Europe and the United States gained the right to have their own property, began to advocate for the right to vote, and were able to attend institutions of higher learning, the idea of the modern family changed yet again, largely because the idea of the "new woman" and the "modern girl" emerged to represent the possibility of women's sexual and bodily liberation that departed from the domesticated wife of the nineteenth century.[34] Rather than the secluded or "private" woman of the middle of the nineteenth century who had few options other than marriage and family, the image of the "new woman" offered the possibility of living without familial expectations. This image was produced through a vibrant press culture, advertising, consumerism, and the urbanization of everyday life allowing the "new woman" to experiment with new clothing (rejecting the corset and wearing pants), new hairstyles (bobs and bangs), and a modern fashion aesthetic that enabled her to enter urban life as someone who could see and be seen in a wider range of public spaces. The "new woman" was mobile, often leaving the home or household

FIGURE 4.4 *The Duchess of Sutherland, Lady Rosemary Leveson-Gower, Miss de Trafford, Miss Millington-Drake, and Lady Sybil Grey, at a sale of crippled girls' work in New Bond Street, London (November 1, 1913). Credit: Topical Press Agency.*

to ride a bus, train, or a bicycle, without a male chaperone.[35] In some places, such as Britain at the turn of the century, the "new woman" represented how "advanced" a nation was, showcasing her ability to be politically active and involved as a citizen in public debates.[36] A photograph of five elite women in England who raised money for disabled workers through sales in a store on New Bond Street in London shows the ways in which women could be good consumers and engaged citizens (Figure 4.4).

In other contexts such as China and Japan, places that had been identified by social theorists as "backward" in their attitudes toward women, the idea of woman's liberation produced anxieties of a loss of sexual respectability. In colonized and semi-colonized parts of the world, such as Egypt or India, the "new woman" was the target of social reforms, such as education, good household management, and the disavowal of superstitions that threatened to make her a poor representative of a reformist national project.[37] By reforming the so-called traditional woman into a "new" kind of gendered subject, the "new woman" flouted cultural norms but perpetuated new ones, transforming how an appropriately gendered female could live her life.

Closely related to the emergence of the "modern girl" (the younger counterpart of the "new woman"), these new forms of womanhood demonstrated the ways in which women's lives had been expanded by the opportunities offered by new technologies, urban life, increased consumer choices, and a modern fashion aesthetic.[38] Young women who identified as "modern girls" could remain unmarried, perhaps work outside the home and avail themselves of the opportunity to explore their individual subjectivities beyond the heteronormative frames of marriage, family, and procreative sex. A new range of cosmetics—including creams to make skin more white and straighteners to make hair less unruly—produced models of female beauty that spread visually through the advertising projects of multinational companies such as Pond's cold cream and Lifebuoy soap or global cinema.[39] The widespread availability of cosmetics was paralleled by the expansion of beauty contests, in which particular attributes of beauty prevailed (slender bodies, pale skin).[40] Even as women were given models for appearing more modern, particularly as they moved through public urban spaces, these models were structured by social demands that women remain respectably circumscribed as sexually moral, middle class, and modest. Cultural anxieties about the newfound freedoms and desires of the "modern girl" were expressed in racial, gendered, and class terms as elites struggled to contain the possible freedoms unleashed by the expansion of multinational companies who found markets across the world for their beauty products.[41] In South Africa, a model of producing "racial respectability" prevailed as writers of the women's pages called for "urban femininity that would distinguish their daughters and wives from the disreputable female figures of the prostitute and beer brewer . . ."[42] Even as the global spread of the cult of the "modern girl" suggests the global empowerment of women, the distinctions made between women instantiated new norms in which the "liberated" woman was seen to be predominantly white, middle-class, and educated, thus conforming to norms of comportment that reinstated the idea that those who identified as women should be sexually restrained.[43]

Coinciding with the emergence of the "new woman" and the "modern girl" was the impetus toward defining nationhood at a range of sites, particularly in places where political freedom and territorial sovereignty had not been achieved. Partha Chatterjee's formulation about the division between the spiritual and the material realms to denote the splitting and gendering of the family structure under colonialism has explained why demands for women's equality were frequently subsumed by demands for nationhood. In what he has called "the nationalist resolution," elite Indian men created the image of an ideal woman/wife who could protect "traditional" cultural norms within the home, even as her bodily habits, dress, and housekeeping skills were reformed in a modern direction.[44] In nationalized spaces from Britain to Egypt, India, and Korea, nationalist elites were compelled to discipline gender and sexual norms in the service of making colonized territories prepared for self-government; a key feature of this gendered management entailed women becoming better mothers, thus ensuring the reproduction of healthy children's bodies.[45] Women's sexuality remained a preoccupation of reformist elites; by promoting a higher age of consent, permitting women to marry and divorce as they wished, political leaders in India and Kenya, both British colonies, were able to signal that they shared the same liberal values as reformers in Britain, while advocating for the defense of traditional gender norms that were seen to defend cultural identity.[46]

Family, state, citizenship, and welfare: A new relationship between women and the state

As the twentieth century unfolded, particularly in the period after each of the world wars, state policies that focused on social welfare have shaped the definition of family. In particular, the definition of a family was reconstituted within the framework of citizenship as social welfare programs were founded to address the hardships of postwar economic depression. National welfare programs to support unemployed men, single mothers, and children proliferated across Europe. The expansion of social welfare for families were predicated on the assumption of gender norms—that the normative family unit was heterosexual, with a man and woman as husband/father and wife/mother—and that they lived in an economically self-sustaining household unit that distributed wages across the family for the greater success of each individual. Under newly restructured national governments, social welfare programs turned to replacing patriarchs who had died or been disabled in the war and could no longer financially support their families.[47] Working from the assumption that wages from the father should support the household and women who bore children should be exempt from laboring outside the home, a system of providing welfare "from cradle to grave" became central to postwar nation-building. The 1946 Beveridge Report that coined this phrase in Britain created new bonds of citizenship that tied individuals to families and thus, to more centralized nation-states.

As decolonization took shape in many Asian and African nations after World War II, new postcolonial states turned to the issue of creating civil laws that could produce social stability in the form of families to form the backbone of new civil societies.[48] Laws declaring that men and women had the right to marry at an appropriate age of consent, to divorce and inherit property as individuals, and to file grievances when they were not adequately compensated for family support proliferated across the world, albeit with different outcomes. The legal rights of individuals and the recognition of citizenship for men and for women remained closely tied to their place in a familial unit. In India, laws, such as the Hindu Marriage Act of 1956, enacted nearly a decade after India's independence, attempted (but failed) to give women the same right to inherit as their male relatives. Hindu women were made into members of joint families, in which a priority was put on preserving the family estate by exempting women from inheriting agricultural land.[49] Yet, in Kenya, supporting women who had children outside marriage became an important feature of the Affiliation Laws that allowed the mothers of so-called "illegitimate" children to sue for paternity and child support. As Lynn Thomas has argued, "the politics of the womb" in postcolonial Kenya gave rise to policies, laws, and practices that enabled the Kenyan government to intervene in maternity and child-rearing, so that the formerly colonized state of Kenya could begin to support the regeneration of the postcolonial nation.[50]

State recognition of its citizens in the twentieth century—born of a growing system of social welfare provisions—depended on the goal of creating family stability by entailing that government welfare replace the family wages that were lost when patriarchs were missing. In this matrix of governmental policies that linked family to the state, women were understood primarily as mothers. Women's reproductive and parenting abilities became critical to a nation's future success. In the United States, women were more likely to be recipients of the Aid to Families with Dependent Children (AFDC) program, commonly labeled "food stamps," while men were more likely to receive unemployment benefits. In Europe and North America the provision of social welfare was seen as an entitlement or benefit for citizens. In areas that had formerly been colonized, however, social welfare was imagined as a development scheme that was a gift to underprivileged women. The discourse of "women and development" (WAD) in the Global South, or the "Third World," as it was known for much of the 1950s and 1960s, targeted social reforms to improve the standards of living for Latin American, Asian, and African children and women.[51] Under welfare and development regimes from the middle of the twentieth century, what women fed their children, where they worked, whether their work outside the home was supported by the state-supported childcare facilities became critical to defining national progress and prosperity. Women across the world were encouraged to vaccinate their children against smallpox, polio, measles, and mumps; they were educated in hygiene and nutrition, at times encouraged to breast feed, at other times, urged to buy formula that was seen to be hyper-nutritious.[52]

As demographers became concerned with managing a growing population, the emergence of "birth control" or "family planning" technologies proved to be an important way in which reproduction became a matter of scientific innovation, cultural transformation, and state intervention. In some parts of the world such as the United States or northern Europe, by using birth control, women were liberated from the fear of unwanted pregnancies so that they could enjoy non-reproductive heterosexual sex; the pill is often credited with spurring the sexual revolution of the 1960s in Europe and the United States in which "free love" between multiple partners was a growing possibility.[53] By limiting pregnancy, families could plan to have fewer children, which meant that the household's income could be concentrated and focused on children and their improvement. Since 1970, when the Population Reference Bureau began to keep track of global birth trends, women are having fewer children, from 4.7 children per woman in 1970 to an average of 2.5 children in 2013. The decline is most pronounced in Asia, Latin America, and the Caribbean, where women averaged giving birth to 5.3 children in 1970 to a low of 2.2 now. In China and India, family planning became a part of state policy to limit the nation's population growth. Of these state policies, China's one-child policy and the sterilization campaigns targeted toward women living in Indian slums have received a great deal of negative attention because the state intruded on the sexual practices of women.

Since 1945, as governments and non-governmental organizations provide social welfare to families, governments and other institutions have become important actors in defining what types of families should be recognized as recipients of support. By recognizing some families and not others, those living in unconventional family structures found they had few legal rights. Because the logic of equal treatment has undergirded constitutions across the world and it is widely assumed that all individuals have the right to have equal recognition from their respective governments, in the last few decades, social movements to legally recognize our family forms, different sexualities, and gendered bodies has produced a great deal of political dissent.

The millennial family

At the turn of the twentieth-first century, definitions of the family, sex, and gender has become more expansive. Although in some parts of the world fewer people are now married and for fewer years than they once were, definitions of marriage and family have been reformulated. "Family" is no longer defined as the nuclear family of a male husband, a female wife, and several children; indeed, marriage is no longer limited to men and women. This process has not been without its disruptions, particularly as vigorous political debates about same-sex marriage, transnational adoption, and the ethics of reproductive technology rage in different parts of the world. The following section is a snapshot of these debates, showing the uneven and inconsistent logics that are mobilized in defining the modern family.

From the 1960s to the present, definitions of the family, gender, and sexuality have been unsettled by the following developments: a) the emergence of sophisticated methods of family planning, which include birth control for those wishing to manage their ability to have children and the emergence of assisted reproductive technologies, such as in-vitro fertilization, artificial insemination using donor sperm, egg donations, and surrogacy, for those wishing to conceive a child; b) campaigns for same-sex marriage; and c) the dramatic expansion of transnational adoption, in which children from the putatively Global South and Eastern Europe have been placed in suitable homes in the Global North. In short, I end this chapter by asking now that it is possible to have a child without having heterosexual intercourse, what does the modern family look like?

Reproductive technologies have expanded in medical sophistication, enabling the birth of many different kinds of families. For instance, assisted reproductive technologies have now made it possible for women to become mothers with their female lovers; male partners have been able to find surrogates to carry their biological children; and women are no longer tied to their so-called biological clocks because their eggs can be frozen and implanted when women are ready to bear children. Major multinational corporations such as Apple, Facebook, Citigroup, and JP Morgan are willing to pay for this healthcare cost, guessing that it will permit young women to work through the years that were previously assumed to be their prime child-bearing years.

The expansion of the practice of national and transnational adoption has also transformed the social pressures to reproduce ourselves biologically. A widely aired insurance commercial for John Hancock Financial Services, which originally aired in 2000, features lesbian mothers who are adopting an Asian child. The 30-second advertisement begins in an airport arrivals lounge where an American flag and several immigration officers are featured prominently. Two white American women, one holding the baby, discuss what it means to welcome the child "home," and then rifle through their bags for the baby's documents to enter the country. One of the mothers declares, "Can you believe this? We're a family," as John Hancock's products flash across the screen (annuities, life insurance). As the scene fades out, the final words are spoken by the mothers to one another, "You're going to make a great mom." "So are you." These final words were excised after right-wing groups in the United States protested to the public nature of an advertisement that appeared to be promoting same-sex marriage to sell insurance, but the idea that they were a family remained.[54]

How might we understand our current historical moment in which families are no longer exclusively defined by a mother and a father? If we "choose our families," "making parents" through social, legal, and political means that are not limited by heteronormative definitions of sex and marriage, what is a family?[55] Although men have long cohabited with other men, and women with other women, the movement for marriage equality has been an important campaign that advocates legal, social, and public recognition for those whose sexuality was hidden in the past. Since the 1980s, campaigns for gay marriage have picked up steam in the United States, France, and other parts of Europe. The growing number of nations and states that have granted gays and lesbians the legal right to marry fuels a growing sensibility that definitions of family no longer need to be limited to defining heteronormative bodies and sexualities. The movement to legally recognize same-sex marriage has allowed those who are not straight to marry, whether they identify as male, female, or neither gender, or whether they are gay or straight; the children of these relationships—whether they are biologically conceived or adopted—have been recognized as legal heirs; and perhaps most crucially, governments that previously banned and criminalized homosexual acts as a form of immorality or public indecency have recognized that the right to privacy should prevail. These debates, however, have proceeded in different ways. As an example, I look at how the movement developed in France and the United States since the 1990s. In France, the legislation has been framed by a demand that all citizens have basic universal rights as subjects of the French republic. In the United States, the movement in favor of gay marriage has become embedded in a language of family values, once promoted by activists on the political right, thus rendering gays and lesbians who marry as "good" citizens who live monogamously. While the French legislation concerns itself with universal rights of each subject to belong to a family, the American legislation is framed around rewarding "good gays" who are willing to marry, thus leaving those who live promiscuously and without family attachments outside the realm of legal recognition.[56]

But same-sex marriage has not been uniformly welcomed as a social possibility. In parts of Africa, Asia, and the Middle East, homosexuality is often seen as a "white disease" that was imported by Europeans when they colonized these parts of the world. In Iran, which had a thriving tradition of homoerotic desire for young men until the nineteenth century, homosexuality has been banned since the Iranian Revolution because it is seen as a practice that is not in accordance with Islamic ideals. In Africa, leaders such as Robert Mugabe, president of Zimbabwe, have challenged recognition of gay marriages with the argument that in "traditional" societies men do not sleep with men, and women do not sleep with women. Scholars of Africa have shown just the opposite—that homosexuality is deeply embedded in African culture.[57] Although South Africa has legalized gay marriages, its practice has been roundly challenged by Christian church groups that are the descendants of colonial missionary activity in the nineteenth century. In India, the Supreme Court recently issued a ruling to uphold Section 377 of the Indian Penal Code that criminalized homosexuality between men. In an ironic twist, the postcolonial Indian state views homosexual acts as "unnatural," and un-Indian. At the same time, the government of India has agreed to have "third gender" be a category on the Indian census, so that those who identify as neither men nor women can be counted as part of the nation's population. These most recent debates about the status of gays, lesbians, and transgender populations demonstrate that how we have sex and who we marry and raise children with remain important barometers for national and social progress, but that there are many tensions and contradictions in how we comprehend social life beyond the heteronormative.

As reproductive technologies and the growing recognition of same-sex marriage as a legal right expand, how we define family and gender is being reformulated. As the large-scale protests against the "Marriage for All" movement in France recently show, the idea of recognizing gay marriage threatens the binary of gender on which being modern is premised. If marriage is allowed for all, critics in France suggest, how are we to identify what is a man or what is a woman?[58] A possible answer, but by no means a resolution, might be found in the figure of Thomas Beatie, a transgendered American who had gender reassignment surgery in 2002. Until then, he identified as a woman (then named Tracy LaGondino). He had a double mastectomy, and started taking testosterone so that his body would look more like a man's. He married Nancy Gillespie the following year, and subsequently, they found out that Nancy could not bear children. So Thomas, who had retained his female reproductive organs, chose to be artificially inseminated and has now given birth to three children. Caricatured in the tabloids as the "pregnant man," Thomas has been featured in the nationally known LGBT magazine, *The Advocate,* as well as the more mainstream *People*; in interviews with Oprah Winfrey and Barbara Walters, Thomas has explained that he is a mother like any other, except that he cannot breastfeed his children. By making his story public, Thomas hopes that the public can imagine the range of bodily and sexual possibilities that exist beyond male/female, gay/straight, and mother/father.

Conclusion

In what appears to be a return to the fluidity of gender categories that used to mark the premodern, the long-presumed biological links between having sex and having a family have been utterly transformed in the twenty-first century. In the contemporary moment, in some parts of the world, same-sex marriage and transgender rights are a political impossibility. In other parts of the world, a new legal, political, and social regime recognizes a larger range of alternative family forms that are accompanied by a wider range of sexualities and bodily performances.

Suggestions for further reading

Butler, Judith. *Gender Trouble: Feminism and the Subversion of Identity*. New York: Routledge, 1990.

Eng, David. *The Feeling of Kinship: Queer Liberalism and the Racialization of Intimacy*. Durham, NC: Duke University Press, 2010.

Engels, Frederick. *The Origin of the Family, Private Property, and the State*. New York: International Publishers, 1972.

Foucault, Michel, trans by Robert Hurley. *History of Sexuality*. New York: Vintage Books, [1978], 1990.

Laqueur, Thomas. *Making Sex: Body and Gender from the Greeks to Freud*. Cambridge, MA: Harvard University Press, 1990.

Modern Girl Around the World Research Group, Alys Eve Weinbaum,
    Lynn M. Thomas, Priti Ramamurthy, Uta G. Poiger, Madeline Yue Dong, and
    Tani E. Barlow, eds. *The Modern Girl Around the World: Consumption,
    Modernity, and Globalization*. Durham, NC: Duke University Press, 2008.
Najmabadi, Afsaneh. *Women with Mustaches and Men Without Beards: Gender
    and Sexual Anxieties of Iranian Modernity*. Berkeley: University of California
    Press, 2005.
Riley, Denise. *Am I That Name?: Feminism and the Category of "Woman" in
    History*. Minneapolis: University of Minnesota Press, 1988.
Pateman, Carole. *The Sexual Contract*. Stanford, CA: Stanford University Press,
    1988.
Rubin, Gayle. "The Traffic in Women: Notes on the 'Political Economy' of Sex," in
    Toward an Anthropology of Women, ed. Rayna Reiter. New York: Monthly
    Review Press, 1975.
Rupp, Leila. *Sapphistries: A Global History of Love between Women*. New York:
    New York University Press, 2009.
Shah, Nayan. *Stranger Intimacy: Contesting Race, Sexuality, and the Law in the
    North American West*. Berkeley: University of California Press, 2011.
Skocpol, Theda. *Protecting Soldiers and Mothers: Political Origins of Social Policy
    in the United States*. Cambridge, MA: Harvard University Press, 1992.
Stoler, Ann. *Carnal Knowledge and Imperial Power: Race and the Intimate in
    Colonial Rule*. Berkeley: University of California Press, 2010.
Weston, Kath. *Families We Choose: Gays, Lesbians, Kinship*. New York: Columbia
    University Press, 1997.

Notes

1   Michel Foucault [1978], *History of Sexuality*, Vol. 1, translated by Robert
    Hurley (New York: Vintage Books, 1990). This may be the *locus classicus*
    for tracing the change from the premodern body to the modern
    body.

2   Key theoretical texts include Frederick Engels, *The Origin of the Family,
    Private Property, and the State* (New York: International Publishers, 1972);
    E. E. Evans-Pritchard, *Kinship and Marriage among the Nuer* (Oxford:
    Clarendon, 1951); Claude Levi-Strauss, *Elementary Structures of Kinship*
    (Boston, MA: Beacon Press, 1969); A. R. Radcliffe-Brown and Daryll Forde,
    eds, *African Systems of Kinship and Marriage* (London: Oxford University
    Press, 1950); Margaret Mead, *Coming of Age in Samoa* (New York: Blue
    Ribbon Books, 1928, 1934). For revisions, see Jane Collier and Sylvia
    Yanagisako, eds, *Gender and Kinship: Essays toward a Unified Analysis* (Palo
    Alto, CA: Stanford University Press, 1987); Sarah Franklin and Susan
    McKinnon, eds, *Relative Values: Reconfiguring Kinship Studies* (Durham, NC:
    Duke University Studies, 2001).

3   Sigmund Freud, *Totem and Taboo: Resemblances between the Psychic Life of
    Savages and Neurotics* (New York: Moffat and Yard, 1918); *Civilization and
    Its Discontents* (New York: W. W. Norton, 2010).

4   Foucault, *History of Sexuality*.

5   Thomas Laqueur, *Making Sex: Body and Gender from the Greeks to Freud* (Cambridge, MA: Harvard University Press, 1990) and *Solitary Sex: A Cultural History of Masturbation* (New York: Zone Books, 2013).

6   Judith Butler, *Gender Trouble: Feminism and the Subversion of Identity* (New York: Routledge, 1990), pp. 72–78; Gayle Rubin, "The Traffic in Women: Notes on the 'Political Economy' of Sex," in *Toward an Anthropology of Women,* ed. Rayna Reiter (New York: Monthly Review Press, 1975); Denise Riley, *Am I That Name?: Feminism and the Category of "Woman" in History* (Minneapolis: University of Minnesota Press, 1988).

7   Available for free at: http://www.wikiart.org/en/jusepe-de-ribera/magdalena-ventura-with-her-husband-and-son-1631 [accessed February 9, 2016].

8   Afsaneh Najmabadi, *Women with Mustaches and Men Without Beards: Gender and Sexual Anxieties of Iranian Modernity* (Berkeley: University of California Press, 2005).

9   Carole Pateman, *The Sexual Contract* (Stanford, CA: Stanford University Press, 1988).

10 Kathleen Brown, *Good Wives, Nasty Wenches, and Anxious Patriarchs: Gender, Race, and Power in Colonial Virginia* (Chapel Hill: University of North Carolina Press, 1996); Nancy Cott, *Public Vows: The History of Marriage and the Nation* (Cambridge, MA: Harvard University Press, 2000); Edward Shorter, *The Making of the Modern Family* (New York: Basic Books, 1975); Lawrence Stone, *The Family, Sex, and Marriage in England, 1500–1800* (New York: Harper Books, 1979).

11 Herbert G. Gutman, *The Black Family in Slavery and Freedom, 1750–1925* (New York: Vintage Books, 1976), which was written as a response to Daniel P. Moynihan's controversial 1965 report, "The Negro Family: A Case for National Action." See also Naomi Tadmor, *Family and Friends in Eighteenth-century England: Household, Kinship, and Patronage* (Cambridge: Cambridge University Press, 2001); Indrani Chatterjee, ed. *Unfamiliar Relations: Family and History in South Asia* (New Brunswick, NJ: Rutgers University Press, 2004).

12 Trevor Bernard, *Master, Tyranny, Desire: Thomas Thistlewood and his Slaves in the Anglo-Jamaican World* (Chapel Hill: University of North Carolina Press, 2004); Peter G. Robb, *Sentiment and Self: Richard Blechynden's Diaries, 1791–1822* (Delhi: Oxford University Press, 2011).

13 Susan Dwyer Amussen, " 'Being Stirred to Much Unquietness': Violence and Domestic Violence in Early Modern England," *Journal of Women's History* 6 (1994): 71.

14 Durba Ghosh, "Household Crimes and Domestic Order: Keeping the Peace in Colonial Calcutta, c.1770–c.1840," *Modern Asian Studies* 38:3 (July 2004): 598–624.

15 The idea of a time lag comes from Dipesh Chakrabarty, *Provincializing Europe: Postcolonial Thought and Historical Difference* (Princeton, NJ: Princeton University Press, 2008), ch. 1.

16 Stephanie Coontz, *Marriage, a History* (New York: Viking, 2005); Jack Goody, *The Development of the Marriage and Family in Europe* (Cambridge:

Cambridge University Press, 1983); Mary Hartman, *The Household and the Making of History: A Subversive View of the Western Past* (Cambridge: Cambridge University Press, 2004); David I. Kertzer and Marzio Barbagli, *The History of the European Family,* vols. 1–3 (New Haven, CT: Yale University Press, 2001–2003).

17 Leonore Davidoff and Catherine Hall, *Family Fortunes: Men and Women of the English Middle Class, 1780–1850* (Chicago: University of Chicago Press, 1987).

18 Jan De Vries, *The Industrious Revolution: Consumer Behavior and the Household Economy, 1650 to the Present* (Cambridge: Cambridge University Press, 2008), ch. 5.

19 Norbert Elias, *The Civilizing Process*, translated by N. Jephcott (Oxford: Blackwell, 1994); Jonas Frykman and Orvar Lofgren, *Culture Builders: A Historical Anthropology of Middle-class Life* (New Brunswick, NJ: Rutgers University Press, 1987).

20 Peter Stallybrass and Allon White, *The Politics and Poetics of Transgression* (Ithaca, NY: Cornell University Press, 1986), ch. 4.

21 Catherine Hall, *Civilizing Subjects: Colony and Metropole in the English Imagination, 1830–1867* (Chicago: University of Chicago Press, 2002); Ramon A. Gutierrez, *When Jesus Came, the Corn Mothers Went Away: Marriage, Sexuality, and Power in New Mexico, 1500–1846* (Stanford, CA: Stanford University Press, 1991).

22 Ann Stoler, *Carnal Knowledge and Imperial Power: Race and the Intimate in Colonial Rule* (Berkeley: University of California Press, 2010); see also Durba Ghosh, *Sex and the Family in British India: The Making of the British Empire* (Cambridge: Cambridge University Press, 2006); Margaret D. Jacobs, *White Mother to a Dark Race: Settler Colonialism, Maternalism, and the Removal of Indigenous Children in the American West and Australia* (Lincoln: University of Nebraska Press, 2009); Damon Ieremia Salesa, *Racial Crossings: Race, Intermarriage, and the Victorian British Empire* (Oxford: Oxford University Press, 2011); Emmanuelle Saada, *Empire's Children: Race, Filiation, and Citizenship in the French Colonies* (Chicago: University of Chicago Press, 2012); Emma Teng, *Eurasian: Mixed Identities in the United States, China, and Hong Kong, 1842–1943* (Berkeley: University of California Press, 2013).

23 Robert Aldrich, *Colonialism and Homosexuality* (London: Routledge, 2003); Stephen O. Murray and Will Roscoe, *Boy-wives and Female Husbands: Studies of African Homosexualities* (New York: St. Martin's Press, 1998).

24 Patricia Seed, *To Love, Honor and Obey: Conflicts over Marriage Choice in Colonial Mexico* (Stanford, CA: Stanford University Press, 1988); Ann Twinam, *Public Lives, Private Secrets: Gender, Honor, Sexuality, and Illegitimacy in Colonial Spanish America* (Stanford, CA: Stanford University Press, 1999).

25 Megan Vaughn, *Creating a Creole Island: Slavery in Eighteenth-century Mauritius* (Durham, NC: Duke University Press, 2005); Matt Matsuda, *Empire of Love: Histories of France and the Pacific* (New York: Oxford University Press, 2005).

26 Ronald Hyam, *Empire and Sexuality* (Manchester, UK: Manchester University Press, 1990); Leila Rupp, *Sapphistries: A Global History of Love between Women* (New York: New York University Press, 2009), especially chs 5–7.

27 Philippa Levine, *Prostitution, Race, and Politics: Policing Venereal Diseases in the British Empire* (New York: Routledge, 2003).

28 Prabhu Mohapatra, "'Restoring the Family': Wife Murders and the Making of a Sexual Contract in Indian Caribbean Colonies," *Studies in History* 11:2 (1995): 227–260; Aparna Vaidik, "Settling the Convict: Matrimony and Domesticity in the Andamans," *Studies in History* 22:2 (2006): 221–251.

29 Ross G. Forman, "Randy on the Rand: Portuguese African Labor and the Discourse on 'Unnatural Vice' in the Transvaal in the Early Twentieth Century," *Journal of the History of Sexuality* 11:4 (2002): 570–609. T. Dunbar Moodie, *Going for Gold: Men's Lives in the Mines* (Berkeley: University of California Press, 1994); Nayan Shah, *Stranger Intimacy: Contesting Race, Sexuality, and the Law in the North American West* (Berkeley: University of California Press, 2011).

30 Elizabeth Kolsky, *Colonial Justice in British India: White Violence and the Rule of Law* (Cambridge: Cambridge University Press, 2010).

31 Robert Beachy, *Gay Berlin* (New York: Alfred Knopf, 2014); George Chauncy, *Gay New York: Gender, Urban Culture, and the Making of the Gay Male World, 1890–1940* (New York: Basic Books, 1995); Deborah Cohler, *Citizen, Queer, Invert: Lesbianism and War in Twentieth-century Britain* (Minneapolis, MN: University of Minnesota, 2014); Matthew Cook, *London and the Culture of Homosexuality, 1885–1914* (Cambridge: Cambridge University Press, 2003).

32 Sharon Marcus, *Between Women: Friendship, Desire, and Marriage in Victorian England* (Princeton, NJ: Princeton University Press, 2009); Carroll Smith-Rosenberg, "The Female World of Love and Ritual: Relations between Women in Nineteenth-century America," *Signs* 1:1 (1975); Martha Vicinus, *Intimate Friends: Women Who Loved Women, 1778–1928* (Chicago: University of Chicago Press, 2004); Jeffrey Weeks, *Coming Out: Homosexual Politics in Britain from the Nineteenth Century to the Present* (London: Quartet Books, 1977). For a global history over a *longue duree*, see Rupp, *Sapphistries*.

33 Harriet Guest, *Small Change: Women, Learning, Patriotism, 1750–1810* (Chicago: University of Chicago Press, 2000), chs 11–12.

34 Martha H. Patterson, ed., *The American New Woman Revisited: A Reader, 1894–1930* (New Brunswick, NJ: Rutgers University Press, 2008); Mary Louise Roberts, *Disruptive Acts: The New Woman in Fin-de-siècle France* (Chicago: University of Chicago Press, 2002).

35 Patricia Marks, *Bicycles, Bangs, and Bloomers: The New Woman in the Popular Press* (Lexington, KY: University Press of Kentucky, 1990); Judith Walkowitz, *City of Dreadful Delight: Narratives of Sexual Danger in Late-Victorian London* (Chicago: University of Chicago Press, 1992).

36 Antoinette Burton, *Burdens of History: British Feminists, Indian Women, and Imperial Culture, 1865–1915* (Chapel Hill: University of North Carolina Press, 1994).

37 Tani E. Barlow, *The Question of Women in Chinese Feminism* (Durham, NC: Duke University Press, 2004); Marianne Kamp, *New Woman in Uzbekistan: Islam, Modernity, and Unveiling under Communism* (Seattle: University of Washington Press, 2006), ch. 5; Dina Lowy, *The Japanese "New Woman": Images of Gender and Modernity* (New Brunswick, NJ: Rutgers University Press, 2007); Barbara Hamill Sato, *The New Japanese Woman: Modernity, Media, and Women In Interwar Japan* (Durham, NC: Duke University Press, 2003); Mona L. Russell, *Creating the New Egyptian Woman: Consumerism, Education, and National Identity, 1863–1922* (New York: Palgrave Macmillan, 2004).

38 The following section is drawn from the edited volume by the Modern Girl Around the World Research Group, Alys Eve Weinbaum, Lynn M. Thomas, Priti Ramamurthy, Uta G. Poiger, Madeline Yue Dong, and Tani E. Barlow, eds, *The Modern Girl around the World: Consumption, Modernity, and Globalization* (Durham, NC: Duke University Press, 2008).

39 *Modern Girl*, chs 1–2.

40 Sarah Banet-Weiser, *The Most Beautiful Girl in the World: Beauty Pageants and National Identity* (Berkeley: University of California Press, 1999).

41 On images of the "modern girl" that unleashed anxieties about a decline in male authority, see *Modern Girl*, ch. 9; or how the "modern girl" had to remain circumscribed with certain notions of whiteness, chs 3, 6, 7, 10; or about the ways how class norms, particularly in a time of revolution, were instantiated, ch. 8.

42 *Modern Girl*, ch. 5, p. 99.

43 *Modern Girl*, chs 6, 10, 11.

44 Partha Chatterjee, "Colonialism, Nationalism, and Colonized Women: The Contest in India," *American Ethnologist* 16:4 (1989): 622–633.

45 Anna Davin, "Imperialism and Motherhood," in *Tensions of Empire: Colonial Cultures in a Bourgeois World*, ed. Frederick Cooper and Ann L. Stoler (Berkeley: University of California Press, 1997); Lisa Pollard, *Nurturing the Nation: The Family Politics of Modernizing, Colonizing, and Liberating Egypt, 1805–1923* (Berkeley: University of California Press, 2005); Insook Kwon, "The New Woman's Movement in 1920s Korea: Rethinking the Relationship between Imperialism and Women," in *Feminisms and Internationalism*, ed. Mrinalini Sinha, Donna Guy, and Angela Woolacott (Oxford: Blackwell, 1999).

46 Mrinalini Sinha, *Specters of Mother India* (Durham, NC: Duke University Press, 2006); Lynn M. Thomas, *Politics of the Womb: Women, Reproduction, and the State In Kenya* (Berkeley: University of California Press, 2003).

47 See Deborah Cohen, *The War Come Home: Disabled Veterans In Britain and Germany, 1914–1939* (Berkeley: University of California Press, 2001); Linda Gordon, *Pitied but Not Entitled: Single Mothers and the History of Welfare, 1890–1935* (New York: Free Press, 1994); Susan Pedersen, *Family, Dependence, and the Welfare State: Britain and France, 1914–1945* (Cambridge: Cambridge University Press, 1993); Theda Skocpol, *Protecting Soldiers and Mothers: Political Origins of Social Policy in the United States* (Cambridge, MA: Harvard University Press, 1992).

48 Rachel Jean-Baptiste, *Conjugal Rights: Marriage, Sexuality, and Urban Life in Colonial Libreville, Gabon* (Athens, OH: Ohio University Press, 2014).

49 Eleanor Newbigin, *The Hindu Family and the Emergence of Modern India* (Cambridge: Cambridge University Press, 2013).

50 Thomas, *Politics of the Womb.*

51 Ester Boserup, *Women's Role in Economic Development* (London: Allen Unwin, 1970).

52 See Lynne Haney and Lisa Pollard, eds, *Families of a New World: Gender, Politics, and State Development in a Global Context* (New York: Routledge, 2003); Seth Koven and Sonya Michel, *Mothers of a New World: Maternalist Politics and the Origins of Welfare States* (New York: Routledge, 1993); Firoozeh Kashani-Sabet, *Conceiving Citizens: Women and the Politics of Motherhood in Iran* (Oxford: Oxford University Press, 2011); Elizabeth Thompson, *Colonial Citizens: Republican Rights, Paternal Privilege, and Gender in French Syria and Lebanon* (New York: Columbia University Press, 2000).

53 Elaine Tyler May, *America and the Pill: A History of Promise, Peril and Liberation* (New York: Basic Books, 2010).

54 David Eng, *The Feeling of Kinship: Queer Liberalism and the Racialization of Intimacy* (Durham, NC: Duke University Press, 2010), pp. 99–101. For the advertisement, visit www.commercialcloset.org.

55 Kath Weston, *Families We Choose: Gays, Lesbians, Kinship* (New York: Columbia University Press, 1997); Charis Thompson, *Making Parents: The Ontological Choreography of Reproductive Technologies* (Cambridge, MA: MIT Press, 2005).

56 Eric Fassin, "Same Sex, Different Politics: 'Gay Marriage' Debates in France and the United States," *Public Culture* 13:2 (2001): 215–232.

57 Marc Epprecht, *Heterosexual Africa?: The History of an Idea from the Age of Exploration to the Age of AIDS* (Ohio: Ohio University Press, 2008); Murray and Roscoe, *Boy-wives and Female Husbands.*

58 Camille Robcis, "Catholics, the 'Theory Of Gender,' and the Turn to the Human in France: A New Dreyfus Affair?" *Journal of Modern History* 87:3 (September 2015).

5

The Persistence of the Gods:

Religion in the Modern World

Tony Ballantyne

One powerful narrative that is often used to explain the characteristics of the modern world is secularization. This suggests that the emergence of sophisticated forms of modern governance, economic behavior, and cultural activity were intimately connected to the diminished political influence, moral authority and cultural weight that were attached to faith. In this view, as modernity took shape, religion had less impact on the public sphere and was either increasingly regulated to being a private matter of individual concern, or, more generally, was dispensed with in the face of the increasing ascendancy of rational and scientific worldviews. This chapter challenges such a view, suggesting that modernity was actually characterized by the increasing systematization of religion and by ongoing clashes around religion's meaning, significance, and its place in public life. These were contests over the legitimacy of faith, the authority of sacred texts, the influence of clerical elites and ritual experts and the validity of popular understandings of the divine and devotional practices. These arguments over religion were never simply waged within and between political officials and religious leaders, rather they were frequently initiated by individuals and groups from the lower social strata—slaves and indentured workers, oppressed laborers, the dispossessed, the colonized, and peasants who felt the brunt of state power. This chapter shows that in the modern age, religion—in all its multiple and contested forms—became increasingly cemented as a central organizing node of popular social life and a key ground for struggles over power in most parts of the world. Religion is pivotal in any understanding of modern histories of dissent and disruption as well as domination: it has been central in shaping modernity from both "above" and "below."

My particular focus here is on the ways in which religion was especially significant in contexts of cross-cultural engagement in light of the pioneering world historian W. H. McNeill's famous axiom that "encounters with strangers" are the "main drive wheel of social change" in human history. From the late eighteenth century on, such meetings became increasingly common. By 1780, the operation of merchant diasporas, the growth of slavery, and the growing reach of both missionary orders and imperial regimes meant that cultural mixing was much more common than it had been in 1580. These processes, which created new forms of interdependence between human communities, were extended, multiplied and accelerated through the nineteenth and twentieth centuries, albeit fitfully and unevenly, as steam power, electricity, fossil fuels, and then digital technologies underwrote expansive economic, political, and cultural regimes. By 2000 cultural mixing was almost ubiquitous; it was no longer primarily characteristic of ports and key marketplaces, but rather was woven into the fabric of most cities. And the circulation of media meant that for even those communities where there was relatively less direct engagement with peoples of different origins, images of other peoples, distant places, and alternative belief systems were ubiquitous.

So one useful way of thinking about modernity is not to see it as an age where gods were banished, but rather as an age where gods and their believers were on the move and, by necessity, had to negotiate the nature and meaning of their co-existence. Against this backdrop of mobility and mixing, religion took on greater significance as a way of making sense of human experience and as a way of organizing social life. Of course, religion was not only concerned with the relationship between humanity and the divine, but was also central in debates over the shape of social life, cultural patterns, and political authority. These exchanges took on a new shape when they were not simply an internal dialogue within homogenous societies but rather often fraught exchanges within, across and between various communities within polyglot, multi-ethnic, and multi-faith societies. Religion has been pivotal in both elite debates and everyday struggles over how society should work and how power should be distributed.

This chapter explores some of these dynamics in three sections. The first section particularly focuses on the ways in which Protestant missionaries, indigenous evangelists and new converts vernacularized Christianity in many parts of the world, often working from the margins of the social order as the poor, impoverished, and exploited embraced the power of new religious ideas and practices to question established political and cultural formations. It also demonstrates how these evangelistic projects stimulated both reassertions of other faith traditions in response and offered powerful templates for religious reform at a global level. The second section of the chapter suggests that these missionary struggles helped cement religion in global political life, while also prompting the increased systematization of many religious traditions and spurring wide-ranging reform movements in the non-Western world. The final part of the chapter shows that this systematization helped ultimately drive a cultural bifurcation, where many male elites had accommodated themselves to the demands of the state to contain religion and as a result experienced increasingly attenuated relationships to popular religion. Their worlds, like that of the state, tended to become disenchanted, whereas the power of the divine continues to be strongly felt by most of the world's populations.

Evangelicalism and the vernacularizing impulse

From 1750 probably the most mobile god was the God of Protestant Christians, largely as a result of a concerted global effort to construct vernacularized Christian communities where the Bible was translated into local languages and missionaries attempted to reshape local cultures in light of biblical teaching and evangelicalism's distinctive stress on the importance of work, the primacy of the family, and the cultural value of literacy. The catalyst for this drive was the evangelical revival. Evangelicals were unified by their belief that the essence of the Biblical narrative was that salvation was made possible by faith in the atoning sacrifice of Jesus Christ's crucifixion. From the 1730s, Protestants in Britain, the German-speaking lands, and North America were caught up in a series of revivals where large numbers of ordinary people had conversion experiences, were energized by their belief in God's redemptive love and an enthusiasm for sharing the gospel, and bringing the joys of new life to others directly rather than through the authority of the established churches. Underpinning these revivals was a doctrinal shift where key thinkers like Jonathan Edwards (the great New England preacher and theologian), George Whitefield (the influential English Anglican preacher), and the founders of Methodism, Charles and John Wesley, stressed that believing Christians were justified by their faith in Christ alone and that assurance of salvation was a common element of a conversion experience.[1]

This new understanding that the converted might feel assured in their own salvation was widely spread through preaching to large audiences, the circulation of printed sermons, and the extensive mobility of these exponents of the Christian message. This religious vision and energy had lasting consequences. In Wales, for example, it fed a Methodist revival, revitalized the other non-conformist traditions (the Baptists and Congregationalists), and helped fortify the Welsh language, while in colonial British America it fed the Great Awakening, which promoted an intense and personal faith while simultaneously stressing the spiritual equality that resulted from the openness of salvation.[2] It also had significant political consequences: it is possible to see, for example, the egalitarian style, energy, and ethos of evangelical preachers and pamphleteers as a key seedbed for the ideologies espoused during the American Revolution and which subsequently shaped the American republican tradition.[3]

It was not until the 1790s that this equality was seen to extend to people beyond Christendom, and many Europeans accepted the idea that European Christians had a responsibility to bring their message of faith and salvation to non-Christians. There had been some significant experiments in bringing the gospel to non-Europeans, particularly by some of the most notable architects of the evangelical revival, including Jonathan Edwards who ministered to Mahican peoples at Stockbridge, Massachusetts and John and Charles Wesley who were optimistic that their teaching would reform the Native Americans they encountered during their sojourn in the colony of Georgia in the 1730s.

Generally, however, European Protestants remained skeptical of the need to minister to non-European peoples and they lagged behind the Augustinians, Franciscans, Dominicans, and Jesuits who took Catholicism to the New World and to Asia during the early modern period. This situation changed rapidly from the final years of the eighteenth century, in the wake of the publication of William Carey's *An Enquiry into the Obligation of Christians to Use Means for the Conversion of the Heathen* (1792), which articulated a new obligation for British Protestants to spread the gospel and constructed this task as a global campaign. Carey's text was molded not only by evangelical enthusiasm, but also by Enlightenment empiricism and he provided a global religious demography that highlighted the urgent need for overseas mission work: he noted that some 420 million lived in "pagan darkness" and argued that the gospel had to be carried to all corners of the Earth.[4] Carey was a Baptist shoemaker from Northampton and was the catalyst behind the Baptist mission to India: his career as an influential advocate for missions, a pioneer in the Indian mission field, and as a groundbreaking translator and printer exemplifies that mission work overseas opened up new opportunities for those whose options were constrained at home and functioned as a key outlet for the activism and energy unleashed by the evangelical revival.[5]

Carey's career dramatizes some of the complex links between evangelical work and empire and reminds us that the roots of the modern global missionary movement lie not in the established Anglican Church or British elites, but amongst dissenters and working class and lower echelons of the "middling sorts." Until the 1830s the operations of Protestant missionaries in India were heavily constrained by the East India Company, which officially followed a policy of "toleration," which saw the Company generally limiting its "interference" in the established "religious usages" of its Hindu, Muslim, and Sikh subjects and, in some instances, taking on a more active role as a patron and protector of Indian traditions. Carey and his fellow missionaries were generally unpopular with the East India Company establishment: their commitment to the critique of non-Christian cultural practices, their aspiration to convert locals, and their "enthusiasm" were all seen as

FIGURE 5.1 *William Carey (1761–1834), English protestant missionary and baptist minister. Engraved by J. Jenkins after Robert Home. From the book* The National Portrait Gallery *(Vol. III published 1820). Credit: Universalimagesgroup.*

potentially destabilizing colonial rule. Company officers and the small Anglican establishment that served the needs of Company men and the small expatriate British community were also often skeptical of missionaries because of their humble origins and unrefined manners. Influential British commentators, such as the Anglican critic and *Edinburgh Review* editor Sir

…issionaries as "raving enthusiasts," critiques that …cism about the cultural capacity of lower-class …ly transmit God's word as well as opposition to … Christianity.[6] Carey's Baptist mission itself was not …y within the British East India Company's ambit after …ed to license missionary activity, but rather was based in …al enclave at Serampore.

B… …gh some colonial authorities such as the East India Company attempte… …onstrain missionary work in early nineteenth century, the empire generally provided an arena for evangelization and a distinct career trajectory for skilled evangelicals from the "respectable" working class and the lower echelons of the "middling sort" who had energy, practical skills, and faith. For William Carey himself it was the extension of Britain's imperial reach into the Pacific that prompted his vision of a global mission: "Reading Cook's voyages was the first thing that engaged my mind to think of missions."[7] Missionary work within the empire in turn shaped British culture at home: cheap or free missionary pamphlets and periodicals were specifically aimed at working-class parishioners, soliciting their financial support for mission work and seeking volunteers for evangelization. It was after reading the account of the death of a pioneering Maori Christian and traveler named Maui, that a Norfolk blacksmith named James Kemp volunteered his services to the Church Missionary Society in 1818; his offer was swiftly accepted and he and his new wife soon found themselves working on the New Zealand frontier at Kerikeri, where they would play influential roles as evangelists, teachers, storekeepers, and cross-cultural brokers.

At the heart of this Protestant missionary drive to bring the gospel to all human communities was a commitment to vernacularizing Christianity, to translating the Bible and making it available for all people to read in their own language, rather than in Latin, which remained the dominant liturgical language of Catholicism until the late twentieth century. Such undertakings required working closely with local peoples to gain the linguistic and cultural knowledge required to make plausible translations. So while the evangelistic initiatives of Protestant missionaries have been very influential at a global level, in all localities these initiatives have been heavily dependent on the knowledge, support and labor of local peoples. Often missions required the patronage and protection of chiefly elites or hereditary rulers and as a result, evangelical teachings subsequently played a significant role in the reformulation of political cultures in much of the Pacific and Africa. But the appeal of Christianity and the Bible was often most keenly felt by those at the bottom of the social order: slaves, war captives, peasants, poor workers, and women with limited economic resources and little or no access to power. Biblical narratives that promised salvation and that divine judgment would be delivered upon the tyrannical and corrupt had a particular appeal to those who were enslaved and colonized: in the American South, for example, Christianity was overlaid with a host of inherited African cosmologies and rites, becoming a distinctive form of faith that offered social and spiritual solace in the form of brutal oppression.[8] The prominence of Protestantism in that region, as both a bulwark of slavery and a refuge for the enslaves, encapsulates the ways in which religion could simultaneously operate from "above" and "below" in molding a social and political order.

Throughout the nineteenth century (and into the twentieth), new Christians were consistently adept at producing localized versions of the Christian tradition that were imprinted by inherited traditions and responsive to social and political pressures. The creativity of converts was at one level the result of the centrality of the vernacular text and reading in missionary pedagogy: individual readers often generated innovative interpretations of texts in ways that surprised missionaries, occasionally delighting them and more frequently worrying them. Of course, the diversity of African and Pacific Protestantisms that emerged also reflected the nature of the Bible itself, a compendium of diverse genres, divergent narratives, and competing voices that provided a vast store of material, which could be read in a multitude of ways. Missionaries and clerics worked hard to shape and discipline the understandings of their converts, but the new denominational traditions that developed at the edges of empires typically were at some variance with those found in Europe: the Methodism of Tonga or the Solomon Islands was not the same as that found in the chapels of London (which in turn varied from that of the valleys of Wales).

In some cases, particularly where the critiques of missionaries and the transformations set in train by empire significantly disrupted traditional social patterns and fomented deep-seated anxiety, prophetic movements emerged that rejected the authority of the claims of missionaries and denominational identities even when the prophet's message was imprinted by Christianity. Prophetic movements often functioned as both powerful rejections of the new orders created by colonialism and capitalism and as a promise of cultural revitalization: they suggested that the wrongs of empire and modernity might be reversed. In the United States, the Ghost Dance movement associated with the teachings of Wovoka, the Northern Paiute prophet, is an excellent example of the ways in which a prophecy could be harnessed against colonialism, drawing powerfully on old ideas and practices as well as new Christian ideas. Wovoka was the son of Tavivo who had himself followed Wodziwob, a Paiute shaman and prophet who talked of a better time to come when whites would be eliminated and the native dead returned. Wokova, who was also known as Jack Wilson, was exposed to Christian teaching while working with David Wilson, a pious rancher in Nevada. During a solar eclipse on January 1, 1889, Wokova had a prophetic vision that saw Europeans and European things being removed from America through an apocalyptic event and that promised the resurrection of the Paiute. These transformations, Wovoka believed, could only be brought about by Native American communities embracing and performing the Ghost Dance, a circular dance, in a sequence of five-day gatherings. Wovoka preached peace, enjoining his followers not to take up arms against white Americans, his prophecy promising that it would be old supernatural forces that would ultimately banish Europeans. These teachings echoed elements of the messages preached by earlier Native American prophets such as Neolin of the Delaware who advocated for a return to traditional ways in the 1760s, Tenskwatawa the Shawnee prophet in the early 1800s who energized resistance against American settlers in the Midwest, and the dreamer-prophets Smohalla of the Wanapum and Skolaskin of the Sanpoil in Washington territory in the 1860s and 1870s respectively.[9] Wovoka's teachings spread quickly among many Native American peoples, including the Cheyenne, Shoshone, and the Lakota who understood Wovoka as communicating the mysterious spiritual powers of the universe, although some Lakota also understood him as being like the Christian Messiah. The Ghost Dance itself was a powerful pathway to visions of the dead and promised ordinary people that they could be active agents in summoning the forces that would restore earlier generations and cast out European Americans and their things.[10]

The Lakota people that embraced Wovoka's teachings were true to his message and never contemplated using armed force to bring about the promised transformation, but they were willing to defend themselves. Moreover, in their commitment to carrying out this ritual that promised to use sacred powers to better the condition of the Lakota people, they were defying the government's systematic oppression of Native American rituals. They were also eschewing Western technologies and opposing government-sponsored boarding schools. The Lakota Ghost Dancers understood that they were challenging the authority of the American state; that authority was anxiously reasserted at the massacre of Lakota Sioux at Wounded Knee in December 1890, which left 153 Lakota dead.[11] Like other prophetic movements—such as the Hauhau movement in New Zealand, the devotees of the spirit-medium Kinjikitile Ngwale or Bokero who precipitated the Maji Maji Rebellion in German East Africa, or the followers of the "wizard" Tavalai who resisted German expansion into the Gazelle peninsula in German New Guinea—the Ghost Dancers believed that divine powers would render devotees immune to industrial Western weapons. But Ghost Shirts, the upraised hand and chants of Hauhau, Bokero's war medicine, and Talavai's bullet-proof ointment did not prove efficacious in the face of assertive colonial states keen to vanquish rival gods and their authority.[12]

Prophetic movements continued to emerge in the twentieth century, often in the contexts of deep social and economic distress and colonial domination. In colonial South Africa, for example, Nontetha Nkwenkwe, a Xhosa widow and mother of ten children, emerged as a prophet after the outbreak of Spanish Flu in October 1918. She interpreted the terrible ravages inflicted by the epidemic as a punishment visited by God on those people who did not follow his laws and as a sign that the end times were near. Drawing on the teachings of the Ethiopian Church of Dwane as well as the missionaries of the American Methodist Episcopal Church, she stressed the importance of obedience to God, the need for people to set aside alcohol and embrace moral improvement. Her teachings were not explicitly anti-colonial, but her encouraging African workers to boycott missionary churches and her growing popularity caused the government considerable anxiety, leading to her being arrested and jailed in 1922, before her commitment to the Fort Beaufort Mental Hospital and subsequently the Weskoppies asylum in Pretoria.[13]

These anxieties had been fed in part by the emergence of the Israelites, an independent church led by the Mfengu prophet Enoch Mgijima. Raised in a large Wesleyan family, Mgijima had a sequence of religious visions that he initially resisted, before being called to prophethood after seeing Halley's Comet in 1910, which he interpreted as a sign of God's calling. He exhorted his followers to return to the ancient religion of the Israelites. Mgijima's association with the African-American Church of God and Saints of Christ (CGSC), founded by William Saunders Crowdy in Kansas in 1896, influenced his thoughts. Crowdy taught that the original Jews were black, and African-Americans and Africans both descended from the lost tribes of Israel. In 1903 Crowdy sent Albert Christian, an African-American sailor who had previously visited South Africa as a Jubilee singer, to act as a missionary amongst South Africa's black communities. Although Mgijima had no direct contact with Albert Christian, he learnt of Crowdy's teaching through various African evangelists connected to Christian, including John Msikinya, the Mfengu teacher who eventually served as the South African bishop of the CGSC. Msikinya appointed Mgijima evangelist-in-chief of the CGSC and Mgijima's reputation was enhanced through this connection: ultimately, however, he was excommunicated as Crowdy was alarmed by reports of Mgijima's vision of an impending war between blacks and whites that would herald the onset of the final days.

By the end of World War I Mgijima had a large following and in 1918 he instructed his followers, many of whom were African Christians who had left the missionary churches because they saw them as intimately connected with white domination, to gather at Ntabelanga to await the final days. Mgijima's teachings resonated with many poor Africans in the Ciskei and Transkei, who had not only suffered under the pressures of increased inflation and taxation during World War I, but who had also been afflicted by a series of environmental disasters, including the loss of large numbers of stock as a result of epidemics, the influenza pandemic of 1918, and a terrible drought in 1919. They gathered at Ntabelanga, Mgijima's New Jerusalem, from where they would be safe from the turbulence that marked the approach of the millennium and they could return to the practices of true religion. In the eyes of colonial officials, however, Mgijima's people were illegally occupying lands and were in open defiance of the South African state.[14] Conflict developed between the Israelites, most of whom had followed Mgijima's injunction to give up their material goods, and the local farmers whose land they had occupied. The Israelites remained steadfast and repeatedly refused to leave the land that they saw as their sanctuary and ultimately took up arms in the face of the large police force deployed against them. With their machine guns and cannon, the agents of the state overwhelmed the Israelites on May 23, 1921, killing approximately 200, wounding more than 100, and arresting 141, including Enoch Mgijima, whose imprisonment marked the demise of the Israelites.

If trans-Atlantic linkages were an integral element to Mgijima's emergence as a prophet, they were even more central in the formation of the Rastafari movement. Rastafari's historical and cultural vision was Afrocentric. Grounded in a belief that the emperor of Ethiopia, Haile Selassie I (r. 1930–67), was Jah Rastafari, an incarnation of God the Father and the Second Coming of Jesus Christ, Rastafari thinkers were fierce critics of Western materialism and colonialism. Denouncing colonial rule, the tyranny of white supremacy, Western culture, and capitalism as "Babylon," Rastafari mobilized a mix of Biblical understanding and Jamaican folk practices in a religious vision that offered hope to Jamaicans who suffered from persistent poverty and racial denigration, experiences that they likened to exile. In the face of the corruption of Babylon, followers of Rastafari looked to Zion, which they understood as Ethiopia, as the birthplace of humanity, the epitome of true civilization, and the "Promised Land." Many

FIGURE 5.2 *Crowds of Rastafarians await the arrival of Haile Selassie I, emperor of Ethiopia, Kingston, Jamaica, April 21, 1966. The day was subsequently commemorated as a Rastafarian holy day known as Grounation Day. Credit: Lynn Pelham.*

Rastafari now identify the great Jamaican thinker and leader Marcus Garvey as their founding prophet. They continue to draw inspiration from Garvey's celebration of the riches of African culture and his "Back to Africa" movement, which imagined the return of the descendants of enslaved Africans to their "Motherland" as a redemptive future that would restore their economic prospects and cultural pride. But even if this return was not eminent, Rastafari could be empowered by exerting their control over fundamental aspects of daily life. One of Rastafari's distinctive features was reimagining the human body as God's true temple and many Rastafari have embraced its distinctive Ital vegetarian diet, the wearing of hair in locks, and the spiritual use of cannabis. Since the 1930s Rastafari has become a global movement, gaining adherents particularly in Africa, including Democratic Republic of Congo, Malawi, Botswana, and South Africa, but also amongst diasporic Caribbean peoples in the United Kingdom and also amongst some Maori communities in New Zealand, who have embraced the teachings of Rastafari as a way of repudiating both Pakeha domination and the authority of long-established tribal structures and established Maori Christian traditions.[15]

The emergence of Rastafari can also be read as a rejection of the Christian churches that have become powerful forces in Jamaican life during the nineteenth century. In other parts of the world, however, evangelical missionaries struggled to initiate conversions, and their impact on popular forms of devotional practice was limited: this was particularly the case where longstanding textual traditions were deeply embedded and where powerful spiritual and ritual elites oversaw complex communities of faith and practice. Thus in much of the Islamic world, South and East Asia, conversion to Christianity occurred on a small scale, often amongst those on the margins of social hierarchies, like tribal peoples and Dalits (outcastes) in India. In China, where the Jiaqing Emperor of the Qing Dynasty (r. 1796–1820) openly opposed all Christian missionary activity as part of his drive to suppress heterodoxy in general (including Buddhist movements), Protestant initiatives were delayed. Catholic missions struggled to survive in the early nineteenth century and depended on the initiative of local converts in small communities of exiles and in isolated locales far from the seats of imperial power.[16] After the Anglo-Chinese War, which effectively opened many coastal cities to Europeans, there was a substantial growth of Protestant missionary work and by the 1860s, some thirty Protestant organizations were evangelizing in China. Some Chinese did embrace and rework the Christian message, particularly through Hong Xiuquan's millenarian Taiping Heavenly Kingdom, but in the longer term, missionaries were perhaps even more influential as institution-builders and educationalists. Missionary organizations built many hospitals, trained nurses and doctors, and established a host of educational institutions and these reached into the interior as Christians enjoyed even greater freedoms from the 1870s. These were important as they provided new opportunities for the peasantry and allowed girls greater opportunities to become literate; they also introduced an important body of "useful knowledge" and new agricultural and technical information. In the long term, Christianity was pivotal in reshaping Chinese institutional infrastructure and in creating new political possibilities for non-elites.[17]

In South Asia, missionary institutions again were of lasting significance and they opened up access to both medicine and education. Like churches, they were also sites of cultural struggle and translation. In Punjab, British but also American and then New Zealand Protestant missionaries worked hard to win converts and to remake Punjabi culture, but they never gained the successes they aspired to in the face of Hindu, Muslim, and Sikh reform movements and a vigorous public sphere. Some Punjabis, overwhelmingly from Punjabi low status and Dalit communities, embraced Christmas or "Bara Din" (the Big Day), illuminated religious texts, and sang vernacular hymns as they wove elements of Christianity into their worldview. Those who fully embraced Christianity, however, were confronted by a maze of cultural tensions, some of which were born out of missionaries believing that "native customs" were difficult to budge. Some Punjabi Christians were perplexed by having to sit on the floor during worship, to read religious texts in Urdu, and to remain barefooted, when they would have preferred to sit on pews, to read the Bible in English, and to wear shoes like British Christians.[18] While the resulting struggles over faith and practice brought many of the fault lines of empire into sharp relief, at the same time many Punjabis came to rely on missionaries to access many of the elements of what they understood to be the foundations of modern life, especially literacy and scientific medicine. In Punjab by the 1930s, Protestant missionaries ran six colleges, twenty-two high schools, and twenty-eight hospitals. These institutions were influential in molding Punjabi culture and were particularly significant in shaping the economic and social position of Punjabi Dalits through the waves of violence and migration that accompanied Punjab's turbulent decolonization into the post-1947 period of independence.

Systematization and its limits

One key consequence of the translations, exchanges and debates initiated by the global growth of missionary work was the emergence of increasingly systematized and uniform understandings of what "religion" was. Missionaries routinely grappled with the difficulties of translation and the weight of cultural difference. Despite their often limited formal education, they were also important ethnographers who recorded, described, and analyzed non-Christian beliefs and practices. Their work as preachers, pamphleteers, and teachers helped transform and fortify European understandings of the very meaning of "religion." The growing reach of empires and the rapid proliferation of mission societies and outposts from the late eighteenth century multiplied and thickened the flows of information about non-Christian beliefs and societies. As missionaries and other Europeans tried to make sense of, control, and transform the peoples they lived amongst, "religion" provided a key analytical lens for the discussion of cultural difference. Europeans, convinced that religion was a universal cultural phenomenon that in fact transcended the bounds of Christendom, searched for the components of religion: a founder, sacred texts, religious experts, and an organized community of believers. Not only was it universal, however, but as a category it was increasingly understood as separable from material culture and other forms of cultural practice—religion could be distinguished from economics or politics.[19]

Empire-building and missionary work in colonial and semi-colonial spaces were central to the emergence of this notion of religion. Encounters with non-Western cultural systems, studying textual traditions in the languages of Asia, the Middle East, Africa, the Pacific, and the Americas, and the creation of relationships with ritual experts and learned authorities opened up large bodies of knowledge for Europeans, within the context of struggles, large and small, over their ability to access, assess, and understand these ways of thinking, speaking, and acting. Even though missionaries and colonial administrators often were fascinated by what they understood as the most sensational elements of these ways of interacting with the Divine and denounced aspects of these longstanding sets of beliefs and practices, they also played key roles in identifying and defining the history, textual framework, and institutional structures of these traditions. In turn, the resulting vision of religion as a self-contained system was reproduced through a range of initiatives pursued by both missionaries and colonial administrators: from engaging with "priestly" experts to military recruitment, from the publication of endless texts on indigenous "religious" traditions to the working of colonial census, religion was an indispensable category within the variegated cultural terrain of empires.

As a cultural technology printing was integral to missionary work and it was also fundamental in nineteenth-century European attempts to identify and define as a "religion" as a fundamental and recurrent aspect of civilization. These European understandings of "religion" privileged the written word and saw sacred texts as the foundations upon which religious systems were built. This textualism reflected the abiding impact of the Protestant reformist tradition, which from the sixteenth century on had insisted that Christianity must be vernacularized through the reading of the Bible in local languages as opposed to Latin and stressed scriptural literacy's fundamental position in belief and practice. The printed word also became a crucial vehicle for debating right thought and action, as a bewildering array of prescriptive tracts outlined orthodoxy and orthopraxy. This disciplinary power of print was important for Evangelicals and humanitarians concerned with lawlessness and impiety amongst male-dominated settler populations and newly converted indigenes. In turn, print's usefulness for circulating prescriptive visions was also embraced by indigenous urban reformers, conservative revivalists, and prophetic leaders who also set about purifying the faith of their fellow believers. Even if the marked extension of literacy, a key feature of the long nineteenth century at a global level, was uneven, by 1900 large numbers of peasants, urban workers, migrants and colonized people were reading both scriptural texts and reformist tracts. Debates over "religion" were almost ubiquitous being driven from "above" and "below," mobilizing opinion across wide swathes of human society.

The shifting networks that composed empires ensured that accounts of missionary work and the proliferating encounters and exchanges between religious traditions circulated widely. Here again print was central: industrial printing and communication technologies combined with the lightness and portability of paper to enable information and opinion to traverse great distances and at greater speeds when the dominance of steam power greatly reduced long-distance shipping times from the middle of the nineteenth century. Cheap or free printed tracts were disseminated by missionary organizations to bring news of missionary work in Africa, Asia, and the Pacific to working-class congregations and increasingly specialized missionary periodicals were produced to cater for the supposedly distinctive tastes of female readers and children. The proliferation of these cheap publications was one key way that the empire was brought home and it was through these texts that many Europeans, whether they were in Ireland, Scotland, Wales, England, France, or the German-speaking lands, gained much of their knowledge about the world and its diversity of environments, peoples, and histories. Missionary literature, often penned by men of humble origins but shaped by educated and influential middle-class editors, was replete with comparisons and parallels that connected the "heathen" and "pagan" peoples of imperial frontiers with the poor at home.[20] Working-class Ulster Protestant readers, for example, consumed texts that suggested the supposed conservative ignorance of their Roman Catholic female neighbors echoed the tradition-bound quality of the women of Asia and Africa.[21]

Struggles over the correct forms of thought and practice and the place of faith in modern societies were a common feature of global life in the decades either side of 1900. Across the globe, reformist movements emerged that sought to purify and regularize people's relationships to the gods and the ways in which religious communities worked. In colonial spaces and in localities where several faiths co-existed, these reformist impulses were often tied up with a desire to define and police religious boundaries. The program of the Singh Sabha, a Sikh reform movement, in colonial Punjab exemplifies this dynamic. The Singh Sabha was formed in part as a response against the extension of Christian evangelization in central Punjab, but more generally it reflected the fears of some Sikhs that in rural areas the Muslim majority dominated the Sikh community and, at the same time, that popular Sikh practice was being distorted by Hindu accretions growing out of the blurred lines between Hindu and Sikh communities. In response, the modernizing

Tat Khalsa faction of the Singh Sabha advocated a clearly delineated Sikh identity and emphasized that Sikhism was entirely independent and distinct from Hinduism. They railed against vestiges of caste, popular "superstition," and the willingness of village Sikhs to offer devotions to Hindu goddesses and Muslim *pir*s, and launched educational campaigns to fortify Sikh understandings of their sacred texts and past. Through a range of manuals as well as polemical literature, Tat Khalsa members set out a series of rites to mark the crucial transitions in life: birth, marriage, and death.[22]

This systematizing drive, which aimed to mark off Sikhs from their Hindu neighbors through a sequence of rituals and through a regime of bodily discipline (most notably, through the maintenance of the "five Ks" and the turban), was also extended through the reworking of the tradition of prescriptive *rahit-nama* texts. A committee established by the Chief Khalsa Diwan, the central committee of the Singh Sabhas, produced a new text that both synthesized key elements of previous *rahit-namas* and codified these new rituals.[23]

This drive to systematize Sikhism was also shaped by a desire to ensure that the colonial state recognized the distinctiveness of Sikhism and afforded legal protection to Sikh identity. Sikhs were generally successful in this project: Sikh reformers and key colonial officials came to agree on the divergence between monotheism and the polytheism of popular Hinduism, the cultural freedoms that came from Sikhism's repudiation of caste and Brahmanical "tyranny," and juxtaposing martial qualities of the "orthodox Sikhs" in contrast to the "effeminate" Hindu. These arguments conferred special status upon Sikhs, a status that generated substantial wealth and influence for groups that were prominent in military service (especially members of the Jat cultivator caste). And most importantly, these discourses also played a central role in enabling the global service of Sikh soldiers and policemen, opening up distant labor markets as well as exposing generations of Sikh men to the risks of injury and death. The colonial state's investment in defining and protecting the distinctiveness of Sikhism was made manifest through legislation, such as the Anand Marriage Act (1909), which recognized the distinctiveness of the new Sikh marriage rite and the Sikh Gurdwaras Act (1925), which offered clear definition of Sikhism as a distinctive, independent, and exclusive religious tradition: "I solemnly affirm that I am a Sikh, that I believe in the Guru Granth Sahib, that I believe in the Ten Gurus, and that I have no other religion."

These kinds of programs to redefine and purify popular belief played out within the Abrahamic faiths as well. European Jews, who occupied diverse economic positions and who had to negotiate with a wide range of political structures, debated the nature of modernity and the relationship between religion and politics within a context where they were politically emancipated but also increasingly expected to assimilate into the developing national cultures of Europe. While some working-class Jews placed little emphasis on their faith as they were drawn to socialism and revolutionary movements, most tried to find a way of balancing their faith and the demands of citizenship. In some parts of Europe, such as Alsace and Lorraine, Jews retained many elements of their traditional culture, speaking Yiddish and playing key roles in the rural economy until the second half of the nineteenth century, when industrialization, urbanization, and the growing influence of state schooling prompted a much greater engagement with French culture and language.[24] In the German-speaking lands and the newly unified Germany (after 1871), Jews were provided with German-medium secular education and were increasingly integrated into urban economies. These dynamics promoted the "Germanization" of Jews and influenced Jewish religious reform in the mid-nineteenth century. Against the backdrop of debates over Jewish legal rights, many advocates of reform suggested that the Jewish liturgy should dispense with references of returning to Zion and re-establishing Jewish sovereignty and that prayers for the rebuilding of the Jerusalem Temple should cease. Other rabbis, such as Zacharias Frankel, were proponents for a much stronger continuity with traditional Judaism. The reformers themselves split over how far reform should go and to what extent the religion should accommodate itself to the German political and cultural context. The most influential of Radical reformers Samuel Holdheim urged sweeping changes: his Berlin congregation used a prayer that diverged sharply from the traditional *siddur* and argued that the Sabbath should move to a Sunday, that circumcision should be abandoned and that Jews should repudiate any claims to having a distinct national identity.

Such radical change had a limited reach and Liberal reformers such as Rabbi Abraham Geiger were more influential. Geiger stressed the value of much tradition and maintained Hebrew for most prayers, but suggested that German Jews should remove those elements from the traditional service that some Germans used to question their loyalty. In the medium term, these changes also reshaped the modern form of Orthodox practice that emerged in Germany: these Neo-Orthodox Jews, who made up about 15 percent of the Jewish community, embraced some elements of secular culture, incorporated German-language sermons and male choirs into their worship, but stopped short of embracing the organ music which was a key marker of German-reformed Judaism. These changes in liturgy and religious organization reflected the deep changes to everyday practice. During the second half of the nineteenth century most working-class Jewish men stopped following the laws that governed the preparation and consumption of food, no longer went to the *mikveh* (ritual bath), and did not observe the restrictions traditionally attached to the Shabbat. German Jewish women, who typically remained within the private world of the home, generally maintained more religious practices for longer, in part because of the weight attached to their role as mothers, who were understood as key reproducers of faith and culture.[25]

The drive to enlarge the reach of religious institutions, strengthen the reach of clerical elites and ritual experts, and to uplift, improve, and reform popular practice was a strong feature of Christianities within the West as well. Within Protestantism there were persistent debates over the correct orders of service and ritual practices (such as baptism and burial). Some of these were driven by the innovations that emerged amongst colonial communities distant from the original "home" of these traditions.[26] In the second half of the nineteenth century, the Roman Catholic Church attempted to tighten the bonds of faith within a global church: here the promulgation of a doctrine of Papal infallibility in 1870 was important as was the ability of Rome to send out large numbers of priests to the frontiers of the Catholic world, especially to Latin America where Protestant expansion and the persistence of folk and indigenous practices were persistent concerns. Most importantly, the winning of independence had strengthened ideas of national culture in South America and states like Colombia, Argentina, and Brazil attempted to redefine the position of the Church, the ability of the state to make ecclesiastical appointments, and the nature of ties to Rome.[27] The creation of Colegio Pio Latino Americano, endorsed by Pius IX as a special college in Rome to train priests from Latin America, strengthened doctrinal and institutional ties between Rome and the largest Catholic communities outside Europe.[28] While the authority and social standing of the priests may have been contested in many parts of Latin America in the second part of the nineteenth century, most urban workers and peasants continued to identify as Catholics while adhering to religious forms that were strongly imprinted by longstanding local beliefs and syncretic innovations.[29]

Projects designed to project centralized authority, such as Rome's attempts to strengthen its influence in South America, worked alongside and interacted with different agendas for reform in various national contexts. Within Europe, the so-called "devotional revolution" in Ireland was the most striking and most successful drive to systematize religious practice. This was simultaneously a campaign to expand the Catholic establishment through an enlargement of the priesthood and the religious orders (especially nuns) to cultivate a new regularity of attachment to the church amongst the laity and to cultivate acceptable devotional practices such as pilgrimage, reading catechisms, and praying the rosary in the place of folk traditions that were seen as tainted by traces of paganism or which spilled over into unrestrained excess (such as wakes). Driven by Paul Cullen, archbishop of Armagh (1850–52) and of Dublin (1852–78), this was an effective program that saw the church significantly extend its provision of education as well as rooting it much more deeply in the both urban and rural regions through its use of "parish missions." Even as older customary and communally focused folk traditions were displaced by a new order grounded in canonical norms, many of the poor embraced the expanded role of the church in the wake of the Famine and in light of the weak provision of welfare by the state.[30]

By the 1870s, the regular practice of key religious observances had been greatly extended with over 90 percent of Catholics regularly attending Mass, in effect ensuring that the vast majority of the Irish population were practicing

Catholics in close connection to the Church.[31] The parish church and a popular devotionalism influenced by Italian and French models became key parts of Irish life as Catholicism moved from being primarily associated with the agricultural bourgeoisie to being a foundation of the social life of a large agricultural proletariat.[32] Irish women from humble backgrounds, who became women religious, were key agents in spreading and popularizing this remade religious culture: they upheld a deeply moral religious vision that was institutionally focused, ultramontane (stressing the powers and prerogatives of the Pope), and canonical (grounded in the rules and laws of the Church) in opposition to popular, folk, and magical beliefs that were common in rural Ireland in 1850. These nuns were able to help propagate this formalized version of Catholicism in part because they worked within traditional gender roles that imagined women as caring and self-sacrificing providers of aid and compassion.[33] These gendered roles were also reproduced through parish-level benevolent and devotional associations that were popular with working-class women: such organizations provided important opportunities for sociability, collective social action and influence at the parish level, both in Ireland and amongst diasporic Irish communities in locations like Toronto.[34] In turn, the reinvigorated authority of parish priests and the work of women religious were integral in cultivating a highly regulated sexual and moral culture that emphasized respectability, the importance of individual faith, and the primacy of the family as a spiritual, social, and economic unit.

While the Catholic establishment directed these transformations, this program was simultaneously championed by pious members of the laity who saw the reinvigoration of their faith as an effective means of shoring up their communities. The "devotional revolution" was a powerful form of dissent, both elite and popular, against the threat of Anglicization: it promoted a growing skepticism of both Protestantism and the state and was a powerful boon to Irish nationalism. Catholicism was foundational to popular visions of Irish nationhood and in the late nineteenth and early twentieth centuries it was hard to envisage Ireland or Irishness without according absolute centrality to Roman Catholicism. These ties between nationalism and faith persisted and consolidated after the Republic of Ireland gained its political independence from the United Kingdom in 1922: Catholicism was integral to visions of Irishness within the Republic and in Ulster, where the Catholic minority strove for a united Ireland and struggled against the centrality of popular Protestantism in Ulster Loyalist traditions.[35]

This devotional revolution was exported overseas, becoming a global phenomenon. It powerfully imprinted the Catholic churches in England and Scotland, which became effectively Irish as a result of the reach of these institutional currents as well as the growing numbers of working-class Irish migrants drawn to urban churches.[36] The influential networks fashioned by Bishop Cullen to British settler colonies such as South Africa, Canada, Australia, and New Zealand also meant that this religious culture was widely reproduced within the Irish diaspora.[37] The reinvigorated allure of the Church also drew increasing numbers of Irish men and women of humble origins into missionary work overseas, both through Continental orders and through the Irish orders established in the early twentieth century: St Columban's Society (or the Maynooth Mission to China) founded in 1916; the Missionary Sisters of St Columban in 1922; the Missionary Sisters of Our Lady of the Holy Rosary in 1924; St Patrick's Foreign Missionary Society in 1932; and the Medical Missionaries of Mary established in 1937.[38] These missionary organizations drew upon significant support from the laity and shaped the ways in which Irish Catholics understood Asian and African societies and their own place in the world as purveyors of the true faith and civilization.[39]

But efforts to systematize practice were limited by the persistence of deeply ingrained traditions, the weight of longstanding social patterns and the willingness of many ordinary people to live with contradiction and ambivalence. In rural Punjab, for example, they never entirely erased heterodox identities. Despite the Tat Khalsa's ability to convince the colonial state of the distinctiveness of Sikh life-cycle rituals, Brahman continued to officiate at some Sikh weddings in the countryside until World War II and such occasions continued to be accompanied by the music, performances by *mirasi*s (popular musicians), and energetic celebrations that worried educated urban Sikhs; and some families continued to contract marriages through the work of *nai* (barbers), influential Hindu intermediaries. Some Sikh peasants only strategically embraced the external symbols of Sikhism that reformers and the British saw as essential markers of an orthodox identity in order to enter into military service, dispensing with their turbans, cutting their hair, and trimming their beards after discharge from the army. Moreover, rural Punjabis confounded the tidy categories promulgated by their urban and literate counterparts and adopted by the colonial state in its census, an instrument that had great political significance as strong ties developed between enumeration and the organization of political representation. In 1901 Punjabis offered over 130 different designations that were then placed into the category "Sikh" within the Census. Many of these designations reflected the kinds of categories that the Singh Sabhas endorsed, but others mediated their Sikh identity through the lens of caste, identifying themselves as "Ramgarhia Sikhs" or "Mazhabi Sikhs," or most strikingly by the Hindu saints (Sakhi Sarvar) and gods they devoted themselves to ("Devi-Dharm," "Baba Mahesh," or "Vaishno"). Over 1,100 defined themselves as "Arya Sikhs," testifying to the ability of some Punjabis to reconcile the ostensibly irreconcilable claims of the competing Arya Samaj and Singh Sabha reform movements.[40]

Within the extensive Sikh diaspora, which developed from the second half of the nineteenth century, the Singh Sabha had even less hold and it was quite common for Sikh migrants to dispense with the physical markers of their faith. On the west coast of North America, some radicalized Sikhs deprioritized their religious affiliations altogether, placing new weight on their status as "workers" or as "Indians" as they were drawn into the revolutionary teachings of the Ghadr movement. Others adopted more radical strategies as they sought ways of staying in North America and purchasing land by marrying into Mexican migrant worker families. As a result of this strategy, communities of mixed descent grew in Arizona, Texas, the valleys of central and northern California, but especially in Imperial Valley along California's border with Mexico: these families typically lost connection with Punjab, embracing Catholicism and the Spanish language.[41]

In Ireland too, there were limits to the reach of the "devotional revolution": in rural areas, some still made pilgrimages to holy wells and maintained other elements of pre-Tridentine folk cosmologies.[42] Even if the institutional church exercised strong control over public morality and the formal practice of religious observances, individual believers exercised considerable creativity and autonomy. The letters of Catholic migrants to America reveal an individual piety focused on a caring God and the experience of transcendence, rather than a deep preoccupation with sin and the importance of external manifestations of faith.[43] And in much of Africa, the authority of missionary churches was often tenuous: local people with the ability to effectively channel supernatural powers in a convincing way—whether they were child prophets, wonder-workers, or traditional healers—often

FIGURE 5.3 *Ghana, Jirapa: Dagaba women weeping over the death of Jesus Christ on Good Friday in a Catholic church. Credit: Ullstein Bild.*

exercised greater cultural influence than foreign missionaries. African Christians themselves displayed a persistent creativity and the ability to localize, rework and fundamentally repackage Christian teaching, reshaping understandings of both the past and the future in the process.[44] More generally, neither Christianity nor Islam dislodged longstanding popular African understandings of honor, beliefs that in some places inflected the forms those world religions took in Africa, while in other places, such as Yorubaland where Christian missionaries struggled in the face of strongly held beliefs about military honor, these old ideas proved durable and resistant to new teaching.[45]

Fault lines and fundamentalisms

The accelerated mobility spawned by empires and modernization created new opportunities for critique and reform even as these connections were seen as integral to the operations of colonial power and the global reach of capitalism. Muslim critics of British rule in India, for example, traveled beyond the boundaries of British sovereignty to important port cities and political centers in Aceh and Burma in the east and to key Ottoman cities, like Istanbul and Jeddah in the cosmopolitan Hijaz region. From these locations, these Muslim preachers and writers like Sayyid Fadl Alawi and Maulana Rahmatullah Kairanwi, who were fugitives from British power in India because of their roles in anti-colonial resistance, were able to observe and critique the operation of different imperial systems (Dutch, British, and Ottoman) and advocate for reform. They drew upon the inclusive traditions of thought that flourished in the Ottoman lands under reformist sultans like Mahmud II and Abdülmecid I, which were designed not only to modernize the Ottoman state but to produce a greater freedom of religion in the hope that the multi-faith and multi-ethnic nature of the Ottoman Empire might be fortified. They also looked back to the influential Delhi Naqshbandi Sufi Shah Waliullah whose vision of a truly unified *umma* (Muslim community) suggested that it was possible for radical and liberal traditions of Islamic thought to co-exist. But the thought of these "fugitive mullahs" in the late nineteenth century was dependent on both the new connections created by steam, steel, and electricity as well as drawing upon much older traditions of Islamic connectivity and cosmopolitanism grounded in the movement of texts and students. Given this mix, it is not surprising that the arguments forwarded by these men were geared towards the cultivation of a modern reformist Islam that would strengthen the ties that linked the global *umma*, a project that emphasized the legitimacy of Scripture while constructively engaging with science, arguments about the rights of the individual, and the challenge of European imperial resurgence.[46]

This form of Muslim internationalism co-existed with the sharper anti-colonial pan-Islamism espoused by Jamal al-Din al-Afghani, the highly mobile Muslim reformer and transnational critic of European colonialism whose career took him from Kabul to Cairo, Istanbul, Iran, Russia, and British India. Al-Afghani stridently defended Islam against the critiques made by Europeans, including colonial authorities and missionaries, and in the face of Darwinian evolution, most notably in his *The Refutation of the Materialists (ar-Radd 'alal-dahriyyin)*. He stressed the primacy of true religion in forwarding progress in human societies and insisted on the strict maintenance of Islamic principles. But he also emphasized the importance of education, the value of self-improvement, Islam's compatibility with modern technologies and much of modern science, and the necessity for political reform, especially in light of what he saw as the prevalence of corruption within Muslim ruling elites. A powerful public speaker, he also recognized the power of print, urging his pupils and supporters to publish newspapers, and reaching broad audiences through his mastery of written Arabic. His willingness to critique Muslim rulers as well as European powers made him a controversial figure: he was exiled from Egypt for making anti-British speeches, expelled from Iran for his criticisms of Shah Naser al-Din (who was later assassinated by one of al-Afghani's followers), and was placed under house arrest after moving to the court of the Ottoman sultan Abdulhamit I. Nevertheless, he was an influential early champion of a modern pan-Islamic vision that drew upon a popular desire for religious and political revival within the Muslim world.[47] Like the Egyptian Islamic jurist Muhammad Abduh and his associate Muḥammad Rashīd Riḍā, al-Afghani was deeply concerned with the need to shore up Muslim communities in the face of European culture and imperial power, while simultaneously arguing that Islam itself was a coherent and robust way of life that could selectively incorporate key elements of the modern world.[48]

In some contexts, the architects of nation states offered very different readings of the place of religion in the modern world. For example, Mustafa Kemal, architect of the Turkish Republic proclaimed in 1923, was convinced that religion should be pushed to the margins of public life. Modern Turkey was born out of fierce fighting between Turks and Greece, defined by an agreement with Lenin to divide Armenia and shaped by the deportation of over one million Orthodox Christians to Greece (which, in return, deported 400,000 Muslims to Turkey): the result was that modern Turkey was much more religiously homogeneous than the old multi-ethnic Ottoman Empire. But Kemal pursued the creation of a secular rather than an Islamic republic: he abolished the position of the Caliph, the successor to the Prophet, who had been understood by many Muslims as the head of the global Muslim community and who had been the focus of a significant political mobilization in many Muslim lands during World War I. More broadly, he initiated the most ambitious set of secularizing reforms undertaken in any Muslim country, abolishing Shari'a, disestablishing madrasas, promulgating Turkish written in Roman script over Arabic, replaced Friday with Sunday as the weekly day of rest, and abolished all Sufi orders, a move that precipitated fierce resistance from the large Kurdish minority in the east of Turkey. These initiatives, which also extended the franchise and the right to hold office to women, greatly extended the earlier reforms, such as the Tanzimat. But this radical program failed to entirely transform popular belief and practice, especially in rural areas, and this produced a significant gulf between urban elites, who generally embraced the opportunities opened up by secular modernization, and the remainder of the population.

In the Arabian peninsular very different political models were pursued. Out of a mix of inter-tribal conquests and skilled diplomacy, 'Abd al-Azīz ibn Sa'ūd drew upon the authority of the Wahhābī tradition to take control of much of the region in the 1920s, including the holy cities of Mecca and Medina. This state was consolidated and recognized as the "Kingdom of Saudi Arabia" in 1932. Its foundations were a rigid and exclusive interpretation of Islam within the Wahhābī tradition. Nomadic groups, who were often seen as infidels, were forced to become sedentary and many popular practices, including those surrounding the culture of Hajj, were suppressed. The realities of managing a large state and balancing competing interests meant that even though the Saudi state was conservative, some Wahhābī *ulama* were convinced that it fell short of fully implementing a pious social order: they were angered, for example, that the state allowed automobiles to be driven and, more seriously, permitted Shiites to complete the Hajj.[49]

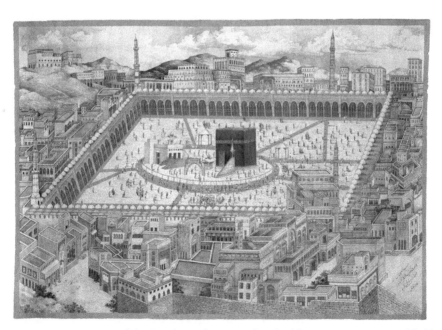

FIGURE 5.4 *View of the Ka'aba and surrounding buildings in Mecca, second half of the nineteenth century. Artist: Mahmud (?–1893/4). Credit: Heritage Images.*

The rise of secular nationalism in the Arab world was seen by some Muslims as a threat to Islam as serious as European colonial domination had been. Gamal Abdul Nasser, the Egyptian leader, was an active modernizer who saw value in socialism and who suppressed the Muslim Brotherhood, the populist Islamist movement established by the school teacher and imam Hasan al-Banna, who drew upon the writings of Muḥammad Rashīd Riḍā to fashion strong critiques of British colonialism and the decay of Islam. By the 1950s the Muslim Brotherhood's popularity with humble Egyptians, which was cemented through its extensive charitable works and social provision, was seen to threaten the primacy of the state. By the time of al-Banna's assassination in 1949, the Brotherhood claimed some 2,000 branches and 500,000 members.[50] After the Brotherhood's attempt to assassinate Nasser failed, he banned the Brotherhood, incarcerating its leaders and attempting to undermine its popularity.[51] Nasser was a dynamic advocate for pan-Arab solidarity, but leading Wahhābī thinkers were deeply concerned by his "materialism."

In the face of the secularizing reforms that were taking root across the Arab world in the 1950s and 1960s, the Saudi state worked closely with Wahhābī *ulama*. One important initiative was the holding of a conference in Mecca to address strategies for combating secularism and socialism in the Muslim world, leading to the establishment of the World Muslim League. This institutional initiative was important because it not only strengthened the ties between Saudi Wahhābīs and the Muslim Brotherhood, but also created strong connections with the reformist but elitist Ahl al-Hadith (India) and the influential advocates of Islamization, Jamaat-i Islami (India and Pakistan). These groups were unified in their commitment to rooting out popular forms of religious devotion, undercutting Sufism, and fortifying Islam in the face of Western culture. This institutional innovation had far-reaching consequences for popular forms of Muslim practice: Muslims in West Africa, especially Nigeria, soon found themselves confronted by the Izala Society, which sought to purify folk culture and challenge Sufism. At the same time, some poor West Africans began to take up scholarships to study at Saudi Arabia's religious universities, another mechanism designated to propagate adherence to pure forms of Islam outside Saudi Arabia.[52]

Saudi Arabia functioned as a key crucible for contemporary Islamic movements in part because of these flows of scholars and teachers from across the Muslim world. Particularly important here was the influx of adherents of the Muslim Brotherhood from Egypt, but also from Iraq and Syria, in the wake of nationalist crackdowns on these movements. Members of the Muslim Brotherhood brought a wider vision of the importance of public religion, which was also sharpened by both anti-colonialism and their critique of the failures of secular Arab regimes: when these concerns gained greater currency within Saudi Arabia, they created a powerful foundation for a new interest in the possibilities of launching modern forms of jihad.[53]

Over the past five decades the Islamic world has generated a succession of new religious movements, many of which have reacted against both the cultural and political influence of the West, the corruption of local elites and the failure of decolonized states to deliver security and the constructive elements of modernization: schools, hospitals, and reliable infrastructure. Some of these have had a fundamentalist sensibility, but contrary to the claim of recent Islamophobic discourse, fundamentalism is not particularly connected to Islam nor, of course, are fundamentalist traditions simply the province of those in the developing world. In fact, some of the strongest movements are deeply embedded in the West, especially the United States: these traditions of dissent forward fierce critiques of modern Western culture from within.[54] The certainties of fundamentalism—whether Jewish, Sikh, Islamic, Protestant, or Hindu—appeal to many who have felt that they are beleaguered.

Fundamentalism allows those who feel economically disadvantaged, oppressed or failed by the state, or who hold beliefs that are at odds with those of the political or economic elite to shore up their distinctive identity or community through a turn to the past. Creatively and selectively mobilizing "old" texts, traditions, and practices that they imagine as fundamental to their faith, they have created an array of movements that re-energize and reimagine their religion. These fundamentalisms are frequently shaped in opposition to what are understood as key elements of the modern world—capitalism, science, and liberalism: in contesting the authority of these markers of modernity, adherents seek to remain true to their faith, and fashion cultural safe havens to protect themselves against lures of secularism. Women who have been drawn into some jihadi movements have explained that they are not only rejecting the materialism of Western capitalism but what they also see as the globalizing and universalizing aspirations of Western feminism.[55] Effectively, these movements often seek to disentangle their followers from the outside world, rolling back those processes of disenclavement that had been powerful engines for modernization, to fashion new enclaves of tightly-bound faith communities.[56]

But fundamentalist movements have themselves often become irreducibly modern in some significant ways, especially in commitment to the articulation of a clearly defined "identity," their concern with textual purity, their often-punctilious regard for technicalities of practice, and their legalistic orientation.[57] While they assert the purity of their own faith, they tend to contribute to disenchantment of the world by excoriating any divergences in thought or ritual. Hindu fundamentalisms, for example, have not only been fiercely critical of the "cultural imperialism" of global cultural flows, but also have consistently rejected many of those elements of popular Hindu belief and practice, especially those associated with fertility and the power of the feminine, echoing many of the critiques articulated by missionaries and indigenous reformers a century or more earlier.

Of course, many states have created legal frameworks and political cultures that attempt to contain religion to the private realm, reflecting a consciousness drive to separate faith and politics and to protect the primacy of national identity from the competing claims of religion. In Britain and France, many citizens who trace their ancestry back to the colonies of Africa and Asia have interpreted these policies as attacks on their faith. In some cases, parts of these "minority" communities retreat into fundamentalist versions of their faith in response, seeking the security of a cultural "enclave"; but others attempt to shift state policy through sustained political engagement as well as finding ways of adopting their faith in light of the demands of their environment. Such dynamics are now frequently complicated by geographical and cultural mobility. Working-class Sikhs in Britain, for example, have worked hard to have the distinctiveness of their religious identity recognized and protected, seeking special dispensation to be able to maintain their turbans on construction sites and motorbikes instead of following laws that make hardhats or motorcycle helmets mandatory. In recent years, particularly after the London bombings of 2005, a small number of British Sikhs have invested considerable energy into public efforts that stress the fundamental incompatibility of Sikhism and Islam and implicitly question the political loyalty of Muslims through their emphasis on the unique loyalty of Sikhs to Britain.[58]

Conclusion

This example underlines the complex fault lines that have developed as people and their gods have been increasingly on the move in the modern age. The place of gods and their believers has been endlessly contested under modernity: these contests have frequently been fierce and violent because not only political power has been at stake, but the favor of the gods themselves. In a world of nation states and secular science, religion may seem to have been pushed to the margins, but if the world has been disenchanted, it has only been patchily so. Sacred texts, religious institutions, preachers, and prophets remain powerful as does the religious commitment of many of the world's ordinary people for whom some kind of faith, some belief in the divine or in the power of the supernatural, helps them navigate the fraught terrain of modern life.

Suggestions for further reading

Alavi, Seema. "'Fugitive Mullahs and Outlawed Fanatics': Indian Muslims in Nineteenth Century Trans-Asiatic Imperial Rivalries," *Modern Asian Studies* 45 (2011): 1337–1382.

Ballantyne, Tony. *Between Colonialism and Diaspora: Sikh Cultural Formations in an Imperial World*. Durham, NC: Duke University Press, 2006.

Bayly, C. A. *The Birth of the Modern World 1780–1914*. Oxford: Blackwell, 2004.

Breuer, Mordechai. *Modernity Within Tradition: The Social History of Orthodox Jewry in Imperial Germany*, trans. Elizabeth Petuchowski. New York: Columbia University Press, 1992.

Cox, Jeffrey. *Imperial Fault Lines: Christianity and Colonial Power in India, 1818–1940*. Stanford, CA: Stanford University Press, 2002.

Dunch, Ryan. *Fuzhou Protestants and the Making of a Modern China, 1857–1927*. New Haven, CT: Yale University Press, 2001.

Edgar, Robert R. and Hilary Sapire. *African Apocalypse: The Story of Nontetha Nkwenkwe, a Twentieth-century South African Prophet*. Athens, OH: Ohio University Press, 1999.

Hefner, Robert. ed. *New Cambridge History of Islam: Vol. 6 Muslims and Modernity*. Cambridge: Cambridge University Press, 2010.

Lamond, Gabriel A., R. Scott Appleby, and Emmanuel Sivan, eds. *Strong Religion: The Rise of Fundamentalism around the World*. Chicago: University of Chicago Press, 1992.

Shilliam, Robbie. *The Black Pacific: Anti-Colonial Struggles and Oceanic Connections*. London: Bloomsbury, 2015.

Notes

1   David W. Bebbington, *Evangelicalism in Modern Britain: A History from the 1730s to the 1980s* (London: Unwin Hyman, 1989), 42–43; Mark A. Noll, *The Rise of Evangelicalism: The Age of Edwards, Whitefield and the Wesleys* (Leicester, UK: IVP [Apollos], 2004), 84–85, 97.

2   G. M. Ditchfield, *The Evangelical Revival* (London: UCL Press 1998), 51–52; Thomas S. Kidd, *The Great Awakening: The Roots of Evangelical Christianity in Colonial America* (New Haven, CT: Yale University Press, 2009).

3   Harry S. Stout, "Religion, Communications, and the Ideological Origins of the American Revolution," *William and Mary Quarterly* 34:4 (1977): 519–541.

4   William Carey, *An Enquiry into the Obligations of Christians, to Use Means for the Conversion of the Heathens* (Leicester, UK: Ann Ireland, 1792), 62–63.

5   Bebbington, *Evangelicalism in Modern Britain*, 2–4, 10–12.

6   Sydney Smith, *The Works of the Rev. Sydney Smith: in Three Volumes* (London: Longman, Orme, Brown, Green, and Longmans, 1839), Vol. 1, 145, 158, 169, 170.

7   Eustace Carey, *Memoir of William Carey D.D.* (London: Jackson and Walford, 1836), 18.

8   Orlando Patterson, *Slavery and Social Death: A Comparative Study* (Cambridge, MA: Harvard University Press, 1982), ch 2.

9   Robert H. Ruby and John A. Brown, *Dreamer-Prophets of the Columbia Plateau: Smohalla and Skolaskin* (Norman: University of Oklahoma Press, 1989); Alfred A. Cave, "The Delaware Prophet Neolin: a Reappraisal," *Ethnohistory* 46 (1999): 265–290; Gregor Evans Dowd, *A Spirited Resistance: The North American Indian Struggle for Unity, 1745–1815* (Baltimore, MD:

Johns Hopkins University Press, 1992); R. David Edmunds, "Tecumseh, The Shawnee Prophet, and American History: A Reassessment," *Western Historical Quarterly* 14:3 (1983): 261–276.

10 James Mooney, *The Ghost-Dance Religion and the Sioux Outbreak of 1890* (Washington, DC: Government Printing Office, 1896), 771–773, 797; Jeffrey Ostler, *The Plains Sioux and U.S. Colonialism from Lewis and Clark to Wounded Knee* (New York: Cambridge University Press, 2004), 250–255, 259–260.

11 Ostler, *The Plains Sioux and U.S. Colonialism*, 260–288.

12 Peter Hempenstall and Noel Rutherford, *Protest and Dissent in the Colonial Pacific* (Suva, Fiji: Institute of Pacific Studies of the University of the South Pacific, 1984), 95–96.

13 Robert R. Edgar and Hilary Sapire, *African Apocalypse: The Story of Nontetha Nkwenkwe, a Twentieth-century South African Prophet* (Athens, OH: Ohio University Press, 1999).

14 Robert Edgar, "The Prophet Motive: Enoch Mgijima, the Israelites, and the Background to the Bullhoek Massacre," *The International Journal of African Historical Studies* 15:3 (1982): 401–422.

15 Nathaniel Samuel Murrell, William David Spencer, and Adrian Anthony McFarlane, eds, *Chanting Down Babylon: The Rastafari Reader* (Philadelphia: Temple University Press, 1998); Robbie Shilliam, *The Black Pacific: Anticolonial Struggles and Oceanic Connections* (London: Bloomsbury, 2015).

16 Lars Peter Laamann, *Christian Heretics in Late Imperial China: Christian Inculturation and State Control, 1720–1850* (London: Routledge, 2006), chs 7 and 8.

17 Ryan Dunch, *Fuzhou Protestants and the Making of a Modern China, 1857–1927* (New Haven, CT: Yale University Press, 2001).

18 Jeffrey Cox, *Imperial Fault Lines: Christianity and Colonial Power in India, 1818–1940* (Stanford CA: Stanford University Press, 2002), 91.

19 S. N. Balagangadhara, *"The Heathen in his Blindness": Asia, the West, and the Dynamic of Religion* (Leiden: E. J. Brill, 1994).

20 Susan Thorne, *Congregational Missions and the Making of an Imperial Culture* (Stanford, CA: Stanford University Press, 1999), 82–83.

21 Andrea Ebel Brozyna, *Labour, Love, and Prayer: Female Piety in Ulster Religious Literature, 1850–1914* (Montreal: McGill-Queen's University Press, 1999), 194–197.

22 Harjot S. Oberoi, *Construction of Religious Boundaries: Culture, Identity, and Diversity in the Sikh Tradition* (Oxford: Oxford University Press, 1994); C. A. Bayly, "From Ritual to Ceremony: Death Ritual and Society in Hindu North India since 1600," in *The Origins of Nationality in South Asia* (Oxford: Oxford University Press, 1999), 133–171.

23 These lifecycle rituals did not feature in earlier rahit namas. See W. H. McLeod, ed., *The Chaupa Singh Rahit-nama* (Dunedin: University of Otago Press, 1987).

24 Vicki Caron, *Between France and Germany: The Jews of Alsace-Lorraine, 1871–1918* (Stanford, CA: Stanford University Press, 1988); Paula Hyman,

The Emancipation of the Jews of Alsace (New Haven, CT: Yale University Press, 1991).

25 Marsha L. Rozenblit, "European Jewry: 1800–1933," in *Cambridge Guide to Jewish History Religion and Culture*, ed. Judith R. Baskin and Kenneth Seeskin (Cambridge: Cambridge University Press, 2010), 177–178; Mordechai Breuer, *Modernity Within Tradition: The Social History of Orthodox Jewry in Imperial Germany*, trans. Elizabeth Petuchowski (New York: Columbia University Press, 1992).

26 Ali Clarke, "Calendars, Cemeteries and the Evolution of Colonial Culture," *Journal of New Zealand Studies*, no. 12 (2011): 125–136.

27 Bayly, *Birth of the Modern World*, 339.

28 John Frederick Schwaller, *The History of the Catholic Church in Latin America* (New York: New York University Press, 2011), 186.

29 "Latin American Theology," in *The Encyclopedia of Christianity: J–O*, ed. Erwin Fahlbusch et al (Amsterdam: Eerdmans-Brill, 2003), 193.

30 D. W. Miller, "Irish Catholicism and the Great Famine," *Journal of Social History* 9 (1975): 81–98.

31 S. J. Connolly, *Priests and People in Pre-Famine Ireland* (Dublin: Gill and Macmillan, 1982); Emmet Larkin, "The Devotional Revolution in Ireland, 1850–75," *The American Historical Review* 77 (1972): 625–652.

32 K. Whelan, "The Catholic Parish, the Catholic Chapel, and Village Development in Ireland," *Irish Geography* 16 (1983): 1–15; Emmet J. Larkin, *The Historical Dimensions of Irish Catholicism* (New York: Arno Press, 1976), 9.

33 Caitriona Clear, *Nuns in Nineteenth-Century Ireland* (Dublin: Gill and Macmillan, 1988), 150, 157, 160, 166.

34 Brian P. Clarke, *Piety and Nationalism: Lay Voluntary Associations and the Creation of an Irish-Catholic Community in Toronto, 1850–1895* (Montreal: McGill-Queen's University Press, 1994), 89–90.

35 Marianne Elliott, "Faith In Ireland, 1600–2000," in *The Oxford Handbook of Modern Irish History*, ed. Alvin Jackson (Oxford: Oxford University Press, 2014), 176; Fergus Kerr and D. Vincent Twomey, "Great Britain and Ireland," in *The Blackwell Companion to Catholicism*, ed. James Buckley, Frederick Christian Bauerschmidt, and Trent Pomplu (Oxford: Blackwell, 2010), 170.

36 Larkin, *Historical Dimensions*, 10.

37 Dáire Keogh and Albert McDonnell, eds, *Cardinal Paul Cullen and His World* (Dublin: Four Courts Press, 2011); Nicholas Reid, *James Michael Liston: A Life* (Wellington: Victoria University Press, 2006), 33–34.

38 E. M. Hogan, *The Irish Missionary Movement* (Dublin: Gill and Macmillan, 1990).

39 Fiona Bateman, "Ireland's Spiritual Empire: The African Mission Field in the Twentieth Century," in *Empires of Religion*, ed. Hilary Carey (Basingstoke, UK: Palgrave Macmillan, 2008); Fiona Bateman, "Defining the Heathen Irish and the Pagan African: Two Similar Discourses a Century Apart," *Social Sciences and Missions* 21:1 (2008): 73–96.

40 Tony Ballantyne, *Between Colonialism and Diaspora: Sikh Cultural Formations in an Imperial World* (Durham, NC: Duke University Press, 2006), ch 2.

41 Karen Leonard, "Flawed Transmission? Punjabi Pioneers in California," in *Transmission of Punjabi Heritage to the Diaspora*, ed. Pashaura Singh (Ann Arbor: University of Michigan, 1996), 98.

42 Michael P. Carroll, *Irish Pilgrimage: Holy Wells and Popular Catholic Devotion* (Baltimore, MD: Johns Hopkins University Press, 1999).

43 Jay P. Dolan, "The Immigrants and Their Gods: A New Perspective on American Religious History," *Church History* 57 (1988): 71–72; Jay P. Dolan, *The American Catholic Experience: A History from Colonial Times to the Present* (Garden City: Doubleday and Company, 1985), 220–240.

44 John Iliffe, *The African Poor: A History* (Cambridge: Cambridge University Press, 1988), 179.

45 John Iliffe, *Honour in African History* (Cambridge: Cambridge University Press, 2005), especially 81–82.

46 Seema Alavi, "'Fugitive Mullahs and Outlawed Fanatics': Indian Muslims in Nineteenth Century Trans-Asiatic Imperial Rivalries," *Modern Asian Studies* 45 (2011): 1337–1382.

47 Nikki Keddie, *An Islamic Response to Imperialism: Political and Religious Writings of Sayyid Jamal al-Din al-Afghani* (Berkeley: University of California Press, 1968); Vernon O. Egger, *A History of the Muslim World Since 1260: The Making of a Global Community* (Upper Saddle River: Pearson, 2007), 342–345; Ahmad S. Dalall, "The Origins and Early Development of Islamic Reform," in *New Cambridge History of Islam: Vol. 6 Muslims and Modernity*, ed. Robert Hefner (Cambridge: Cambridge University Press, 2010), 144.

48 Dalall, "The Origins and Early Development of Islamic Reform," 142–147.

49 David Commins, *The Wahhabi Mission and Saudi Arabia* (London: I.B.Tauris, 2009), 78.

50 Robin Wright, *Sacred Rage: The Wrath of Militant Islam* (London: I.B.Tauris, 2001), 179.

51 Carrie Rosefsky Wickham, *The Muslim Brotherhood: Evolution of an Islamist Movement* (Princeton, NJ: Princeton University Press, 2013), 30–40.

52 Commins, *Wahhabi Mission*, 151–153.

53 Gilles Kepel, *The War for Muslim Minds: Islam and the West* (Cambridge, MA: Belknap Press, 2006), 173–174

54 Mary Ann Tétreault, "Contending Fundamentalisms: Religious Revivalism and the Modern World," in *Gods, Guns & Globalization: Religious Radicalism and International Political Economy*, ed. Mary Ann Tetreault and Robert Allen Denemark (Boulder, CO: Lynne Rienner, 2004), 1.

55 Martin E. Marty and R. Scott Appleby, *The Glory and the Power: The Fundamentalist Challenge to the Modern World* (Boston, MA: Beacon, 1992), 30, 33–34, 134–135.

56 Gabriel A. Lamond, R. Scott Appleby, and Emmanuel Sivan, eds, *Strong Religion: The Rise of Fundamentalism Around the World* (Chicago: University of Chicago Press, 1992), 30–33.

57 Lamond et al., *Strong Religion*, 232.

58 Tony Ballantyne, "Migration, Cultural Legibility and the Politics of Identity in the Making of British Sikh Communities," in *Punjab Reconsidered: History, Culture and Practice*, ed. Anshu Malhotra and Farina Mir (Delhi: Oxford University Press, 2012).

6

Global Mobilities[1]

Clare Anderson

Spanning Europe and the Atlantic, Indian, and Pacific Ocean worlds, this chapter writes world history from below through the prism of global mobility: the movement, migration and circulation of enslaved people, indentured laborers, convicts, displaced persons, and labor migrants, from the fifteenth century to the present day. First, the chapter brings European nations and their colonies into an integrated framework of analysis with other polities, to take a global perspective. Second, it suggests that a focus on slaves and ordinary people on the move disrupts our Global North-centric understanding of migration as a largely European phenomenon, usually with a "start" and "end" point. Third, it opens out to view the importance of coercion in effecting the journeys that networked distant parts of the world, and the labor exploitation that ultimately underpinned global expansion. Fourth, this history of mobility from the bottom up challenges the idea that European migrants were largely free, and global "others" were largely unfree. It lays stress on the importance of slave, subaltern, and subject peoples' dissent too, for mobility was not only contested, it could also be generative of particular modes of resistance and rebellion. If people connected the world together, they could also become vectors in the production of moments and forms of *dis*connection. Finally, the chapter challenges teleological, progressive interpretations of the history of migration, which presume a long-term transition from "forced" migration in the past to "free" migration today. It argues rather for considerable continuities in the coercive texture of global mobility in the world in which we live.

The great irony of mobility in the age of European expansion is that although it emerged within a global context of enhanced technologies of communication and movement—most importantly in the nineteenth century steam ships, telegraphs, submarine cables, and railways—it was often secured through the captivity, confinement, and restriction of subject peoples, and not through freedom of movement. Their response to these modes of control was, however, far from passive; they mutinied on board ships, revolted on plantations, escaped from penal settlements, refused to work, feigned sickness, and went on hunger strike. These were sometimes expressions of individual or collective protest against the particular living and working conditions that were associated with the organization of coerced labor. But these subordinated yet mobile subjects sometimes also carried with them—or became exposed to—new types of insurgency or anti-colonial sympathies on arrival in new places, lending their actions an explicitly political dimension. Whilst the movement of people and ideas took the same routes as the movement of capital and modes of colonial governance, a focus on the drama of their resistance, and its spread around Empire, therefore offers a point of intersection for the meeting of subaltern and global history. It is through this meeting point that the chapter stresses the prevalence of disruption and dissent amongst mobile peoples and their importance in making world history. It also provides perspectives on how insurgency moved across and around metropolitan and imperial spaces.

Indigeneity, slavery, coerced labor

Indigenous destruction and world history

Since *homo sapiens* "came out of Africa," human mobility has been a feature of human life, of community formation, and ultimately of the making of polities, nation-states, and empires. And yet migration is often represented as a relatively recent or new phenomenon; as a feature of modern globalization that upsets finely calibrated societies rooted originally in indigeneity, or authentic, native belonging to particular places. Sometimes, of course, as in the Americas and Australia, European expansion effected through enslavement, the use of convict labor or other means in what became white settler colonies had a devastating effect on Indigenous peoples. In places like Australia, many Aborigines died in outbreaks of newly introduced diseases against which they had no resilience, or were rounded up and confined on islands or in reserves, or died during what colonial administrators were fond of calling "skirmishes"—in other words violent and armed resistance against invasion.[2] The demographic, economic, social, and cultural legacies of such colonization remain with us today, in the social, cultural, and economic exclusion of Indigenous peoples from settler-descended societies, and in associated activism and rights movements.[3]

Notwithstanding the importance of acknowledging that migration has always been a feature of human life, and the urgency of recognizing the Indigenous devastation often wrought by imperial expansion, what does migration mean for those of us who are interested in writing world histories from below? This section of the chapter centers on how understanding mobility through the movement of subaltern or subject people offers a way of foregrounding three key phenomena of world history. First, it opens out to view something of the fundamental ambivalence of migration—that colonized subject peoples, and the European poor and in other ways socially disadvantaged, could also be colonizers. Second, it enables an appreciation of the intra-imperial and sometimes circulatory character of migration. This rebalances the importance of sojourning alongside that of settlement when considering the politics and patterns of movement and (re)location.[4] Third, and in relation to this second point, it facilitates a shift in focus beyond the nation-state as a "natural" spatial unit for understanding world history. Rather, it stresses the significance of other spatialities, borders, and borderlands. All three allow us to inject social hierarchy (and class) into world history, and also to understand it as more than the sum of Europe-centered histories, or as a story solely of Europe expanding outwards to disastrous Indigenous effect. I shall return to the importance of viewing migration as a feature of all societies in my discussion of the legacies of global mobilities, below. Meantime, here I draw on the examples of the Atlantic slave triangle, slavery in the Indian Ocean, convict transportation to and between the Americas, Africa, Asia, the Pacific, and the Antipodes, indentured labor in the Pacific and the Caribbean, and the migration of Indian laborers across the Bay of Bengal.

Enslavement

From the sixteenth to nineteenth centuries, the European powers shipped some 12.5 million slaves from Africa to the Americas, and around half a million around the Indian Ocean (Tables 6.1 and 6.2). Though slave labor in the Americas was used extensively on sugar plantations, slave trading in the Indian Ocean was distinctive in its employment of slaves in households or small industries in places like the Cape Colony and Mauritius, and the ownership of slaves by so-called free coloreds, and not solely Europeans. If

Table 6.1: The Trans-Atlantic Slave Trade

Period	No. of Slaves
1501–1600	277,506
1601–1700	1,875,631
1701–1800	6,494,618
1801–1866	3,873,580
Total	12,521,336

Source: Slave Voyages: The Trans-Atlantic Slave Trade Database. http://www.slavevoyages. org/assessment/estimates (accessed March 27, 2015).

Table 6.2: Estimated Minimum Number of Slaves Traded by Europeans, Indian Ocean, 1500–1850

Powers	No. of Slaves
Portuguese	41,875–83,750
Dutch	43,965–66,465
English	10,525–12,539
French	334,936–384,040
Total	**431,301–546,794**

Source: Richard B. Allen, "Satisfying the 'Want for Labouring People': European Slave Trading in the Indian Ocean, 1500–1850," *Journal of World History* 21:1 (2010): 45–73 (64).

we include those exported by other polities from sub-Saharan Africa in the Indian Ocean totals, the number of enslaved peoples in the region likely exceeded those transported in captivity across the Atlantic. Despite its huge scale, the history of slavery is still marginalized in migration history despite its prevalence in area studies based historiography.

It is well established that slave labor was vital for the economic success of European empires and their successor states in Latin America, particularly in places like Brazil, the southern United States, and the Caribbean. But it is important not to lose sight of human stories and sufferings in these vast global mobilities. Enslaved people wrote and spoke about their experiences with a residual textual regularity that is perhaps surprising. In the United States context, authors included Olaudah Equiano, who detailed his childhood kidnap in West Africa and enslavement in Barbados and Virginia; as well as Frederick Douglass and Harriet Jacobs, African-Americans who escaped from slavery to inspire and to lead the abolitionist movement. Even where enslaved women and men did not write or publish autobiographies, though heavily mediated, glimpses of their attitudes to their enslavement, their labor, and their affective and intimate lives, can be found in a careful reading between the lines of the official record.

It is also evident that even after abolition, slavery endured in numerous other guises. Most notable, perhaps, was the transition from slavery to emancipation in most colonies in the British Empire. A further period of so-called apprenticeship was enforced on recently freed slaves in the 1830s. Envisaged as a transition to freedom, they were tied as workers to their former owners for a fixed number of years. Of equal notoriety was the indenturing of illegally trafficked slaves ("Prize Negroes" captured by the Royal Navy after Britain's abolition of the slave trade in 1807). They were put out to work, sometimes in African colonies like Sierra Leone or the

ON BOARD A SLAVE-SHIP.

FIGURE 6.1 *Captives being brought on board a slave ship on the West Coast of Africa (Slave Coast), c.1880. Although Britain outlawed slavery in 1833 and it was abolished in the USA after the defeat of the Confederacy in the Civil War in 1865, the transatlantic trade in African slaves continued. The main market for the slaves was Brazil, where slavery was not abolished until 1888. Credit: Print Collector.*

Cape, or on Caribbean islands like Tortola (some 40,000 went to the West Indies alone). Though the British called them "liberated Africans," their conditions of servitude often resembled those of their chattel forebears.[5] They felt the similarities keenly too. Working with Saidiya Hartman's description of the larger context of slave trade abolition as "the story of an elusive emancipation and a travestied freedom," Anita Rupprecht analyzes the mediated voices of liberated Africans in British parliamentary papers to demonstrate how they understood the distinctiveness of their fate from promises of citizenship and freedom, providing vital insights into the below, in the historical record.[6]

In numerous other contexts, including for and in African polities, and in pre-colonial and colonial South and Southeast Asia, slaves were not particularly mobile. Indeed, enslavement has complex meanings within a world history frame. Beyond the Atlantic, it was often situated within complex and locally defined forms of bondage that were not necessarily connected with either empire or mobility, present or ancestral, but rather with culture, poverty, and above all, debt. This is especially evident in South

Asia.[7] Anthropologist-turned-fiction writer Amitav Ghosh articulates brilliantly the historical accidents through which their presence might be noted in official records. The title of his intervention is unequivocal: "The Slave of [archival document no.] Ms. H.6." This deliberately and pointedly reminds us that in colonial archives, the subaltern is not always accorded the dignity of a name.[8]

Convict labor

Accompanying the development of our understanding of the importance of enslavement in the making of the modern world across various contexts, including most recently in the economic, cultural, and social development of metropolitan Europe,[9] has been the growth in appreciation of the significance of other unfree labor flows for imperial expansion, in the period before, after, and during slavery. Historians of imperialism have investigated bonded labor migration of various kinds, including European servitude, military impressments, penal colony work, and Asian indentured labor. So prevalent were these labor forms that, notwithstanding the crucial importance of slavery for imperial expansion, if we are to write world history from below, we ought to add "Coercion" to the established list of the "Three Cs of Empire": Christianity, Commerce, and Civilization.

Many of the first North American European settlers were what have been described as "colonists in bondage."[10] Some were sent across the Atlantic under contracts of indenture. On arrival, they undertook service of various kinds, including domestic and agricultural work. In the eighteenth century, before the War of Independence, British convicts were also transported to the Americas, particularly to the Chesapeake. Positioned competitively against indentured servants, they were usually sold into indenture for the period of their sentence, and put to work in identical occupations. Prisoners sometimes awaited shipment for several years. Gwenda Morgan and Peter Rushton recount the case of one woman convicted in the northeast of England who was kept in jail so long that she gave birth twice, and died before embarkation. British convicts sometimes worked alongside slaves and Indigenous Americans on plantations; only later did "race" emerge as a principle of organizing labor in the British imperial context.[11] These eighteenth-century Atlantic flows of indentured servants and convicts converged not only with the slave trade, but with the circular mobility of mariners who worked both slave and passenger ships. Impressed or inveigled into service, or seeking an escape from poverty or adventure at sea, these highly mobile, multinational "motley crews" were one element of the "many-headed hydra" of Peter Linebaugh and Marcus Rediker's conceptualization of the revolutionary Atlantic; vital carriers of news and information between Europe and the Americas.[12]

Britain was far from alone in its use of convict transportation to satisfy the mutually compatible aims of getting rid of criminal offenders and using

FIGURE 6.2 *Convict ship ready to sail from England to Australia, parts of which Britain used as a penal colony. Friends and relations having said farewell, probably for ever, wave from the shore. Early nineteenth-century engraving. Credit: Universalimagesgroup.*

their labor to expand the frontiers of Empire. Indeed, unlike slaves, who constituted valuable property, convicts did not represent a financial investment, and so were expendable and easy to replace. All the major European powers—Dutch, Portuguese, Spanish, British and French—transported convicts overseas, both from metropole to colony, and (what is often lost in penal history and of especial relevance to our interest here in the spatiality of mobility) between colonies. At the very lowest estimate, over 2 million convicts were sent overseas (Table 6.3). This figure rises to tens of millions if the great twentieth-century overland political

Convict Transportation and European Empires: Principal Flows, 1415–1939

Origins	Destinations	Period	Estimated Total
Portugal	Goa, Brazil, São Tomé, Timor, Mozambique, Angola	1415–1932	92,000
Spain, New Spain, Cuba and Philippines	Cuba, Puerto Rico, New World/ N. African *presidios*, Fernando Po	1550–1911	110,000
UK, Ireland, British colonies and British India	American and Caribbean colonies, Australian colonies, Bermuda, Gibraltar, Mauritius, Straits Settlements, Burma, Aden, Labuan, Andaman Islands	1615–1939	376,000
France & French colonies	New France, Louisiana, French Guiana, Algeria, New Caledonia	1552–1939	100,000
European Russia	* Siberia	1590–1920	1,900,000
Total			2,578,000

* Period following 1823 only; generally poor data means that this is almost certainly an underestimate.

Source: Clare Anderson and Hamish Maxwell-Stewart, "Convict Labour and the Western Empires, 1415–1954," in *The Routledge History of Western Empires*, ed. Robert Aldrich and Kirsten McKenzie (London: Routledge, 2013); Timothy J. Coates, *Convict Labour in the Portuguese Empire, 1740–1932: Redefining the Empire with Forced Labour and New Imperialism* (Leiden: Brill, 2013); Stephen Nicholas and Peter Shergold, "Transportation as Global Migration," in *Convict Workers: Reinterpreting Australia's Past*, ed. Stephen Nicholas (Cambridge: Cambridge University Press, 1988), 30.

transportations are taken into consideration. In the case of the movement of convicts between colonies, including the British West Indies, Cape Colony, and Australia, transportation had additional functions: the putting down of native resistance or insurgency and the consolidation of imperial authority. It also effected massive labor movements that entirely circumvented Europe in shifting colonized peoples around the contours of the imperial globe.

It is interesting that in some places—Portuguese Angola and French Guiana, for example—into the twentieth century, European transportees worked side by side with Africans and, in the latter case, Indochinese and other imperially transported French convicts. This appears anomalous to increasing racial bifurcation in other imperial sites, for instance turn-of-the-century "White Australia," South Africa, and North America. Marilyn Lake and Henry Reynolds have brilliantly articulated this as the drawing of a global color line.[13] Nevertheless, these exceptions that prove the rule are important reminders of both the unevenness of empire—John Darwin characterizes empire as a many-tentacled "project"—and the importance of injecting class and social status in discussions of economy, society, and imperialism.[14] It warns against assuming shared experiences across *empires* too. We are compelled here also to recognize the importance of incorporating the poor whites of imperial expansion into our world histories from below.[15]

The beginning of penal transportation in the imperial age can be dated to 1415, when the Portuguese first used convicts to establish a North African fort (*presidio*) at Ceuta. The Portuguese later sent convicts from and between Europe and Goa (western India), Brazil, São Tomé, and its African colonies Angola and Mozambique, with transportation enduring to 1932. The Spanish Empire from the seventeenth century was characterized by remarkable convict circularity, as transported felons flowed from Cadiz to and between *presidios* across the American coasts, Mexico, and the Philippines. There were important overlaps with the army, for some of the Spanish convicts flowed into the military labor market, joining soldiers in their new destinations. The Dutch shipped convicts between the East Indies and the Cape Colony during the same period.

Following the loss of the American colonies in 1785, the British Empire sent a few felons to the slave forts of West Africa, but after most died, the British settled on Botany Bay in Australia as the new destination for convicts. As well as New South Wales, convicts were later sent to Van Diemen's Land (Tasmania). Most originated in Britain and Ireland, but a few had been convicted and sentenced in Britain's Caribbean, African, and Mascarene colonies, notably Jamaica, the Cape Colony, and Mauritius. The two youngest ever convicts sent to New South Wales, for example, were enslaved children from Mauritius, Elizabeth and Constance. They had been convicted of attempting to poison their mistress. Of British offenders, after important changes to the penal system were effected in the 1830s and 1840s, convicts also served out their sentences on hulks in Bermuda and Gibraltar, and in Western Australia. In each colony, convicts undertook important public works projects, including the construction of a huge naval dockyard in the navy's small but strategically vital Atlantic outpost.

Though a few colonially convicted offenders were transported to the Australian colonies, the British largely pursued a policy of reserving them for "white" convicts. Thus, the much larger number of convicts from the jewel in Britain's crown, India, was shipped not to the Antipodes but to penal settlements in neighboring Southeast Asia and across the Indian Ocean. They included in the first part of the nineteenth century Penang,

Malacca and Singapore (known together as the Straits Settlements), Burma, and Mauritius. One man of African origin, George Morgan, had an extraordinary journey across Britain's penal archipelago. Convicted in Calcutta, in India's Bengal Presidency, he was first shipped across the Bay of Bengal to one of the East India Company's penal settlements in Burma. Escaping from the transportation ship when it docked on the Rangoon River, he was rearrested in Madras. From there, he was sent back to Calcutta, where he was retried and shipped to Van Diemen's Land. He soon escaped, never to be seen again.[16] After some of the Indian settlements refused to accept offenders convicted in the aftermath of the Great Uprising ("Mutiny") of 1857, the British renewed their earlier interest in consolidating trade routes in the Bay of Bengal, and established the Andaman Islands as a penal colony. The Andamans received convicts from India and Burma, and endured as a penal colony until the Japanese occupied in 1942, opened the gates of the cellular jail, and liberated the remaining convicts.[17]

The French also used transportation between colonies routinely and extensively. After an early disaster in the establishment of a late eighteenth-century penal colony in Guyane in South America, when most of the convicts died of fevers and other diseases, after 1858 *bagnards* were transported to a second settlement there, and *communards* to the Pacific colony of New Caledonia. Receiving convicts from the French colonies, including Indochina, French Guiana remained open until World War II. The penal colony acquired a dubious reputation for its incarceration of celebrated political convicts, like Albert Dreyfus (1859–1935), whose conviction for treason resulted in his confinement on the notorious Devil's Island. In the first decades of the twentieth century, journalists wrote damning accounts of its unique system of *doublage*, which obliged time-served convicts (*libérés*) to remain in the colony, often for the rest of their lives. These accounts were sometimes based on the writings of *libérés* themselves. American roving reporter Richard Halliburton, for instance, paid French convicts for the production of materials that later formed the basis of his book on the penal colony, *New Worlds To Conquer*. His New York-based literary agent wrote: "The stories the men wrote themselves . . . Of course they are frightfully rough, frightfully vulgar in spots . . . it is the only material of its particular kind in the world."[18] After the decision was made to close down the penal colony, the French metropolitan government called on the assistance of the Christian association, the Armée du Salut (Salvation Army), to assist with repatriation, largely to France and Algeria.[19]

Finally amongst the European powers in the nineteenth century, Russia shipped convicts to *kátorga*, expanding its frontiers in the Baltic in Central Asia and Siberia in the Russian Far East, and forming the precursor of the vast *gulag* archipelago of Soviet labor camps and colonies established for political purposes in the twentieth century. These forced relocations were part of larger efforts to remove opponents, and particular ethnic or religious groups, and to populate internal or imperial frontiers. As was the case in other penal colony contexts, only literate convicts left accounts of their transportation, which are atypical in their very existence, but fascinating nonetheless. A different published account, staggering in is detail, is Anton Chekhov's *Sakhalin Island*. This study of one of the Siberian penal colonies in the Russian Far East might be described as one of the first modern social surveys.[20] Guards also wrote about (and sometimes drew representations of) life in the Russia colonies, including (famously) Danzig Baldaev, who in the twentieth century also compiled an encyclopedia of convict tattoos.[21] However, despite the richness of all these sources, only with the opening up of the archives of the former Soviet Union since Gorbachev's period of *Glasnost* in the second half of the 1980s are historians beginning to understand the full extent of this forced mobility. It is almost impossible to reach an appreciation of the total number of convicts sent to Russian *kátorga* and *gulag*, though it almost certainly reached many tens of millions. Anne Applebaum calculates that 24 million people were either sent to the *gulag* or exiled to remote locations between 1929 and 1953.[22]

An important feature of penal mobility during this 500-year period was the gradual transition from blended flows of coerced labor, where—as in the Americas, Straits Settlements, and Philippines—convicts joined those of other unfree workers, to the establishment of discrete penal colonies, containing only (or mainly) convicts. The latter included the Andaman Islands, Sakhalin in the Russian Far East, and Île Nou, New Caledonia. Across both periods, convict work included land clearance, the construction of basic infrastructure like roads and bridges, agricultural cultivation, forestry, and mining. On occasion, and even in discrete colonies, convicts could be employed alongside other types of laborers, including slaves and indentured workers. They were also employed in penal service: as warders, clerks, grooms, cooks, and servants. It is noteworthy too that the European powers were not alone in their employment of convict labor for frontier expansion. Mid-Qing China used convicts for colonization purposes from the mid-eighteenth to early nineteenth centuries. After 1800, newly independent Latin American states set up penal colonies, including in Mexico and Argentina. With the Meiji Restoration of 1868, when Japan turned to the West in a bid to "modernize," it consulted on British and French penal colonies, and sent convicts to the northern island of Hokkaido.[23] Across global contexts, then, convicts were sent as worker-settlers to remote locations; usually places that were so isolated that they did not attract free settlers. But even where free settlers would migrate, convicts were preferred as an expendable and pliable (i.e. easy-to-move) workforce. The fact that convicts moved across long distances in conditions of confinement and constraint into the middle decades of the twentieth century constitutes one of the deepest ironies of global mobility. Indeed, it reminds us that if we are to avoid teleological interpretations that celebrate the transition from enslavement to freedom in world history, in many ways that history can *only* be written from below.

Asian indentured labor

Another significant form of global mobility, beginning in the nineteenth century, was Asian indentured labor, which was used extensively in British and French colonies in the Indian Ocean and Caribbean. It was introduced first in the British Empire in Mauritius in the 1830s, at the moment of the abolition of slavery, as slave owners sought an alternative form of coerced labor to enslavement, mainly for work on sugar plantations. For this reason, at the time indenture was critiqued as a new system of slavery. Trinidad, British Guiana, and Fiji also received substantial numbers of indentured migrants and, as in Mauritius and the French colonies of Réunion Island, Martinique, and Guadeloupe, they mainly worked as plantation labor. Some indentured workers sent to Uganda, Tanzania, and Kenya in East Africa, in contrast, were put to work in railway building. Most indentured laborers were from India, many were hill tribals (*dhangars*), and a significant minority was from China. Sometimes called "coolies," migrants signed contracts of indenture for defined periods, their return passage paid. The total number of indentured workers who were shipped to British colonies during the period to 1920 when the system ended was close to 1.5 million—almost one third of whom went to Mauritius (Table 6.4). In the Pacific, Europeans exploited existing socio-economic structures to use the offer of "trade boxes" to indenture approximately 300,000 Melanesian migrants, many in Australia's tropical Queensland. In that place, the powerlessness and alienation felt by Indigenous people forced into labor coercion has been described as Aboriginal slavery.[24]

Indenture produced massive demographic changes. Within just a few years, for instance, the island of Mauritius, which had no Indigenous population, transitioned from a largely African-descended (formerly enslaved) population to one of largely Asian origin. This underpinned remarkable changes in culture and society in migrant destinations. In Mauritius it created new forms of community and identity; and led to the increased marginalization of slave-descendants. Anthropologists today call this *le malaise créole* (the creole malaise).[25]

Though historians debate whether the character of indenture was more coerced than free, it is perhaps productive to note that early incidents of kidnapping and misleading migrants gave way to increased regulation during the nineteenth century. Migrant letters written home to India from the colonies reveal a complex experiential picture.[26] Also, from contemporary enquiries in the rural districts of north India we know that potential migrants framed their prospects in the colonies through what appears to have been a wide knowledge of contemporary penal transportation. This suggests that subaltern perceptions of various kinds of migration perhaps blurred their character more than we might suppose. In one report on emigration, it was noted that the term *kala pani* (black waters) was a well-understood metaphor for the cultural degradation of crossing of the oceans into *either* penal

Table 6.4: Indentured Migrants, British India and China to British Colonies, 1834–1916

Destination	Period of Migration	Total
Mauritius	1834–1900	453,000
British Guiana	1838–1916	239,000
Malaya	1844–1910	250,000
Trinidad	1845–1916	144,000
Jamaica	1845–1913	36,000
Grenada, St Lucia, St Kitts & St Vincent	1856–1895	10,000
Natal	1860–1911	152,000
Réunion Island (French)	1861–1883	27,000
Surinam	1873–1916	34,000
Fiji	1879–1916	61,000
East Africa	1896–1921	39,000
Seychelles	1904–1916	6,000
Total		**1,451,000**

Source: Brij V. Lal, ed., *The Encyclopaedia of the Indian Diaspora* (Singapore: Editions Didier Millet, 2006), 46.

transportation *or* indentured migration. One government official writing in the 1880s reported the response of potential indentured workers to recruiting magistrates' use of the words: "Says the coolie to himself, when he hears a Magistrate Saheb talking to him of *kala pani*—'Kya! Ham ne kya kasur, kiya ke ham ko kala pani sunate hain?'" ("What! What wrong have we done, that [he] speaks to us of *kala pani?*") It is also interesting that some ex-convicts, returning home from penal settlements in the Straits, Burma, or Andamans to find property destroyed or land appropriated by others, on occasion signed contracts of indenture and on-migrated to the sugar colonies. There were significant overlaps, then, between these apparently distinct labor regimes.[27]

A variant of indenture, the *kangani* system, through which trusted Indian workers recruited migrants on behalf of their employers, prevailed in Southeast Asia after 1910, where many such laborers worked on coffee and rubber plantations. As Sunil Amrith has shown recently, migration around the Bay of Bengal by indentured and other workers was so extensive that in the century after 1840 perhaps as many as 28 million Indian and Chinese

FIGURE 6.3 *"Coolies at worship," Jamaica, c.1905. Group portrait of Indian immigrants who came to the island as indentured workers. Illustration from* Picturesque Jamaica, *by Adolphe Duperly & Son (England, c.1905). Credit: Print Collector.*

people migrated to Ceylon, Malaya, and Burma. For them, cultural similarities were more significant than imperial political borders or colonial projections of their difference. This staggering Bay of Bengal mobility far outnumbered other contemporary migrations, including the better known European flows to the USA, Canada, Australia, and New Zealand. One reason for the lack of historiographical focus on Indian and Chinese workers is that they often moved back and forth between places. This urges us to decenter Global North assumptions about the character of mobility as migration from one place to another, and to take seriously Global South patterns of circularity.[28] The global mobilities of the British Empire were not characterized so much by the *settlerism* of "Angloworld," as James Belich has suggested recently,[29] as the *sojournerism* of its imperial "others." The writing of bottom-up world histories of mobility demands, to use the eloquent language of Dipesh Chakrabarty, that we provincialize Europe.[30]

Men, women, and children

Many population flows and migration streams were homosocial in character, as administrators sought fit, young men to work at various kinds of productive labor. In some penal colonies, for example, the number of female migrants was nil, in others it was small or miniscule. The pre-Andamans Indian penal settlements received only a handful of female convicts; French Guiana a few hundred only; and the Bermuda and Gibraltar hulks (prison ships) none at all. Colonial administrators were greatly exorcised by the sexual disorder that was said to result from the prevalence of men, and fears about the practice of both solitary masturbation and sex between men in penal colonies and hulks was often a central feature of abolitionist discourse. Indeed, the Indian Jails Committee of 1919–20 even compared the alleged "immorality" of the Andamans in this respect to that claimed for the Australian colonies of a near-century earlier.[31]

Otherwise, it is interesting that the Indian Ocean slave trade incorporated much larger numbers of women and children than was the case for the Atlantic Ocean. This was to do with the particular economic demands of a region that was not so dominated by plantation labor. In turn, because they were often captured in the Indian Ocean, women and especially children made up a relatively large proportion of the liberated Africans who were taken from slave vessels off the African coast and apprenticed in West Africa and the Caribbean.[32]

Despite or perhaps because of early gender ratio imbalances in Asian indentured labor, over time the idea that migrant laborers were best managed for work from within family units became central to their organization across a range of contexts. After a series of gruesome murders in Fiji, for instance— characterized as "coolie wife murders" provoked by arguments over women— regulations developed on the ratio of women to men on indentured ships, and during the second half of the nineteenth century, women were shipped to plantations in much larger numbers than was previously the case.[33] There is, then, an important gender dimension to mobility and world history.[34] In South Asia, ideas about supposedly ideal communities developed, grounded in families and households. Model villages were established in settings as far apart as the canal and railway colonies of the Punjab and United Provinces of northern India, and Ferrargunj in the Andamans. A so-called hereditary criminal tribe—the Bhantus—was sent in family groups for "rehabilitation" under the direction of the Salvation Army.[35] Each constituted an element of the politics of colonial intimacy and the swirling of imperial "bodies in contact," as established by Tony Ballantyne and Antoinette Burton.[36]

Periodization and the Global South

Writing about global mobilities from below also suggests, as Adam McKeown has argued, that we challenge the overstatement of transatlantic (European/New World) mobility in the usual periodization of 1914 as the historical moment at which mass migration ended. This does not work for global history. Many millions of people migrated trans-oceanically after World War II, with millions more journeying between and around Africa and western Asia. Moreover, much migration in the Global South—including the Pacific, China, and South and Southeast Asia—was seasonal, inter-regional and temporary. These labor movements are not easily captured in the archives from which migration figures are drawn; archives which overstate the comparative extent of Global North, or European, migration.[37]

If we are to be attentive to the often-coerced character of mobility, and take seriously the world outside of Europe in the Global South, it is also important to include the mass population displacements that accompanied and were often generative of the character of geopolitical shifts during the last century in our characterization of "migration." The *gulags* of Soviet Russia, discussed above, are important examples of this. Others can be drawn from the mass movements of people produced by European decolonization. Indeed, one of the great forced migrations in history was effected during the Partition of India, following Independence in 1947, when over 30 million British Indian subjects—Hindus and Muslims—were forced to move across the religious lines of the new nation states of India and Pakistan.[38]

Journeying, identity, and protest

The historiographies of enslavement and coerced migration more generally have engaged with important questions of colonial domination, individual and collective experience, and resistance and identity formation, in a range of contexts. In this section of the chapter, I will explore their relationship with global mobility specifically. As we will see, journeys were key sites for the establishment of coercive practices as well as for community formation, and the staging of individual or collective, violent or everyday protest. I will draw here on the significance of ideas about shipmates and brotherhood in coerced labor streams; examples of shipboard mutiny from the mid-eighteenth to mid-nineteenth centuries; and on incidents of unrest at sea connected to the sexual exploitation of migrant women. Writing world history from below reveals the nature and extent of resistance to coerced mobility, as well as some of the ways in which—perhaps somewhat surprisingly—it was productive of new forms of social affiliation and belonging.

Discipline and kinship

In the "age of sail," dating roughly from the fifteenth to the mid-nineteenth centuries, discipline at sea was notoriously harsh, with ships' captains declared "lords of the seas." Their authority was unquestionable, and reprisals against those who challenged it were swift and violent. All those who were confined below deck—slaves, convicts, and indentured migrants—shared the rhythm of the ship, which over time grew to include a disciplinary repertoire of "dancing" (exercise), working, and medical surveillance. The entire ship was gathered to watch spectacles of flogging, which were displays encompassing both punishment and deterrence. Sailors too—some of whom were impressed into involuntary service by press gangs operating in port cities all over the world—were subject to equally strict regimes at sea, if not the inhumanity of routine chaining. Like soldiers, they constituted a transnational, circulatory labor force.

The close confinement of oceanic journeys was undoubtedly productive of new forms of identity, kinship, and social affiliation. Arguably, the "shipmate" relationship as it developed between slaves became what Sidney W. Mintz and Richard Price have described as "a major principle of social organization" in the new world. In Jamaica, it appears to have been used in the same way as "brother" or "sister." And, it had a genealogical afterlife that led children to call the shipmates of their parents "uncle" and "aunt."[39] In other contexts, journeys were vitally important in producing new forms of kinship, including "mateship" in the Antipodes, which originated in convict transportation. And, as I have argued elsewhere, Indian convicts transported to Mauritius on the same transportation ships called each other *bhai* (brother).[40] I will return to the importance of these new social bonds vis-à-vis the theme of mobility and the spread of subject resistance in a moment.

Mutiny and unrest

In a recent review of new work on unrest at sea, the apparently high incidence of mutiny was declared "perfectly astonishing." Warships, merchantmen, whalers, slave vessels, and convict ships all experienced greater unrest than has been previously recognized—perhaps as many as 10 percent of all slave ships broke out in mutiny. Moreover, in the great Age of Revolution (1760s–1840s) the oceans worked as spaces of incubation and as vectors for the diffusion of political radicalism. Adding further support to the earlier work of Linebaugh and Rediker, which had envisaged the early modern Atlantic world as characterized by collectivism, anti-authoritarianism, and egalitarianism, the sea is placed at the heart of what is usually seen as a history of land-based nations and empires. Solitary or collective, maritime resistance ranged from complaining to downing tools, sabotage to assaults on officers. Onshore, sailors played key roles in the American, French, and Haitian revolutions.[41] Eighteenth-century ships lay at the center of a sphere of circulation that exploited labor capital, and they were both engines of capitalism and spaces of resistance.[42] Once again, here we see the importance of class.

Ships carrying slaves, convicts and indentured workers all experienced outbreaks of various kinds, including but not limited to mutiny. The most recent historiography has added rich ethnographic detail regarding individual incidents to earlier calculations of the extent of mutiny on Atlantic slave ships, and has shown that ships were one means through which revolutionary struggle could spread around the region.[43] During the first half of the nineteenth century, there were several outbreaks on Indian convict vessels, sailing to or from India, Mauritius, Burma, Singapore and the Andaman Islands. The convicts sometimes carried insurrectionary sentiment or protest to new locations, with subsequent outbreaks in the penal colonies on occasion connected both to pre-transportation local struggles and to connections forged in Indian prisons or on transportation ships.[44] Lascars, Indian Ocean sailors who hailed from all over the region and sometimes manned transportation ships, also contested shipboard authority and routine, through refusing to work, assaulting their superiors or outright mutiny. In what historians sometimes call everyday forms of resistance, they also maintained various cultural practices, including religious festivals.[45] Crossing the line (equator) ceremonies are particularly interesting in this respect. They were inversions of the usual hierarchy of the ship, led by ordinary sailors. A long-serving seaman dressed up as Neptune, and questioned, ridiculed, rubbed paint on and even shaved the beards of the ship's officers.[46]

Gender and race at sea

Historian Verene A. Shepherd has presented a moving account of the rape and death of a female passenger, an indentured laborer known to us only as Maharani, on her way to British Guiana in 1885 as a means of exploring the phenomenon of what she terms shipboard "sexploitation."[47] As Shepherd shows, during the nineteenth century there were a number of violent incidents that revolved around Indian protests against crews' assaults of or disrespect towards women, together with fragmentary and uncertain evidence of the existence of what we might term a shipboard sex trade. If indentured ships were gendered spaces, they were racialized ones too. During the 1880s and 1890s, officials decried the relative merits of European and Indian lascar crews. Lascars were cheap, but unfit for cold weather, "cowardly," and sexually predatory. Europeans were less culturally sensitive, but no more deferential to shipboard authority or female propriety.[48] Commonly it was a breakdown in the authority of captains and surgeon superintendents (often as a result of violent drunkenness) that led to more general lapses in shipboard discipline, and their associated consequences for the health and safety of indentured laborers. In one case, Surgeon Superintendent Jacob Anthony was tried before the Mauritian Supreme Court for "criminally and willfully inflicting certain wounds in and upon the body of one immigrant (name unknown)." According to witnesses who testified against him, Anthony had tied the man up by his thumbs for "making a mess" between decks. He was being treated for dysentery at the time, and later died. At the same time, Captain J. C. Wilson and Chief Mate Joseph Ninton were fined for throwing the body of an almost dead coolie overboard to avoid the ship being forced into quarantine.[49]

Migration, circulation, anti-colonialism, and proto-nationalism

Journeys were a space of identity formation and resistance, and they were also the means through which protest spread to other areas of the globe. We have already seen something of the political dynamics of shipboard revolt, and here I would like to extend this analysis through a discussion of how the migration or circulation of ordinary people helped to shape the spread of anti-colonial or proto-nationalist ideas. For instance, enslaved people in the Caribbean protested about their conditions through revolt, including after the British abolition of the slave trade in 1807, when it became clear that their emancipation was in fact to be a condition of apprenticeship and not freedom. Asian laborers too protested against the conditions of plantation indenture; feigning sickness, downing tools, or assaulting their overseers. In extreme circumstances, including after the British shipped *sipahi* (soldier) convicts to Burma following the Great Indian Revolt of 1857, and again in the early twentieth century when they sent political prisoners to incarceration in the Cellular Jail in the Andaman Islands, individuals or groups of workers went on hunger strike, refusing to eat and during the later period suffering forced feeding.

Such actions were sometimes a response to the peculiarities of specific conditions, associated with the organization of coerced labor, but in some cases mobile subjects became exposed to new forms of insurgency or anti-colonial sympathies, and this could inspire action that was more directly political. Recently, Uma Kothari has described how imperial opponents were exiled to various places in the Indian Ocean. She argues that although they were supposed to lose their political associations in spaces of isolation, in important ways exile enhanced and deepened anti-colonial networks. Exiles carried ideologies of resistance with them, and inspired political agitation amongst the people that they met.[50] We find similar examples for the Bay of Bengal. They include soldiers transported from India in 1854 following British victory in the Anglo-Sikh Wars, who led a mutiny on board a ship called the *Clarissa*. They killed several crewmembers, took control of the ship and sailed to Burma, marching inland in the mistaken belief that they could offer themselves for the anti-colonial army of an as yet imperially unincorporated rajah. Unfortunately, they were two years too late. The ensuing criminal court proceedings involved so many (convict) defendants that the trial had to be held in Calcutta's Town Hall.

Legacies and continuities

Creolization, cultural syncretism, and cosmopolitanism

Despite its often-coercive features, global mobility generated cultural creativity of various kinds: through the production of particular social and cultural practices, in the formation of communities, and in the making of postcolonial identities. In former slave colonies, this creativity is sometimes referred to as "creolization," and in these and other contexts as cultural syncretism or hybridity. It might include the emergence of distinct forms of religious worship, language, music, dance, and food, as place-specific blends of African, Asian, and European influences. Examples are the Mauritian Kreol language, the Bermudan Gombey dance, and the Louisiana dish Jambalaya.[51] In recent years, in Mauritius, there have been calls for the concept of "coolitude" to join that of *créolité* (which emerged first in mid-twentieth-century French Martinique as a counter to the Pan-African ideal of *negritude*) as a means of explaining the process of cultural production, and incorporating the experience of Asian indentured migration specifically.

Further concepts employed by historians are those of "cosmopolitanism," where different cultures live side-by-side, or "diaspora," which is seen as a means of explaining the peculiar social and cultural formations of groups of people with shared cultures and values living outside their or their forebears' place of origin. For sociologist Robin Cohen, it is possible to distinguish various diasporic typologies, including that of the "victim diaspora," those who were forced to migrate, including the descendants of slaves.[52] Scholarly critique includes skepticism as to whether social diversity amongst migrants can be captured in such an apparently all-embracing and cohesive term, as well as its underlying assumption that there are two kinds of populations: those which are static, and those which are mobile. As I suggested at the beginning of this chapter, over the long history of the world, migration has been a feature in the formation of all societies. A focus on the emergence of distinct cultural forms masks the way in which societies are continually in flux, and are made and remade as ordinary people move around and bring cultures into contact with each other. Such encounters range from the political to the intimate, and as we have seen the latter elevates the importance of gender and sexuality to the center of our analysis of global movement.

History and the present

Moreover, the tendency to celebrate the apparent cultural creativity and syncretism of parts of the postcolonial world today has the perhaps unanticipated double effect of glossing over their origins in disruption, dissent, and contestation, and of turning our vision away from the significant continuities in patterns of global mobility today. One feature of the historiography of migration has been the viewing of forced labor as what Patrick Manning has eloquently described as "a significant and painful step in the creation of the modern world economy."[53] I have already suggested the significance of coercion in effecting global mobility, and of recognizing the importance of Global South circular labor flows, and in so doing of foregrounding both resistance and domination in world history. I would also like to restate the value of looking beyond teleological interpretations of the historical "place" of forced labor and towards an appreciation not just of its effects, or legacies, but of its ongoing significance and importance. Without wishing to flatten historical difference or distinctiveness over time or across regions, borderlands, nations and/or empires, it is evident that forced labor and slavery remain features of the contemporary world, and that there has not been a seamless or total historical shift from coerced to free migration. A less Eurocentric understanding of labor mobility enables us to think of unfree migration, I would like to propose, as a form of human circulation that might never end.

Nowhere is this better represented historically than by juxtaposing the idea of Indian indenture as "a new system of slavery," as critics argued in the 1830s, with Indian nationalist M. K. Gandhi's celebration of its abolition in 1916. Though no new workers were indentured for overseas service thereafter, it was some years before those already in the colonies had served out their contracts. Moreover, even after the abolition of indenture, Indian migrant workers continued to play an important role in the global economy. They still do in the twenty-first century. The denial of citizenship and various other rights in some sites of migrant labor might be viewed as a direct legacy of earlier modes of coerced labor mobility. This includes, in the case of Indians working in places like Singapore without voting rights, the political deprivations of transported Indian convict labor.[54]

The feminization of migration

A second key element in modern overseas migration from Global South to Global North has been the feminization of international migration, and the development of a transnational sexual division of labor. Women from India and other countries in the Global South, including the Philippines, work overseas as nurses, nannies, or maids. Many of the women who stay behind migrate long distances from their homes, to work in factories or export processing zones geared to meet the material desires of Europe and the United States.[55] Debt bondage, forced labor, enslavement, and human trafficking remain features of many modern societies too. British campaign groups estimate that there are 13,000 people living in slavery in the United Kingdom alone. When we research and write about the abolition of the slave trade and of enslavement, in the earlier age of imperialism, we would do well to appreciate their seemingly enduring character.[56]

Suggestions for further reading

Allen, Richard B. *European Slave Trading in the Indian Ocean, 1500–1850*. Athens, OH: Ohio University Press, 2015.

Amrith, Sunil S. *Migration and Diaspora in Modern Asia.* Cambridge: Cambridge University Press, 2011.

Anderson, Clare and Hamish Maxwell-Stewart. "Convict Labour and the Western Empires, 1415–1954." In *The Routledge History of Western Empires,* ed. Robert Aldrich and Kirsten McKenzie. London: Routledge, 2013, 102–117.

Ballantyne, T. "Mobility, Empire, Colonisation," *History Australia* 11:2 (2014), 7–37.

Bush, M. L. *Servitude in Modern Times.* London: Polity, 2002.

Cohen, Robin. *Global Diasporas: An Introduction.* Abingdon, UK: Routledge, 2008.

Cohen, R. and P. Toninato, eds. *The Creolization Reader: Studies in Mixed Identities and Cultures.* London: Routledge, 2009.

Heuman, Gad and James Walvin, eds. *The Slavery Reader.* London: Routledge, 2003.

Eltis, D. ed. *Coerced and Free Migration: Global Perspectives,* Stanford, CA: Stanford University Press, 2002.

Harper, M. and S. Constantine. *Migration and Empire.* Oxford: Oxford University Press, 2010.

Hoerder, D. *Cultures in Contact: World Migrations in the Second Millennium,* Durham, NC: Duke University Press, 2002.

McKeown, Adam. "Global Migration, 1846–1940," *Journal of World History* 15:2 (2004): 155–189.

Manning, P. *Migration in World History.* London: Routledge, 2005.

Northrup, D. *Indentured Labor in the Age of Imperialism, 1834–1922.* Cambridge: Cambridge University Press, 1995.

Strasser, U. and H. Tinsman. "Engendering World History," *Radical History Review* 91 (2005): 151–164.

Notes

1 The research leading to these results has received funding from the European Research Council under the European Union's Seventh Framework Programme (FP/2007–2013) / ERC Grant Agreement 312542. The Economic and Social Research Council funded work on Indian convict transportation in the Indian Ocean, including the Andaman Islands (Grant Nos R000271268/ RES-000-22-3484).

2 Martin Daunton and Rick Halpern, eds, *Empire and Others: British Encounters with Indigenous Peoples, 1650–1800* (London: University College London Press, 1999); Benjamin Madley, "From Terror to Genocide: Britain's Tasmanian Penal Colony and Australia's History Wars," *Journal of British Studies* 47:1 (2008): 77–106.

3 Emma Battell Lowman and Adam Barker, *Settler: Identity and Colonialism in 21st Century Canada* (Halifax: Fernwood Press, 2015).

4 Prabhu Mohapatra, "Eurocentrism, Forced Labour, and Global Migration: A Critical Assessment," *International Review of Social History* 52 (2007): 110–115.

5   Daniel Domingues da Silva, David Eltis, Philp Misevich, and Olatunji Ojo,
    "The Diaspora of Africans Liberated from Slave Ships in the Nineteenth
    Century," *The Journal of African History* 55:3 (2014): 347–369; Marina
    Carter, V. Govinden, and S. Peerthum, *The Last Slaves: Liberated Africans in
    19th Century Mauritius* (Port Louis, Mauritius: Centre for Research on Indian
    Ocean Societies, 2003); Bronwen Everill, *Abolition and Empire in Sierra Leone
    and Liberia* (Basingstoke, UK: Palgrave, 2012).

6   Anita Rupprecht, "'When he gets among his Countrymen, they tell him that he
    is free': Slave Trade Abolition, Indentured Africans and a Royal Commission,"
    Slavery and Abolition 33:3 (2012): 435–455 (citing Saidiya V. Hartman, *Scenes
    of Subjection: Terror, Slavery, and Self-Making in Nineteenth-Century America*
    [Oxford: Oxford University Press, 1997], 10).

7   Indrani Chatterjee and Richard Eaton, eds, *Slavery and South Asian History*
    (Bloomington: Indiana University Press, 2006); Peter Robb, "Introduction:
    Meanings of Labour in Indian Social Context," in *Dalit Movements and the
    Meanings of Labour in India*, ed. Peter Robb (New Delhi: Oxford University
    Press, 1993), 1–67.

8   Amitav Ghosh, "The Slave of Ms. H.6," in *Subaltern Studies, Volume VII*, ed.
    P. Chatterjee and G. Pandey (New Delhi: Oxford University Press, 1993),
    159–220.

9   Catherine Hall, Nicholas Draper, Keith McClelland, Kate Donington, and
    Rachel Lang, *Legacies of British Slave-ownership: Colonial Slavery and the
    Formation of Victorian Britain* (Cambridge: Cambridge University Press,
    2014).

10 Abbot Emerson Smith, *Colonists in Bondage: White Servitude and Convict
    Labor in America 1607–1776* (Chapel Hill, NC: University of North Carolina
    Press, 1947).

11 Gwenda Morgan and Peter Rushton, *Banishment in the Early Atlantic World:
    Convicts, Rebels and Slaves* (London: Bloomsbury, 2013), 120. See also: Roger
    Ekirch, *Bound for America: The Transportation of Convicts to the Colonies,
    1718–1775* (Oxford: Clarendon Press, 1987).

12 Marcus Rediker and Peter Linebaugh, *The Many-Headed Hydra: Sailors,
    Slaves, Commoners, and the Hidden History of the Revolutionary Atlantic*
    (London: Verso, 2000).

13 Marilyn Lake and Henry Reynolds, *Drawing the Global Colour Line: White
    Men's Countries and the International Challenge of Racial Equality*
    (Cambridge: Cambridge University Press, 2008).

14 John Darwin, *The Empire Project: The Rise and Fall of the British World
    System 1830–1979* (Cambridge: Cambridge University Press, 2011)

15 Harald Fischer-Tiné, *Low and Licentious Europeans: Race, Class and "White
    Subalternity" in Colonial India* (New Delhi: Orient Longman, 2008).

16 Clare Anderson, *Convicts In The Indian Ocean: Transportation from South
    Asia to Mauritius, 1815–53* (Basingstoke, UK: Macmillan, 2000); Clare
    Anderson, *Subaltern Lives: Biographies of Colonialism in the Indian Ocean
    World, 1790–1920* (Cambridge: Cambridge University Press, 2012).

17 Clare Anderson, Madhumita Mazumdar, and Vishvajit Pandya, *New Histories of the Andaman Islands: Landscape, Place and Identity in the Bay of Bengal, 1790–2012* (Cambridge: Cambridge University Press, 2016).

18 Princeton University Library, Department of Rare Books and Special Collections: C0247 Richard Halliburton Papers: Box 22 (Devil's Island Correspondence for *New Worlds to Conquer*, 1929–33), Folder 46: Jean Wick (Mrs. Achmed Abdullah, author's agent and advisor) to Tom Davin, October 11, 1933. Of crucial importance in bringing international attention to bear on Guyane a decade earlier was Albert Londres, *Au Bagne [In the Penal Colony]* (Paris: Albin Michel, 1923).

19 Charles Péan, *Devil's Island* (London: Hodder and Stoughton, 1939).

20 Anton Chekhov, *Sakhalin Island* (London: Alma Books, 2013) [first published in Russian, 1895].

21 Danzig Baldaev, *Drawings From The Gulag* (London: Fuel, 2010).

22 Anne Applebaum, *Gulag: A History* (New York: Doubleday, 2003).

23 Chaki Oguchi, "The Formation of Some Towns Having Prison (*Shujikan*) in Hokkaido and the Images for the Prison by the Inhabitants," *Rekishichirigaku Kiyo* (March 1983): 43–70; Osamu Tanaka, "The Labour Form of the Initial Stage of Capitalism in Hokkaido: With a Focus on Convict Labour," *Keizaironshu* (March 1955): 67–112; Ricardo D. Salvatore and Carlos Aguirre, "Colonies of Settlement or Places of Banishment and Torment? Penal Colonies and Convict Labour in Latin America, c.1800–1940," in *Global Convict Labour*, ed. Christian G. De Vito and Alex Lichtenstein (Leiden: Brill, 2015); Joanna Waley-Cohen, *Exile in Mid-Qing China: Banishment to Xinjiang, 1758–1820* (New Haven, CT: Yale University Press, 1991).

24 Raymond Evans, "'Kings in Brass Crescents': Defining Aboriginal Labour Patterns in Colonial Queensland," in *Indentured Labour in the British Empire 1834–1920*, ed. Kay Saunders (London: Croom Helm, 1984), 183–212. See also Adrian Graves, *Cane and Labour: The Political Economy of the Queensland Sugar Industry, 1862–1906* (Edinburgh: Edinburgh University Press, 1993).

25 Rosabelle Boswell, *Le Malaise Créole: Ethnic Identity in Mauritius* (Oxford: Berghahn, 2006). See also: Patrick Eisenlohr, *Little India: Diaspora, Time, and Ethnolinguistic Belonging in Hindu Mauritius* (Berkeley: University of California Press, 2006); Thomas H. Eriksen, "Nationalism, Mauritian Style: Cultural Unity and Ethnic Diversity," *Comparative Studies in Society and History* 36:3 (1994): 549–575.

26 Marina Carter, *Lakshmi's Legacy: The Testimonies of Indian women in C19th Mauritius* (Rose-Hill: Mauritius, 1994); Marina Carter, *Voices from Indenture: Experiences of Indian Migrants in the British Empire* (London: University of Leicester Press, 1996).

27 Clare Anderson, "Convicts and Coolies: Rethinking Indentured Labour in the Nineteenth Century," *Slavery and Abolition* 30:1 (2009): 93–109.

28 Today, fully one-quarter of the world's population lives in countries bordering the Bay of Bengal: Sunil S. Amrith, *Migration and Diaspora in Modern Asia* (Cambridge: Cambridge University Press, 2011), 30. See also Sunil S. Amrith,

Crossing The Bay of Bengal: The Furies of Nature and the Fortunes of Migrants (Cambridge MA: Harvard University Press, 2013).

29 James Belich, *Replenishing the Earth: The Settler Revolution and the Rise of Angloworld* (Oxford: Oxford University Press, 2011).

30 Dipesh Chakrabarty, *Provincializing Europe* (Princeton, NJ: Princeton University Press, 2000). For the century after c.1850, see also Adam McKeown, "Global Migration, 1846–1940," *Journal of World History* 15:2 (2004): 155–189.

31 *Report of the Indian Jails Committee, 1919–20* (London: HMSO, 1921), 277–279.

32 Gwyn Campbell, Suzanne Miers, and Joseph C. Miller, eds, *Women and Slavery, Volume I: Africa, the Indian Ocean World, and the Medieval North Atlantic* (Athens, OH: Ohio University Press, 2007); Gwyn Campbell, Suzanne Miers, and Joseph C. Miller, eds, *Women and Slavery, Volume II: The Modern Atlantic* (Athens, OH: Ohio University Press, 2007); Gwyn Campbell, Suzanne Miers, and Joseph C. Miller, eds, *Children in Slavery Through the Ages* (Athens, OH: Ohio University Press, 2009).

33 Brij V. Lal, "Veil of Dishonour: Sexual Jealousy and Suicide on Fiji Plantations," *The Journal of Pacific History* 20:3 (1985): 135–155.

34 See also Ulrike Strasser and Heidi Tinsman, "Engendering World History," *Radical History Review* 91 (2005): 151–164.

35 Anderson, Mazumdar, and Pandya, *New Histories of the Andaman Islands;* Laura Bear, *Lines of the Nation: Indian Railway Workers, Bureaucracy, and the Intimate Historical Self* (Columbia, NY: Columbia University Press, 2007); William J. Glover, "Objects, Models, and Exemplary Works: Educating Sentiment in Colonial India," *Journal of Asian Studies* 64:3 (2005): 539–566.

36 Tony Ballantyne and Antoinette Burton, eds, *Bodies in Contact: Rethinking Colonial Encounters in World History* (Durham, NC: Duke University Press, 2005). See also Tony Ballantyne and Antoinette Burton, eds, *Moving Subjects: Gender, Mobility and Intimacy in an Age of Global Empire* (Champaign: University of Illinois Press, 2008).

37 McKeown, "Global Migration, 1846–1940."

38 Prashant Bharadwaj, Asim Khwaja, and Atif Mian, "The Big March: Migratory Flows after the Partition of India," *Economic and Political Weekly*, August 30, 2008: 39–49.

39 Sidney W. Mintz and Richard Price, *The Birth of African-American Culture: An Anthropological Perspective* (Boston, MA: Beacon Press, 1992), 43.

40 Russel Ward, *The Australian Legend* (Melbourne: Oxford University Press, 1958). For a review of this important historian's work, see the special issue of the *Journal of Australian Colonial History*, ed. Frank Bongiorno and David Andrew Roberts (no. 2, 2008); Clare Anderson, "The Bel Ombre Rebellion: Indian Convicts in Mauritius, 1815–53," in *Abolition and Its Aftermath in Indian Ocean Africa and Asia*, ed. Gwyn Campbell (New York: Routledge, 2004), 50–65.

41 Niklas Frykman, Clare Anderson, Lex Heerma van Voss, and Marcus Rediker, "Introduction," *International Review of Social History* 58, Supplement S21

(2013): 1–14 (quote at 3). See also Emma Christopher, Cassandra Pybus, and Marcus Rediker, eds, *Many Middle Passages: Forced Migration in the Making of the Modern World* (Berkeley: University of California Press, 2007); Marcus Rediker, *Between the Devil and the Deep Blue Sea: Merchant Seamen, Pirates, and the Anglo-American Maritime World, 1700–1750* (Cambridge: Cambridge University Press, 1987); Marcus Rediker, *The Slave Ship: A Human History* (London: Vintage, 2007); and David Richardson, "Shipboard Revolts, African Authority, and the Atlantic Slave Trade," *William and Mary Quarterly* 58 (2001): 69–92.

42 Rediker, *Between the Devil and the Deep Blue Sea*, ch. 2; Rediker and Linebaugh, *The Many-Headed Hydra*, 144.

43 Marcus Rediker, *The Amistad Rebellion: Atlantic Odyssey of Slavery and Freedom* (London: Verso, 2013); Anita Rupprecht, "'All We Have Done, We Have Done for Freedom': The Creole Slave-Ship Revolt (1841) and the Revolutionary Atlantic," *International Review of Social History* 58, Supplement S21 (2013): 253–277.

44 Clare Anderson, "'The Ferringees are Flying—the ship is ours!' The Convict Middle Passage in Colonial South and Southeast Asia, 1790–1860," *Indian Economic and Social History Review* 41:3 (2005): 143–186; Clare Anderson, "The Age of Revolution in the Indian Ocean, Bay of Bengal, and South China Sea: A Maritime Perspective," *International Review of Social History* 58, Supplement S21 (2013): 229–251.

45 Ravi Ahuja, "Mobility and Containment: The Voyages of South Asian Seamen, c.1900–1960," in *Coolies, Capital, and Colonialism: Studies in Indian Labour*, ed. Rana P. Behal and Marcel van der Linden (Cambridge: Cambridge University Press, 2006), 111–141; Aaron Jaffer, "'Lord of the Forecastle': Serangs, Tindals, and Lascar Mutiny, c.1780–1860," *International Review of Social History* 58, Supplement S21 (2013): 153–175; Amitav Ghosh, "Of Fanás and Forecastles: The Indian Ocean and Some Lost Languages of the Age of Sail," *Economic and Political Weekly* 25 (2008): 56–62; James C. Scott, *Weapons of the Weak: Everyday Day Forms of Peasant Resistance* (New Haven, CT: Yale University Press, 1987); James C. Scott, *Domination and the Arts of Resistance: Hidden Transcripts* (New Haven, CT: Yale University Press, 1992).

46 National Maritime Museum, WEL/40: Diary of Richard Joyce of H.M. gun brig RICHMOND 1810–16, and afterwards midshipman of H.E.I.C. David Scott; JOD/5: Robert Ramsay, "Journal of a Voyage from Gravesend to Calcutta by a Cadet in 1825."

47 Verene A. Shepherd, *Maharani's Misery: Narratives of a Passage from India to the Caribbean* (Mona, Jamaica: University of West Indies Press, 2002).

48 India Office Records, British Library (henceforth IOR) L/PJ/6/37 File 538: Enquiry . . . into certain complaints made by the immigrants of the ship "Ellora" (1881); IOR L/PJ/6/96 File 640: Enquiry into circumstances on the emigrant ship "Hesperides" (1883); IOR P/691: Nos 4–5: Complaint against the Dover Castle while employed in conveying emigrants from Calcutta to British Guiana (1872); IOR L/PJ/6/119 File 424: Emigration to Fiji and West Indies: question of employing lascar crews on vessels (1884); IOR L/PJ/6/309

File 2017: Emigration to Fiji and West Indies: lascar crews (1891).

49 IOR P/188/64 India (Public) January 14, 1861 nos 31–3: Misconduct of doctor seaman on ship Thomas Hamlin; IOR P/188/70 India (Public) February 2, 1865 nos 9–13: Regarding ill treatment of coolie passengers on board emigrant ship Rajasthan.

50 Uma Kothari, "Contesting Colonial Rule: Politics of Exile in the Indian Ocean," *Geoforum* 43 (2012): 697–706.

51 Robin Cohen and Paola Toninato, eds, *The Creolization Reader: Studies in Mixed Identities and Cultures* (London: Routledge, 2009).

52 Robin Cohen, *Global Diasporas: An Introduction* (Abingdon, UK: Routledge, 2008).

53 Patrick Manning, *Migration in World History* (London: Routledge, 2005), 133.

54 Anoma Pieris, *Hidden Hands and Divided Landscapes: A Penal History of Singapore's Plural Society* (Honolulu: University of Hawai'i Press, 2009).

55 Bridget Anderson, *Doing the Dirty Work: The Global Politics of Domestic Labour* (London: Zed Books, 2000).

56 See http://www.antislavery.org/english/slavery_today/default.aspx (accessed March 11, 2015).

7

The Anthropocene from Below

Nancy J. Jacobs, Danielle Johnstone, and Christopher S. Kelly

We live in an extraordinary time. The year 2015 was the hottest on record and the increase in Earth's mean surface temperature between 1880 and 2012 has been measured at 0.85°C (1.53°F).[1] Weather is becoming more erratic. Many places are becoming hotter and drier, others wetter, and a few places are becoming more temperate. More severe storms are occurring. Seasons are shifting and changing in length. Polar ice is melting and sea levels are rising. This is far more than a matter of changing weather: The global profile of life is being transformed.[2] Societies are being challenged in new ways, humanity is facing shared environmental problems that are affecting different peoples and places in different ways, and these challenges are making global inequalities starker. The world is being forced to confront a fact: Current global climate change, likely unprecedented in its rate, will impose unequal burdens on the world's people.

Thinking about the magnitude of this change in the context of "world histories from below" requires stretching our conceptions of its history. It demands that we look at climate change from below the elite level, considering perspectives from the Global South and mapping experiences of climate against a human history that is built on a scaffolding of inequality. It also demands that we look at history from below the surface of the earth, considering how natural systems have submitted to human influence. A history of climate change from below considers the transformations of the planet by a deeply uneven global society, the transformations of society by this changing Earth, and the new politics that are emerging.

Physical and biological scientists have suggested that these transformations will constitute a new era. In 2000, Nobel laureate and chemist Paul Crutzen and biologist Eugene Stoermer made the first formal published proposal that Earth has entered a new condition—a contemporary period of a transformed climate. They called this epoch the "Anthropocene," a neologism based on the Greek word for humanity: "anthro."[3] They were not the first scientists to propose that Earth had entered a new era, but writing at a moment of increasing recognition of climate change, they framed a new way of thinking. Central to this paradigm is the contention that the currently recognized geological epoch—the Holocene, the most recent "interglacial" in Earth history—is over. If the next global glaciation is forestalled due to human impact on the climate, this argument goes, geological time keeping should reflect this new development.[4]

This is no casual proposition: the Anthropocene Working Group of the International Union of Geological Scientists is now studying and debating the end of the Holocene. In 2016, this committee of stratigraphers (the scientists who study the geological record) is due to decide whether or not to endorse the new epoch and to rule on which dates and markers define it.[5] This is a difficult matter because stratigraphers must follow formal criteria. They prefer to set their break points at global-scale changes recorded by precise physical markers, called "golden spikes," which can be dated to a year or a decade and complemented by auxiliary evidence of associated widespread changes. The matter is complicated because, while geological evidence of human impacts sometimes dates to different times in different places, a recognized geological age must begin all over the planet at once. Specialist debate and close attention to standards of evidence will determine the recommendation of the Anthropocene Working Group and the decision of the larger body to which they report.[6]

While the Anthropocene would be a geological epoch, it is also of interest to social scientists. It raises questions about the scope and scale of our understanding of the history of humans on this planet. The definition of the Anthropocene will have a great influence on what is accepted as "natural," on what caused the departure from it, and on what should be done about it. Historians do not have the evidence or methods to comment on the golden spikes sought by stratigraphers. This chapter takes climate change seriously, but does not set out to make the case for a new epoch. Our purpose is to explore which human processes may have been powerful enough not just to "make history," but to make geological epochs. Framing climate change within human history invites us to approach it from below.

Drawing on the disciplines of geology, history and contemporary social sciences, this chapter discusses the geo-physical processes of recent climate changes in the context of the driving forces of world history. It narrates human–climate interactions from the very deep past to the present, touching down at several crucial moments that have been associated with environmental transformation on a global scale. We review four leading theories, each positing different opening points for the Anthropocene: the agricultural revolution, the global encounters following the voyage of Columbus, the Industrial Revolution, and the transformations of the mid-twentieth century sometimes referred to as the "Great Acceleration."[7] These theories are represented on Figure 7.1, which conveys their different beginning points.

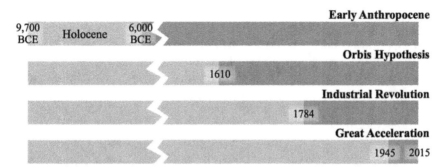

FIGURE 7.1 *Four proposed opening points for the Anthropocene. Credit: Bruce Boucek, Brown University Library. Used with Permission of the Brown University Library.*

Evidently, the Anthropocene means different things to different people, which explains much about its broad appeal. Yet, the vagueness in its definition has stirred disquiet among some natural scientists, who feel political debates have hijacked their discussion about geological periods. More to the point of this chapter, however, some social scientists feel that in fact the framing of human society has been hijacked by natural science. The first objection is philosophical, having to do with the nature of humanity. Social scientists have observed that the emphasis on the "human" in the concept of the Anthropocene inscribes ideas of the exceptionalism of our species, obscuring our position in a wider web including other life forms and the material world. As we will see, pathogens feature prominently in some theories of the Anthropocene, illustrating the tensions in defining the epoch in human terms. The human body is itself an assemblage of organisms, a point that is lost by thinking of humanity as an autonomous agent.[8] A second, sociological critique has more to do with the goals of this book, of approaching history from below. The Anthropocene's packaging of the human species as a single unit erases matters of power and inequality.[9] This chapter takes the problem of social holism as its starting point. The goal is to explore different actors in its causation and different experiences of its effects, with an emphasis on what can be seen from below. We attempt this by explaining the history of climate change as the intersection of two types of systems: the Earth System and the global economic system.

First, the "Earth System" refers to planetary interactions among the atmosphere, soil, rocks and water of the physical Earth and the organisms inhabiting it. Study of the Earth System is interdisciplinary, involving climatologists, chemists, physicists, and oceanographers, who draw together their understandings of many different processes and cycles. The history of the Earth System is expressed in geological periods starting with the Precambrian supereon and extending through units technically divided into eons, eras and periods. This deep past, which saw the development of our planet and the evolution of life, is sometimes referred to as "geological" time, but the focus here is on more than rocks. It is a system of interactions among the atmosphere, the oceans, solid rocks, and evolving organisms. The forces include everything from solar radiation, to microorganisms and volcanoes. Their influence continues into the most recent past, although so slowly as to be imperceptible to our modern eye.[10]

Second, the "global economic system" refers to the consolidation of previously local economies through trade and capital flows. Global economic patterns are the brief of historians, sociologists, anthropologists, and economists who explore how wealth drawn from every region accumulated in centers and was reinvested in ways that further enriched those centers. The global economy grew up in the wake of exploration and conquest by Europeans after 1500. It consolidated through merchant and later industrial capital and developed a worldwide reach through empire. Economic growth and environmental impacts achieved an unprecedented rate with the creation of mass consumer societies in the mid-twentieth century. At the turn of the new millennium, economic power began to decenter from the Global North. Still, much of the world remains relatively underdeveloped.

While the tendency toward social holism in theories of the Anthropocene is real, we find that many understandings of anthropogenic climate change also point toward political and economic forces. Theories of the Anthropocene have already made room for social considerations and we track those topics over the long term. Legacies of inequality remain strong and the chapter closes with a discussion about the present and the future, as disparate experiences of climate change between the global haves and have-nots become yet starker and more uneven.

The Earth System before the Holocene

Climate has changed radically over the course of Earth's history; it has ranged from ice-cover at the equator to tropical conditions at the poles. Until now, the most rapid known period of change was during the Paleocene–Eocene Thermal Maximum (PETM) roughly 56 million years ago, when the rate was an increase of 0.025°C per 100 years. Figure 7.2 compares the rate today with that during the PETM and shows that contemporary global warming is unprecedented in its rate.[11] During the PETM, a tipping point in deep ocean temperature caused a mass release of carbon, previously sequestered at the bottom of the seafloor, into the atmosphere. The resulting change in the Earth system was profound, wholesale, and long-lived. The effects were eerily similar to those predicted for our future: acidification of the oceans, vast migrations and extinctions of animals and plants, and a lengthy 200,000-year recovery to "normal" conditions. As then, the current transformation entails a reversal of conditions created over nearly unimaginable time scales through the interchange between solid earth and

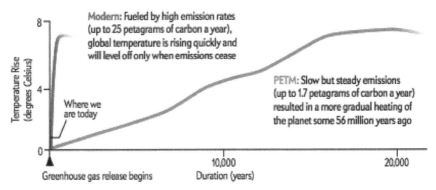

Global temperature is rising much more quickly today than it did during the PETM

FIGURE 7.2 *Global temperature rise, today (left) and during the PETM (right). Lee R. Kump, "The Last Great Global Warming,"* Scientific American *305:1 (2011): 59. Used with Permission of Scientific American.*

atmosphere. Then and now, the release of carbon from the solid earth into the atmosphere involved a resurrection of the chemical composition of ancient atmospheres. A historical perspective informs us that the warming we are facing has precedents, but the current rate is unprecedented.

In tracking climate and life through time, we must follow elements, chemical compounds, biological organisms and geophysical forces. It is impossible to talk about modern life on Earth without mentioning two elements: oxygen and carbon. Oxygen is key to the cycle of respiration and photosynthesis, processes on which modern life depends. Carbon is continually cycled between the atmosphere, the soil, and the oceans and fossilized minerals. Over the very long term, carbon exchange among rocks, the ocean, and the atmosphere determines the composition of atmospheric gases and, consequently, the mean global temperature and Earth's habitability. Carbon cycle accounting is complicated because the element assumes a variety of chemical forms in different reservoirs on Earth. In the ocean, it can be stored in organic (living) compounds, such as bacteria, algae, clams, fish, or dolphins, or it can be in an inorganic (non-living) form, such as carbonic acid or bicarbonate. It can be in mud or rocks, on both land and in the sea. Carbon is stored on land in organisms, such as humans, bacteria, robins, or oak trees. In the atmosphere, carbon is present in a variety of molecules, but most principally, it is in the greenhouse gases carbon dioxide (CO_2) and methane (CH_4). If carbon and oxygen are the building blocks for life on Earth, the Sun is our collective energy source. A third vital ingredient for life, liquid water, requires temperatures between 0 and 100°C. Fortunately, this temperature requirement is satisfied through a combination of the Sun's incoming solar radiation and an atmosphere rich in greenhouse gases, which traps and re-radiates this energy within the Earth System. These heat-saving properties earn "greenhouse gases" their name and provide a habitable planet for life on Earth. Indeed, without greenhouse gases, Earth's mean annual temperature would be −18°C, well below the freezing point of water.[12]

Carbon budgets are essential to planetary history; the balance between processes of CO_2 emission and consumption has helped to prevent a "runaway" hothouse or icebox climate. If the climate had been too hot, the result would have been a Venus. If it had been too cold, a Mars. Earth was in some respects like Goldilocks; its position from the Sun, in addition to its active tectonics and dynamic atmosphere, was just right for life to blossom. And blossom it did, in fits and starts. Earth began as a barren rock planet, punctuated by intermittent lava flows and bombardment by objects from space. The atmosphere was mostly carbon dioxide and nitrogen gas. Oxygen (O_2) was notably in very low concentrations, based on evidence from minerals that cannot form under oxygenated conditions. Gazing out at this environment, an extraterrestrial visitor might not have guessed that in four billion years this desolate sphere would become a highly habitable planet, with a cascade of carbon-based life.[13]

Regardless of how life first arose, fossilized evidence of its beginning dates to about 3.5 billion years ago in the form of thick mats of marine microorganisms.[14] Still, the earth remained fairly unwelcoming to most forms of life until much later. Arguably the first step toward the habitability we relish today occurred 2.7–2.4 billion years ago with the mass emergence of cyanobacteria, marine microorganisms that evolved photosynthetic capabilities and began producing O_2 on an unprecedented scale. Geologic indicators point to the beginnings of an oxygenated atmosphere at this time, with reduced concentrations of atmospheric CO_2.[15] This development, sometimes called "The Great Oxygenation Event" likely produced a cooler climate from 600 million to two billion years ago than had existed during the preceding two billion years of Earth's history.[16] The full transition to an oxygenated atmosphere marked the beginning of the Proterozoic Eon.[17]

Concentrations of oxygen in the atmosphere rose to the present level of approximately 19 percent about one billion years ago: the first multicellular organisms evolved after that. The "explosion" of life 540 million years ago, known as the Cambrian, brought the Earth into its current eon, the Phanerozoic, from which all other subdivisions are carved. Subsequently, all forms of modern life evolved.

The death of organisms usually led to a recycling of their hydrogen, carbon and oxygen into the environment. But in some cases this organic material was preserved. Plant matter lay stagnant in ancient swamps and was eventually subjected to heat and pressure that compacted it into dense, carbon and hydrogen-rich material. Over enough time and appropriate conditions, coal was formed. The oceanic equivalent was the constant "rain" of dead microorganisms from the top of the sea to the very bottom. Oil and natural gas were formed through hot compression of microscopic marine organisms. Coal, oil, and natural gas are collectively known as "fossil fuels" due to their common origin as ancient dead plants and animals. Many fossil fuels date to hundreds of millions of years ago.[18] So much coal was formed that the geologic period of 350–300 million years ago is called the "Carboniferous." These processes are well understood as carbon *sequestration*; that is, carbon is stripped out of the atmosphere through the formation and subsequent burial of organisms into rocks. When humans burn fossil fuels today, they are instantly returning to the atmosphere carbon that had been drawn into solid form over eons.

After the climatic (and CO_2 and CH_4) oscillations in the Phanerozoic, the dominant trend from the end of the dinosaurs 65 million years ago until very recently has been one of cooling. During this period of cooling more than 30 million years ago, ice sheets formed on Antarctica. The changeover from a warmer Pliocene Epoch to the colder Pleistocene when ice sheets grew on Greenland occurred 2.5 million years ago. (The most recent geological epochs are represented on Figure 7.3.) This was a tumultuous time in Earth's history: CO_2 dropped from roughly 380 to 280 parts per million (ppm), the climate cooled accordingly, the genus *Homo* evolved, sprawling ice sheets waxed and waned, and the extent of tropical ocean waters contracted.[19] In the terminology of popular culture, this was the "ice age."

More accurately, though, "ice age" should be plural—the Pleistocene was riddled with many glacial periods. The magnitude of changes in climate from glacial and back again was tremendous; just since our most recent glaciation (roughly 19,000 years ago), Earth's mean surface air temperature has risen 3–8°C.[20] Regular changes in Earth's orbit gave rise to periodic cycles in Earth's climate that occur over tens of thousands of years.[21] The manifestation in Earth's climate system of these variations resembles a saw tooth pattern: slow descent into glacial time periods and rapid thawing periods known as interglacials. CO_2 and CH_4 also varied according to the glacial–interglacial beat; CO_2 fluctuated from 180 ppm during glacials to 260–280 ppm during warmer periods, while CH_4 rose from 350 ppb to 700 ppb in a similarly cyclic manner.[22]

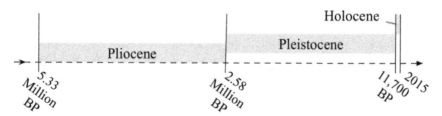

FIGURE 7.3 *Recent geological epochs. Credit: Bruce Boucek, Brown University Library. Used with Permission of the Brown University Library.*

The interglacial Holocene as the Early Anthropocene

After the last glacial age, the earth moved into a time of climatic stability reflected in pivotal climatic and human developmental hallmarks. Around 10,000 BCE (Before Common Era), a shift occurred, from the Pleistocene to the Holocene in geologic ages. In human terms, an "agricultural revolution" took place. These stages were connected since a combination of an increase in temperature and shifting rainfall patterns allowed cultivation to become a reliable option for the human diet. In a process lasting millennia in some parts of the globe, crops and domesticated animals became replacements for wild foods and enabled the development of concentrated population in larger numbers than ever before.[23]

A magisterial history of climate change by John L. Brooke provides a clear and useful synthesis of the history of human habitation and impact on the environment. In larger societies, diseases emerged and circulated, so population growth was gradual. Episodic climate variations, including those caused by volcanic eruptions, led to crop failure and famine. Death rates were high, but because fertility rates outpaced them, human population grew from an estimated seven million people before the development of agriculture to 38 million at around 3,000 years ago, when societies in the eastern Mediterranean started to use metal tools.[24] Concurrent with these events, the climate slowly settled into the system that we now think of as "normal" climate (i.e. moving toward approximately 14°C mean annual temperature, 280 ppm CO_2, 715 ppb CH_4).[25]

This observation that all the social, political, and technological developments of interest to historians have occurred within the Holocene underscores the revolutionary nature of Anthropocene theories. But, the difference between the two epochs is debated. The first theory, of the "Early Anthropocene" (represented on the top bar on Figure 7.1) implies that the entire period now understood to be the Holocene was a human creation. The theory is associated with paleoclimatologist William Ruddiman, who implicates humans in increased carbon dioxide as early as 8,000 years ago when agricultural settlements first appeared in Eurasia.[26] Ruddiman argues that that CO_2 had been trending lower, but people reversed this by burning forests to clear farmlands and causing a net transfer of carbon from biomass to the atmosphere. Additionally, the domestication of stock and the inception of rice paddy irrigation and population growth in Southeast Asia increased atmospheric methane concentrations around 5,000 years ago because of plant decay and biochemical processes among people and livestock.[27] Ruddiman's argument is that anthropogenic climate change started with the conversion of the earth's biomass, long before mass combustion of fossilized carbon.

The implications of mass agriculture were undeniably revolutionary for human society. Technology, political organization, and social formations all changed. Population also grew, but slowly. Over most of human history, a regime of high fertility was offset by mortality that was nearly as high. This near-balance kept population change at gradual growth. At the beginning of the Common Era (CE) the world's human population was about 252 million. The 1,300 years that followed saw agricultural innovation but also famines and episodic plagues. Estimates are that global population grew slowly over these centuries, to an estimated 442 million in 1340.[28] The Black Death, which had already begun in Asia, was responsible for a decrease in global population by as much as a quarter. Following the Black Death was the "Little Ice Age," a globally cooler period experienced primarily in the northern hemisphere beginning around 1450 and considered by some to have endured until as late as 1850.[29] Ruddiman argues the fourteenth-century spread of the plague and the concomitant decrease in food production actually caused the Little Ice Age by slowing anthropogenic emissions of CH_4 and CO_2.[30] Other scientists argue for non-human causes, including volcanic eruptions, a decreased abundance of sunspot activity, and changes in ocean circulation.[31]

Climate scientists continue to debate the relative effect of agriculture on greenhouse gases, but many are not convinced by evidence for human causation or satisfied that a sufficient golden spike for an early start to the Anthropocene exists.[32] If the long slow growth of human population, fed by the clearance of forests and the construction of rice paddies did occur on a global *scale*, the *rate* of this change does not compare with that seen in recent centuries. Thus many scientists find it is more convincing to define the Anthropocene around an extraordinary increase in the rate of climate change, rather than around the presence of human influences at all, as argued by the Early Anthropocene theory.[33]

The Columbian "Orbis" as the onset of the Anthropocene

Before 1500 CE, as we have seen, Earth's climate underwent extreme changes and humans were among the influences. But the 500 years since then have been a period of unprecedented acceleration in the rate of climate change: currently, it is more than ten times faster than the most rapid geological analogue.[34] Those who accept that we are now in a new age, therefore, face common problems of historical interpretation: causation and chronology. Because they require a physical marker to justify the opening of a new period, stratigraphers grapple with when exactly this new geologic period began. This question is not important to historians, but the competing chronologies of the Anthropocene are interesting to them because of different analyses of the forces responsible. Humans were critical in setting off climate change and so historians' understandings of the political and economic contexts are relevant. Inequality and territorial aggression has characterized the past 500 years and for that reason all three theories of the recent Anthropocene foreground processes that can be seen from below.

The latest theory of the Anthropocene, published in a provocative article by Simon Lewis and Mark Maslin in *Nature* in 2015, is the "Orbis" theory.[35] The term "Orbis" is Latin for "world" and thus conveys the importance of intercontinental connections in the history of climate change. This work helpfully fills a gap in Anthropocene histories, between the agriculture- and industry-based explanations and explicitly addresses matters of human inequality. Hearkening back to the Early Anthropocene theory, it associates the warm climate of the Holocene with human conversion of the earth's forests and grasslands for agricultural uses. Both hypotheses argue that human interaction in biological processes made an impact on the physical planet. They differ in where they locate the disruption to the climate. The Early Anthropocene puts it in the origins of agriculture, but the Orbis theory puts it at a sharp disruption of agricultural systems. The Orbis theory concentrates on the "collision of the Old and New Worlds," meaning Eurasia and the Americas, which occurred through European voyages of exploration and creation of empires around 1500. Lewis and Maslin do not use the term, but we follow convention by characterizing that moment of contact as "Columbian," named for the pioneering explorer of the Atlantic, Christopher Columbus.

The aftermath of the Columbian encounter was revolutionary across the globe. In the sixteenth century, silver from South America, sugar from the Caribbean, furs from northeast Asia and North America, and captive laborers from Africa circulated from their origins to other continents. Violence, confiscation of wealth, and enslavement of people put previously self-sufficient and autonomous communities in positions of economic dependence as well as political subjugation.[36] Imperial and mercantilist networks gained influence, even among people who were not impoverished or defeated. Wanting the manufactures purveyed by traders, they dedicated more of their economic capacities to producing commodities desired elsewhere. Yet, Europe was not the only rising region. A historian of China, Kenneth Pomeranz, has worked through careful and extended comparisons of wealthy areas of East Asia and northwest Europe and sees no advantages in Europe before the end of the eighteenth century.[37]

The Columbian encounter is foundational to world history and it sets us up to see centuries of asymmetrical relations. Through intercontinental contact between Europe and the other continents, especially the Americas, diseases circulated through regions where they were never known before. Such introduced microbes had a particularly devastating impact in the Americas, where they contributed to social and political crisis and military defeat. In the Orbis theory, much of the human impact resulted from the introduction of opportunistic pathogens to new places and new populations. The mortality in the Americas—in 1650 perhaps only six million survived of the 61 million before contact—caused the landmasses of North and South

America to reforest. Fewer people farming meant reforestation and the conversion of atmospheric carbon into biomass. This caused a drop in the level of atmospheric CO_2 now evident in the strata of Antarctic ice to about 272 ppm. Lewis and Maslin offer this development as an opening to the Anthropocene, suggesting 1610 as a possible date (see the second bar on Figure 7.1). Most distinctive about this theory, it is of an anthropogenic *depression* rather than of an *increase* in greenhouse gases (as recorded in ice core samples).[38]

Responses to the Orbis theory have credited Lewis and Maslin for drawing attention to key historical intervals and to the issues involved in boundary selection, but have criticized the 1610 date for several reasons. First, the decrease was perhaps due to natural variation; it cannot be shown to have been caused by population decrease in the Americas. Second, while a dip in CO_2 is evident in 1610, this does not qualify it as a break point in the functioning of the Earth System. Clive Hamilton explains that "the Anthropocene concept holds only if it can be shown that humans have had a detectable impact on the functioning of the Earth System." As he puts it: "Nothing happened to the Earth System in 1610."[39]

The drop in global population after the Columbian encounter may not account for a transformation of the Earth System, but the history of subsequent population growth is critical to other understandings of the Anthropocene. The demographic history of this period is difficult because of the paucity of data, but social scientists have developed plausible models. Population losses in the Americas were offset by the transportation of enslaved people from Africa and by free and indentured immigration from Europe. Food crops from the Americas—corn, manioc, sweet potatoes, and potatoes—supported population growth on the rest of the planet.[40] Africa is a large and diverse continent, so generalizations are difficult, but as a whole it was always relatively underpopulated and the slave trade probably slowed overall growth.[41]

The end of the Little Ice Age created better conditions for global population growth, but around then the high-fertility/high-mortality pattern had started to shift in some regions of Europe. The so-called "demographic transition" first involved a drop in mortality, as effective prevention of disease developed. Following the increased life expectancies came a drop in fertility. This new pattern appeared first in northwest Europe. In other areas of the globe, a similar shift to longer lives and fewer births followed economic expansion driven by industrialization.[42]

The Industrial Revolution as the onset of the Anthropocene

According to the most influential hypothesis proposing the new epoch of the Anthropocene—the one first proposed by Crutzen—the Industrial

Revolution transformed the physical earth as well as society and economy. This theory is represented by the third bar on Figure 7.1. It points to James Watt's refinement of the steam engine in 1784 as a watershed, because that invention spurred the consumption of fossil fuels.[43] By the early nineteenth century, "dark satanic mills" were transforming England from an agrarian to an industrial economy. The making of a new working class has long been recognized as one of its effects;[44] another was increasingly smoky skies (Figure 7.4). The argument is that the unforeseen and remarkable repercussion of the consumption of coal, petroleum, and natural gas that began with the Industrial Revolution has been a reversal of ancient geological processes: the carbon that hardened into rocks hundreds of millions of years ago, in processes lasting millions of years, is being returned to the atmosphere in a matter of a few centuries. The result has been abrupt, human-caused climate change.

Some Anthropocene thinkers, most notably Oreskes and Chakrabarty, hold that the burning of fossil fuels during the Industrial Revolution transformed humanity from the biological agents they had always been into geological agents.[45] But many climate scientists, including Ruddiman, have made good cases that agriculture had already affected atmospheric

FIGURE 7.4 *The iron foundry at Coalbrookdale, Shropshire, where good quality pig iron is produced by smelting iron ore with coke instead of charcoal. Original Artwork: Engraving by William Pickett after a drawing by Philippe Jacques de Loutherbourg (pub. 1805). Image: Getty 2635961.*

composition before 1500. The turning point of the Industrial Revolution was not that people first had impact on the composition of the atmosphere. The change in human impact during the Industrial Revolution had to do with time scales: while farmers had produced greenhouse gases by inserting themselves in seasonal and cyclical biological processes, industrialists reached beneath the surface of the earth for carbon that had been drawn down from a paleoatmosphere and sequestered for eons. The new source of energy accelerated the emission of carbon dioxide and methane, which, in large part, dictate Earth's mean annual temperature. Remarkably, the very greenhouse gases (carbon dioxide, methane) that allow for a habitable earth began to grow very rapidly to levels that have likely induced a geologically unprecedented rate of global climate change. As temperatures continue to track rising concentrations of greenhouse gases, we as humans are in for "too much of a good thing."

The Industrial Revolution theory has drawn vigorous criticism that extends to the concept of the Anthropocene itself. This debate connects squarely with the project of seeing the epoch from below. Naming a new era for the age of humanity collectively could be a conceptual error, a political ploy, or possibly even a moral evasion. The objection is that the Industrial Revolution hypothesis locates the origins of the new age in only a few regions undergoing a unique and extreme economic transformation. If only a subset of the world's regions and classes caused the industrial transformation, what then justifies proclaiming it as the opening of a new age of humanity as a whole? Writing on this point, Malm and Hornborg home in on the production of carbon dioxide in particular regions and classes: "Steam engines were not adopted by some natural-born deputies of the human species: by the nature of the social order of things, they could only be installed by the owners of the means of production." Climate change, Malm and Hornborg therefore argue, is not "anthropogenic"—caused by the undifferentiated species of humans—but "sociogenic"—caused by social forces.[46] They review other authors who have proposed that an epoch defined by climate change would more appropriately be named for phenomena responsible for the new energy regime, the capitalist economy, for example "Ecocene," or "Capitalocene."[47]

These critiques underscore the necessity of making consideration of power and politics between regions and classes central to analyses of climate change. Understanding the Industrial Revolution entails exploration of political, economic and social history. As Pomeranz has shown, in the late eighteenth century a "great divergence" did occur between England and eventually the rest of Europe, on one hand, and the lower Yangzi Delta and the rest of China on the other. One essential difference was a local English resource: rich coal supplies that enhanced the use of steam engines and allowed the English economy to develop far beyond that in China. But relations between regions also mattered. Claims on the natural resources of the Americas and enslaved labor from Africa provided the English economy with advantages beyond what was available to Chinese centers from Asian hinterlands. Joseph Inikori supplements this understanding of geopolitical advantage with his assertions that trade with Africa and the enslavement of Africans as laborers were critical to economic expansion and eventually to the Industrial Revolution.[48]

We do not argue that geopolitical advantage is a sufficient explanation for widespread industrialization in England, in the rest of Europe, or in North America. Neither do we assert that it offers a sufficient explanation for poverty in the Global South. The histories discussed above remind us that the Industrial Revolution unfolded on a global scale and that development outcomes were contingent upon world conditions. As it took place locally, industrialization acquired a global reach through its need for resources and for markets for manufactured goods and this intensified the politics of empire. Aspirations for economic expansion ranked high among the motivations for rapidly expanding European empires in the late nineteenth century. Through the seizure and application of power in Africa and Asia, Europe fed its industrial development. Empires structured asymmetrical exchange, underwrote the creation of wealth, and impeded similar industrial development in the colonies. The historic legacy of empires contributed to the underdevelopment of the world's poorer countries, now known as the Global South. (They have also been called the "Third World" or the "developing world.") Walter Rodney summarized the stagnation of African economic and technological development under European rule: "the vast majority of Africans went into colonialism with a hoe and came out with a hoe." Mike Davis has argued that climate stress impoverished India, China, and Brazil and this vulnerability created conditions for subsequent empire building.[49] In Africa and Asia, the countries of South Africa (where white settlers held political power) and Japan (which was itself an empire) have the highest life expectancy and income. These are literally the exceptions that prove the rule about colonial status and unequal economic development.[50]

The argument that the past two centuries contain a watershed is powerful. Through fossil-fuel-driven production, the Industrial Revolution did introduce a human element into geological dynamics that date back to before the species evolved. But, like the Early Anthropocene, the Industrial Revolution lacks an obvious golden spike (globally apparent geological evidence of wholesale Earth System change). Atmospheric carbon dioxide concentrations rose only gradually, from 279 ppm in 1775 to 289 ppm in 1885. Because change was gradual, stratigraphers have struggled to define transformation according to precise standards.[51] But, even if it falls short as one compressed moment of planetary history, industrialization was a pivotal process in world history. Anthropocene theorists have been increasingly observing connections between political and economic processes and planetary effects. Holding center stage, the interrelations of economic and climate history justify approaching the Anthropocene from below.

The Great Acceleration as the onset of the Anthropocene

The ecological manifestation of global disparity became particularly evident after the mid-twentieth century, when the result of the asymmetrical application of power and the movement of resources created a markedly lopsided global pattern of greenhouse gas emissions. The "Recent Anthropocene" theory places the beginning of the epoch in this moment of intensified production and consumption, especially of fossil fuels, at the middle of the twentieth century.[52] In the years since the first proposal for an Anthropocene, some thinkers have focused on a "second phase," when the gradual processes set in motion around 1800 intensified. In the 2000s Will Steffen and a set of co-authors characterized the post-World War II trajectory as the "Great Acceleration" (see the bottom bar on Figure 7.1). Their work effectively conveyed acceleration through graphs of dozens of indicators, all showing simultaneous upward lurches around 1950. These graphs became iconic in understandings of the Anthropocene. Because long slow incline interrupted by a steep short upward movement has been called a "hockey stick," that term now holds a specific meaning in discussions on climate change. The illustrations below reproduce the 2015 version of these graphs, covering Earth System trends (Figure 7.5) and socio-economic (Figure 7.6) from 1750 through 2010.

By 2015 this argument for the late twentieth century as the beginning of the Anthropocene had won significant support from the scientific community, including from the Anthropocene Working Group. Members of that committee co-authored an article that concluded:

the significance of the Anthropocene lies not so much in seeing within it the "first traces of our species", but in the scale, significance and longevity of change to the Earth system. . . . With the onset of the Industrial Revolution, humankind became a more pronounced geological factor, but in our present view it was from the mid-20th century that the worldwide impact of the accelerating Industrial Revolution became both global and near-synchronous.[53]

This emphasis on a dramatic acceleration of change rather than the origins of human impact ameliorates concerns, explained above, that the theory of the Anthropocene is one of human exceptionalism, with no place for interrelationships with other species and planetary forces.

Figure 7.5 conveys that a mid-twentieth-century global environmental watershed was not just a matter of greenhouse gas emissions. One possible marker of the new age is that species are disappearing at rates that might qualify as the age of the Sixth Great Extinction. Or, the global human impact can be seen in plastics that are now ubiquitous on land and in the oceans.

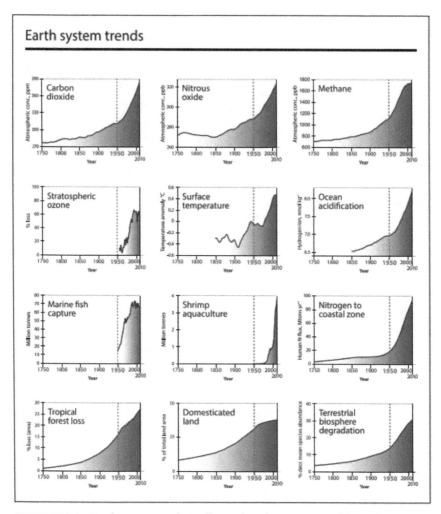

FIGURE 7.5 *Earth system trends. Steffen et al., "The Trajectory of the Anthropocene: The Great Acceleration," 7. Used with permission of* The Anthropocene Review.

Carbon is not the only element whose presence on the planet has been transformed by people: intensive agriculture, necessary to supply the growing population, has also greatly affected the distribution of two elements present in fertilizers: nitrogen and phosphorus. Artificial fixation of nitrogen has increased the concentrations of that element in soil and water, while agricultural applications have drawn down supplies of essential and limited phosphate compounds. Runoff of nitrogen and phosphorus-containing substances degrades fresh water and marine environments by causing algal blooms, often followed by the death of fish.[54] A further dramatic human impact is the radioactive fallout from nuclear weapons that has circulated the entire globe since 1945. Leading scientists have argued that the radioactive isotopes deposited around the world by early atomic bombs created a sufficient boundary in the geological record to mark a new era.[55] But greenhouse emissions are directly implicated in climate change and thus remain central to any understanding of human impact. Atmospheric carbon dioxide rose above 400 ppm in 2014, a level higher than any in the last 800,000 years on Earth, signaling our entry into uncharted climate space.[56]

Steffen and his co-authors credit historians as having recognized the revolutionary character of the late twentieth century before climate scientists did.[57] The changes in this period were enormous. To summarize: it began with decolonization and American-led economic growth. The Cold War spurred state investment in research and development, fostering a revolution in biotechnology and computing systems and economic expansion. Fossil fuel use and an explosion in consumer goods defined daily life in richer countries. Figure 7.6 reproduces what climate scientists have taken from social scientists about socio-economic trends. The data expose the breadth of the causes of the planetary transformation after the mid-twentieth century.

In their original publications, Steffen and his co-authors implied that the "hockey sticks" belonged to humanity as a whole. Critics countered that the case against a holistic treatment of the human species, if anything, becomes stronger as the inclines grow steeper. Malm and Hornborg put it forcefully: "uneven distribution is in fact a condition for *the very existence* of modern, fossil-fuel technology."[58] To their credit, Steffen and his collaborators took the critique seriously. Their 2015 update on the Great Acceleration hypothesis features a section describing "the profound scale of global inequality" and includes graphs that distinguish between developed and developing countries. Countries with the smallest economies (those not in the OECD or BRICS) have about a third of the world's population but register disproportionately low in water use, transportation, and fertilizer consumption.[59] Rich nations are also disproportionately responsible for carbon emissions.[60] And so, the "from below" approach to Anthropocene history has registered among Earth Systems scientists. If they choose to endorse the new epoch, stratigraphers will not draw on social data, but it is no longer an outside position that inequalities between people have been operative in planetary history. As Hamilton wrote, atomic markers

> have nothing directly to do with the Anthropocene. They do, however, have a great deal to do with it indirectly, because they signaled unambiguously the dawn of the era of global economic domination by the United States of America, which was intimately tied to the economic boom of the post-war years and so the rapid increased in greenhouse gas emissions and associated warming.[61]

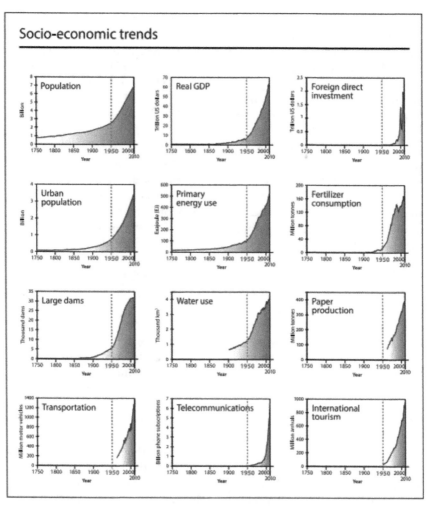

FIGURE 7.6 *Socio-economic trends. Steffen et al., "The Trajectory of the Anthropocene: The Great Acceleration,"* 4. *Used with permission of* The Anthropocene Review.

Human population was among the factors taking a steep upward climb during the Great Acceleration. Population growth has been unprecedented, perhaps even unimaginable. It not only grew, but at greatly increasing rates. At the beginning of the Industrial Revolution, in 1800, the global population was 954 million people, which had risen to more than 2.5 billion in 1950. In 2000, the total surpassed 6 billion. In the second half of the eighteenth century the rate of global population growth was 0.41 percent; in the second half of the twentieth century, it had risen to 1.75 percent per year.[62] More people require more agriculture and cause an increase in the production of carbon dioxide and of methane, the greenhouse gas released (among other ways) through conversion of forest to farmland, livestock production, and rice paddy cultivation.[63] In contrast to the CO_2 emissions, poorer regions lead richer ones in population growth rates.[64] What is to be made of this accounting of the human impact on the planet? Could a sort of equivalence in causation between Global North and South be in effect, between high-consuming and high-reproducing populations? Malm and Hornborg flatly dispute the significance of growing populations, asserting that attention to them obscures the social inequalities that remain pivotal in creating climate change.[65]

On the other hand, the contemporary profile of population growth can be seen as another function of historical global inequality. As children became expensive in the urban and high-consuming North, adults chose to have fewer of them. But the "demographic transition" in industrializing societies described above (characterized by a drop first in mortality rates and then in fertility rates) has not occurred at the same pace everywhere. Mortality probably increased with the establishment of European empires in sub-Saharan Africa but declined after a few decades because of improvements in medicine and the food supply and a decrease in war. But overall fertility rates did not follow the downward trend until the twenty-first century. Economic causes have dominated many explanations for the demographic transition. For example, the historian John Iliffe's explanation for continuing high fertility rates in the late twentieth century was that in Africa children "became economic assets" and having many "increased the chance that one of them might be spectacularly successful and they gave parents some guarantee of support in old age."[66] Demographers have cautioned against understandings of direct economic effects on fertility rates. Tim Dyson argues that mortality decline is the ultimate cause of fertility decline and that a set of intervening factors—education, government policies, the availability of contraception, and economic trajectories—shape different histories of demographic transitions.[67]

The economic dominance of Europe and North America began to recede in the late twentieth century. Through a set of causes too complex and debated to recount here, former colonies—especially in Asia—began to break out of the pattern of enduring poverty. Economic growth was marked in the 1960s in Hong Kong, Singapore, and South Korea. By the end of the century, the two most populous countries in the world, India and China, had become economic powerhouses with improved life expectancies. As a rule, sub-Saharan Africa, did not achieve the developmental success witnessed in much of Asia.[68]

The uneven distribution of wealth that has increased since the Industrial Revolution is changing in the new millennium; wealth and industrial production and the center of gravity in the world economic system are moving "south." An increasing proportion of greenhouse gas emissions are moving with them. China overtook the US as the largest emitter in 2005. India sits poised soon to surpass the US and by some estimates even China in the coming decades.[69] Historically, the Global North is responsible for a far greater proportion of greenhouse gases, but recently we have seen a greater globalization of carbon emissions. This is not to say that inequalities—including those within countries—have evaporated. But the possibility of poorer countries at last achieving development through industrialization and consequent use of fossil fuels and production of greenhouse gases has created tension. Developing countries are prone to make the point that the Global North achieved wealth at the expense of the atmosphere. Cleaner technologies and conservation can be a drag on economic growth. Because it brings disadvantages that had no precedent during the Northern Industrial Revolution, countries in the process of industrialization contest regulation.

Experiences of climate change from below

The actors in Anthropocene narratives are often modern nation-states because of the disparate ways these "imagined communities" industrialized. For example, Chakrabarty writes of the "common but differentiated" responsibility between the increasingly post-industrial nations of Europe and North America who hold "retrospective guilt" and the industrializing nations of the developing world, especially in East and South Asia, who hold "prospective guilt."[70] But beyond the developed and rapidly developing nations, however, are the poorest countries of the Global South, which have not been able to overcome the disadvantages of their colonial pasts. These nations face the worst consequences of climate change, despite being the least responsible for CO_2 emissions. Climate change is bearing down on the most vulnerable.

Models of contemporary society illustrate how economic inequality shapes experiences of climate change. Roberts and Park have examined historical data on vulnerability to extreme weather and extrapolated from them to hypothesize about vulnerability to climate change, which is likely to increase the instances and strength of extreme weather events. They note that "hurricanes may strike wealthy nations, but they do not kill many people when they do."[71] This can be explained through an examination of how vulnerability has been defined. It is important to note that vulnerability is determined by "not only the system's sensitivity, but also its ability to adapt to new climatic conditions"[72] and to respond to and recover from the effects of a changing climate. On the most basic level, it is evident that a lack of capital would lead to diminished financial capacity to adjust (both on the micro scale of household adaptation to new realities and on the macro scale of infrastructure development to educate these households and strengthen the landscape). Jesse Ribot associates this lack of capacity with access to "entitlements"—that is, poor communities in the Global South do not have the political ability to access assets and protections that relieve their vulnerability because they do not have any influence on the global political economy. Ribot defines vulnerability as "social precarity found on the ground when hazards arrive" and posits that vulnerability (as well as climate change itself) is anthropogenic because it is shaped by social history and the constructed global economic system.[73]

Climate change has only recently been recognized and understandings of its effects on the poor are still emerging. It is always difficult to say how recent and current news will be written into history. We may not yet see the most important developments and may be distracted by others that turn out to have less influence. While we perceive recent climate change as a Great Acceleration of human impact, its grinding effect on poor people, who will innovate, migrate, and struggle to survive, unfolds more gradually. Because of this, some social scientists describe environmental concerns like climate change as a type of "slow violence"[74] enacted on the poor through an unbalanced global economic system. Yet, many stories already illuminate the reasons that climate change differentially affects certain people, and these reasons are deeply tied to poverty and the unequal nature of the global economic system.

First, poor nations tend to have significantly resource-dependent populations, typically forming a single cash-crop economy. In communities dependent on subsistence farming, changes in climate can result in threats to life, and survival requires adjustments in agriculture—something that many of these communities are ill-equipped for, having used the same seed to plant the same crop for decades. Similarly, the national economy that relies on a single crop faces economic collapse when climate change undermines that crop's yield. As regions that are already warm and dry experience heightened temperatures and decreased precipitation due to climate change, existing difficulties faced in agriculture will become even more burdensome. Already, subsistence farmers in Tanzania, Uganda, and other sub-Saharan African countries are reporting drastic changes in seasonality that devastate their harvests.

Fish-dependent societies face a similar challenge. Climate change has caused shifts in ocean temperature or acidity, which has affected reproduction. Industrial-scale foreign fishing exacerbates the crisis. For communities that are dependent on fishing for survival, the resulting changes or depletions in fish populations are disastrous. Populations of island nations like Madagascar are suffering from the struggle to maintain the fishing industry on which they are reliant. Madagascan fishers link depletions in fish and sea cucumber supplies to the differences in climate conditions compared to what they remember them being only a few decades ago.[75]

Second, poor communities lack vital infrastructure that is critical to mitigating the effects of climate change. Climate change brings changes to the disease environment that will disproportionately affect those without access to healthcare infrastructure. There have been considerable concerns about how a warming climate in Latin American countries like Ecuador and Colombia may drive *Anopheles* mosquito populations into areas of higher elevation.[76] This could lead to instances of malaria infection in isolated mountain villages that lack the resources to deal with this as-yet-unexperienced disease. Furthermore, as the geographic range of certain species of plants shift, communities without hospitals or orthodox clinics may experience difficulty in accessing herbs needed for local medical practices. In countries where healthcare is minimal, the health risks related to climate change are almost impossible to combat. Similarly, where sanitation infrastructure is not in place, flooding due to sea level rise or climate-related disasters can lead to a proliferation of waterborne diseases.[77] In this way, countries that already face health threats because of limited infrastructure are vulnerable to the most tragic effects of climate change on human health.

Third, poor people are often confined to live in dangerous places and participate in activities that actually increase their vulnerability. Roberts and Parks highlight how Hurricane Jeanne had remarkably different effects in Florida and in Haiti—one of the poorest nations in the Western Hemisphere. Haiti experienced a vast death toll, largely caused by mudslides in the flood-ridden aftermath of the hurricane. They attribute this to the "desperation that lead the poor to deforest"—the fact that Haitians, lacking electricity, deforested the land in order to get firewood and charcoal, thereby clearing trees that would have helped to prevent mudslides.[78]

In fact, even within countries, we can see the potential for disproportionate effects of climate change according to wealth. In Nigeria, poor migrants moving from rural areas to Lagos settle in the only accommodations they can afford, which are often coastal slums in areas most vulnerable to sea level rises.[79] Even in the United States, Hurricane Katrina was most catastrophic to poorer communities in New Orleans because they lived in newer and cheaper parts of the city that lay at a lower elevation than the wealthier French Quarter.[80] When the storm struck these geographically exposed areas, the inhabitants had little chance of escape—many of them did not have transportation to evacuate.

This promise of climate change to disproportionately affect poor communities is driven not by the "bad luck" of poor communities being in geographically susceptible areas, but by societal and economic reasons. Their poverty influences both their geography and their capacity. Cases of "extreme vulnerability" (such as low-lying islands in the Pacific) are extreme not only because of their geography, but because their narrow economies and limited resources undermine their capacity for response and adaptation. In this way, climate-change-related food and water scarcity, flooding damage, extreme weather casualties, and health issues promise to devastate the poorest people in the world long before they become catastrophic to the Global North.

Politics of climate change in the United States

At first, climate change and other anthropogenic alterations in the environment appeared to be a politically uncontroversial issue. It is now one that divides right and left. We have identified the cause of climate change in economic history and the politics around it are now inextricable from those of economic policy.

The genesis of the climate change environmental movement came with the so-called "Earth Summit" in Rio de Janeiro, in 1992. This UN Conference on Environment and Development resulted in the UN Framework Convention on Climate Change (UNFCCC), which acknowledged that "change in the Earth's climate and its adverse effects are a common concern of humankind," while also noting that historical and current greenhouse gas emissions largely originated from developed countries. Signatories accepted a consciousness of climate change and a sense of global (but undirected) responsibility for preventing its worst effects. Environmentalists gained a legal launching board for their demands and a space where they could participate as observers at annual meetings in the high politics of international environmental negotiation.

The UNFCCC identified the importance of sustainable development, the unequal contribution of countries to global concentration of greenhouse gases and the fact that specific countries would face vastly different effects— mostly to establish universal concern as an institutionalized truth. It did not set specific goals and did not establish clear delineations on who should be burdened with the goals. Such assigning of responsibility was to be left until the Kyoto Protocol of 1997, which complemented the UNFCCC by allotting direct emissions-reduction commitments to the developed world. Although the treaty defined a set of global norms, effective action required some kind of coercion or persuasion of individual states.[81] And so, the UNFCCC launched an environmental movement that, anchored in international law, needed a quorum of aligned politicians in the most powerful nations in the world—most notably the United States—in order to be effective in concrete policy building.

Climate change was not always a partisan issue. However, in the early 2000s, as environmentalists searched for a reliable political base, presidential hopeful Al Gore took the issue of global warming as a distinct platform for his campaign. When Gore lost the election to George W. Bush, the deep feeling of loss experienced by many loyal Democrats took the direction of environmentalism. To this group, the idea that Bush had "stolen" the election became deeply tied to the idea that the president was undermining the future of the Earth—a view that Bush only seemed to corroborate with his 2001 announcement that the United States was not going to ratify the Kyoto Protocol. Bush's defense of this decision was economic—the US economy could not afford to reduce fossil-fuel dependence.[82] At this point, the line was drawn in the sand. Climate change became a distinctly liberal issue, which reverberated in it becoming a conservative anti-issue articulated through Bush's language about a rift between environmental policy and a pro-business economy. Clive Hamilton argues: "In the 1990s views on global warming were influenced mostly by attentiveness to the science; now one can make a good guess at an American's opinion on global warming by identifying their views on abortion, same-sex marriage and gun-control."[83]

Through this polarization, climate change skepticism became an ingrained part of the political culture of the American right, deeply linked to capitalist, laissez-faire ideologies. Climate change became a matter of doctrine rather than science or policy. Suspicion ranged from an assumption of exaggeration (we may be altering the climate, but we don't know why or how and we shouldn't endanger our economy until we do) to one of conspiracy (liberals have "bought off" the scientific community to undermine American conservative values and distract from criticism of the Democrats). The ideological polarization was to determine the US political response to climate change for the known future.

In 2005, the weather began to create ripples of understandings of climate change as a distinct, post-polar, human concern; this incremental realization made space for the intellectual conception of environmental justice to move into the mainstream. Social scientists and advocates had been making the case that the poorest communities of the world would be most adversely affected by climate change since before the 1992 Earth Summit. But, for most Americans, it came as a shock when Hurricane Katrina hit New Orleans and revealed not only that the United States could be affected by extreme weather and other projected effects of climate change, but also that the poor would be damned by it. Because of the large costs, poor communities were unable to recover their homes after destruction, to afford sufficient medical attention, or even to evacuate.[84] By the time the financial collapse of 2008 came around, people were ready to "occupy" the issue of climate change, and the recession provided the opportunity to criticize a capitalist system that was complicit, if not *to blame*, for vast inequality.

Environmental issues began to be attached to movements against inequalities and capitalist structural violence and concerns about climate change became commonly included in the publicity materials and action plans of many non-profit or non-governmental organizations. Climate change was no longer a "nature" issue; it was a women's issue, an indigenous people's issue, a racial issue and, perhaps most importantly, a poverty issue (Figure 7.7).[85] Environmentalists embraced this humanized view of the problem and the idea of "climate justice" (richer, industrialized nations paying for emissions reductions and adaptation efforts, allowing poorer nations with low emissions histories to develop) became a central narrative.

FIGURE 7.7 *Members of the Munduruku community in Brazil rally at the Ministry of Mines and Energy in Brasilia, June 2013. Indigenous people in Brazil called for legislation that would include them in decisions about the building of the Belo Monte Dam. Image: Getty 170334525.*

Global dissent over the climate

While in the United States mainstream discourse around climate change has been politically polarized and has tended towards a distancing of nature from human life, this has not been true of the entire world. For instance, surveys of trends in China have shown that although 75 percent of those interviewed believed that scientists do not truly understand what they are saying about environmental issues, 91 percent believed that the world was facing environmental disaster unless habits were severely altered—meaning that many people in China had strong environmental concerns despite having a level of mistrust for environmental science and scientists.[86] Global studies showed many of these apparent contradictions in other nations, implying that the politicized understanding of climate change and environmental policy that prevails in the US is far from universal.

Many of these differences in understanding can be explained through the legacies of historic inequalities. In the Global South, the foundations of economic and environmental justice were part of public discourse about climate change long before they became a pillar of the environmentalist movement in the United States. In these developing countries, ideas of global justice were at the center of grassroots movements in defense of the environment, such as women's groups working against gas flaring by Shell in the Niger River Delta.[87] The reason for the embrace of this discourse is not only because these poor nations are the first and most affected victims of climate change, but also because of existing understandings of the inequalities of the global economic system. Experiences of colonization have created deep-founded political mistrust of the Global North, meaning that the climate justice project ties environmental concerns to the ideals of liberation and independence—ideals that many ruling parties claim as their own. Skepticism in these developing countries, when present, manifests itself in suspicion of Western science, its link to colonial domination, and how it may relate to the political motives of industrialized countries that dominate the global landscape (Figure 7.8).

The fight for agency in the governing of the atmosphere has produced a great variety of everyday understandings of climate change and related policies. For some, this is denial in the face of calls to limit industry and traditional routes of economic development, while for others it is the adoption of justice discourse that demands accountability in the international community. For others still, it is a challenge to the conception that climate change is simply an elite industry-caused problem that can, therefore only be greeted with elite industry regulation.

Efforts to adapt to a changing climate, for example, are exposing citizens of the Global South not as passive victims, but rather as agents of positive change. These agents include women in Bangladesh, arguably amongst the most vulnerable to global-warming-related flooding and extreme weather, because flood-related deaths in Bangladesh disproportionately affect women.

FIGURE 7.8 *Protesters marching in Durban in December 2011, during UN climate talks in Durban. Non-governmental organizations and local, grassroots groups led the protests. Credit: AFP Photo/ Alexander Joe. Image: Getty 134611147.*

Gana Unnayan Kendra, a Bangladeshi NGO working with Oxfam, has started a grassroots effort to prepare women for extreme weather. The organization runs disaster-preparedness training and helps women to invest in improving the resilience of their homes.[88]

In other parts of the developing world, agency comes in the form of what is perhaps a surprising embrace of the universality of responsibility for climate change. In the Marshall Islands, for instance, local communities dismiss the government's focus on climate justice in favor of more localized and immediate forms of accountability.[89] In this low-lying archipelago, which is one of the territories facing the most serious of threats from climate change-induced sea level rise, individuals use universal language of "us" and "we" to assign responsibility. When pressed for more detail, islanders prefer to blame themselves and their neighbors rather than point to foreign industry, thus creating their own agency in being able to shame their communities into personal accountability on the household scale. In this way, the most vulnerable stand in an environment determined by an unequal global history, using universality to assert their humanity in the face of the Anthropocene.

Acknowledgments

We thank readers who have contributed various scientific, social scientific and historical expertise to this document, including: the editors, our fellow "World Histories from Below" workshop participants, Bruce Boucek, Meredith Hastings, James M. Russell, Edward Melillo, Allison Shutt, Sara Weschler, and participants in the BELLS program at the Rhode Island Adult Correctional Institution. We also thank the National Science Foundation Graduate Research Fellowship Program and the Brown University Presidential Fellowship Program for ongoing graduate student support.

Suggestions for further reading

Brooke, John L. *Climate Change and the Course of Global History: A Rough Journey*. New York: Cambridge University Press, 2014.

Chakrabarty, Dipesh. "The Climate of History: Four Theses," *Critical Inquiry* 35:2 (2009): 197–222.

Crutzen, Paul J. "Geology of Mankind," *Nature (London)* 415:6867 (2002): 23.

Gapminder: A Fact-Based Worldview. http://www.gapminder.org.

Kolbert, Elizabeth. *Field Notes from a Catastrophe: Man, Nature and Climate Change*. New York: Bloomsbury, 2006.

Lewis, Simon L. and Mark A. Maslin. "Defining the Anthropocene," *Nature* 519:7542: 171–180.

McNeill, John Robert. *Something New under the Sun: An Environmental History of the Twentieth-Century World*. New York: W. W. Norton & Company, 2000.

Malm, Andreas and Alf Hornborg. "The Geology of Mankind? A Critique of the Anthropocene Narrative," *Anthropocene Review* 1 (2014): 62–69.

Oreskes, Naomi. "The Scientific Consensus on Climate Change," *Science* 306:5702 (2004): 1686.

Ribot, Jesse. "Cause and Response: Vulnerability and Climate in the Anthropocene," *Journal of Peasant Studies* 41:5 (2014): 667–705.

Roberts, J. Timmons and Bradley C. Parks. *A Climate of Injustice Global Inequality, North-South Politics and Climate Policy*. Cambridge, MA: MIT Press, 2007.

Ruddiman, W. F. *Plows, Plagues and Petroleum: How Humans Took Control of Climate*. Princeton, NJ: Princeton University Press, 2005.

Rudiak-Gould, Peter. "Climate Change and Accusation: Global Warming and Local Blame in a Small Island State," *Current Anthropology* 55:4 (2014): 365–386.

Stratigraphy, Subcommission on Quaternary. "Working Group on the 'Anthropocene'." http://quaternary.stratigraphy.org/workinggroups/anthropocene/.

Steffen, Will, Wendy Broadgate, Lisa Deutsch, Owen Gaffney, and Cornelia Ludwig. "The Trajectory of the Anthropocene: The Great Acceleration," *Anthropocene Review* 2 (2015): 81–98.

Zalasiewicz, Jan, Colin N. Waters, Mark Williams, Anthony D. Barnosky, Alejandro Cearreta, Paul Crutzen, Erle Ellis et al. "When Did the Anthropocene Begin? A Mid-Twentieth Century Boundary Level Is Stratigraphically Optimal," *Quaternary International* (2014): np.

Notes

1   "Climate Change 2014 Synthesis Report: Fifth Assessment Report," Summary for Policymakers," 2. http://ar5-syr.ipcc.ch/topic_summary.php. National Oceanic and Atmospheric Information, "Global Summary Information—December 2015," http://www.ncdc.noaa.gov/sotc/summary-info/global/201512.

2   Scientists are in overwhelming agreement about climate change. Naomi Oreskes, "The Scientific Consensus on Climate Change," *Science* 306:5702 (2004): 1686. Below, we discuss how the heated politics of the 2000s created doubt over the extent and causes of climate change.

3   Paul J. Crutzen and Eugene F. Stoermer, "The 'Anthropocene'," *IGBP Newsletter* 2000, 17–18. See also: Paul J. Crutzen, "Geology of Mankind," *Nature* 415:6867 (2002): 23.

4   Subcommission on Quaternary Stratigraphy, "Working Group on the 'Anthropocene'," http://quaternary.stratigraphy.org/workinggroups/anthropocene/.

5   "Anthropocene," http://quaternary.stratigraphy.org/workinggroups/anthropocene/.

6   At the time of writing, this debate is ongoing. For the latest updates see "Anthropocene," http://quaternary.stratigraphy.org/workinggroups/anthropocene/. Papers cited below convey the issues in this discussion, which will build until an official decision is rendered, at the earliest by 2016.

7   We follow Lewis and Maslin in inserting the Orbis hypothesis into a discussion that until recently has been dominated by the other three theories. For example: Will Steffen et al, "The Anthropocene: Conceptual and Historical Perspectives," *Philosophical Transactions of the Royal Society A: Mathematical, Physical and Engineering Sciences* 369:1938 (2011).

8   Dipesh Chakrabarty, "The Climate of History: Four Theses," *Critical Inquiry* 35:2 (2009): 197–222. Julia Adeney Thomas, "History and Biology in the Anthropocene: Problems of Scale, Problems of Value," *American Historical Review* 119 (2014): 1587–1607.

9   Chakrabarty, "The Climate of History," 215–218; Richard Monastersky, "Anthropocene: The Human Age," *Nature*, March 11, 2015, 144–147; Andreas Malm and Alf Hornborg, "The Geology of Mankind? A Critique of the Anthropocene Narrative," *Anthropocene Review* 1 (2014): 62–69.

10 Geological time is delineated into more specific, higher resolution units. The longest periods are supereons. Other, progressively shorter units are eons, eras, periods and epochs. Even recent epochs are still, however, "deep time" as far as historians are concerned, some lasting millions of years.

11 Thomas F. Stocker et al, "Climate Change 2013: The Physical Science Basis," in *Intergovernmental Panel on Climate Change, Working Group I Contribution to the IPCC Fifth Assessment Report (AR5)* (New York: Cambridge University Press, 2013); Lee R. Kump, "The Last Great Global Warming," *Scientific American* 305:1 (2011).

12 "Global Warming: Heating by the Greenhouse Effect," http://ase.tufts.edu/cosmos/view_chapter.asp?id=21&page=1.

13 Lee R. Kump, James F. Kasting, and Robert G. Crane, *The Earth System* (Upper Saddle River, NJ: Prentice-Hall, 2004), 187, 214–217.

14 Kump et al, *The Earth System*, 202.

15 Kump et al, *The Earth System*, 214.

16 Stephen Porder, "World Changers 3.0," http://www.naturalhistorymag.com/features/232772/world-changers-30.

17 As a primer on geological time, see International Commission on Stratigraphy, *International Chronostratigraphic Chart* (2015).

18 Wolfgang K. Seifert and J. Michael Moldowan, "Paleoreconstruction by Biological Markers," *Geochimica et Cosmochimica Acta* 45:6 (1980): 785; Jane R. Eggleston, Thomas M. Kehn, and Gordon H. Wood, Jr., "Chapter 36, Anthracite," in *The Geology of Pennsylvania*, ed. Charles H. Schultz (Harrisburg: Pennsylvania Geological Survey, 2002), 459.

19 Osamu Seki et al, "Alkenone and Boron-Based Pliocene pCO_2 Records," *Earth and Planetary Science Letters* 292:1–2 (2010): 201; A. V. Fedorov et al, "Patterns and Mechanisms of Early Pliocene Warmth," *Nature* 496:7443 (2013): 43; Kaye E Reed, "Early Hominid Evolution and Ecological Change through the African Plio-Pleistocene," *Journal of Human Evolution* 32:2 (1997): 289.

20 V. Masson-Delmotte et al, "Information from Paleoclimate Archives," in *Climate Change 2013: The Physical Science Basis. Contribution of Working*

Group I to the Fifth Assessment Report of the Intergovernmental Panel on Climate Change, ed. T. F. Stocker et al (Cambridge: Cambridge University Press, 2013), 40.

21 James D Hays, John Imbrie, and Nicolas J Shackleton, "Variations in the Earth's Orbit: Pacemaker of the Ice Ages," *Science* 194:4270 (1976): 1121–1132.

22 D. Luthi et al, "High-Resolution Carbon Dioxide Concentration Record 650,000–800,000 Years before Present," *Nature* 453:7193 (2008): 380; M. Delmotte, "Atmospheric Methane During the Last Four Glacial-Interglacial Cycles: Rapid Changes and Their Link with Antarctic Temperature," *Journal of Geophysical Research* 109, no. D12 (2004): 3.

23 John L. Brooke, *Climate Change and the Course of Global History: A Rough Journey* (New York: Cambridge University Press, 2014), 121–242.

24 Unless otherwise cited, population estimates in this chapter are taken from Brooke. *Climate Change and Global History,* 118, 37 and especially 259. These are broad and provisional estimates but devised through the same method, they can support comparisons over time. On the method: Brooke, *Climate Change and Global History,* 118.

25 Working Group I: The Physical Science Basis, "Human and Natural Drivers of Climate Change," https://www.ipcc.ch/publications_and_data/ar4/wg1/en/spmsspm-human-and.html; National Center for Atmospheric Research/University Corporation for Atmospheric Research, "What Is the Average Global Temperature Now?" https://www2.ucar.edu/news/what-average-global-temperature-now.

26 W. F. Ruddiman, *Plows, Plagues, and Petroleum: How Humans Took Control of Climate* (Princeton, NJ: Princeton University Press, 2005), 84–87.

27 Ruddiman, *Plows, Plagues, and Petroleum,* 76–78. Agricultural methane increase occurs because in paddies, like wetlands, decaying plants release the gas. Additionally, ruminants produce it by burping (no joke). Furthermore, the excrement of humans and their animals contributes.

28 Brooke, *Climate Change and Global History,* 259.

29 Masson-Delmotte et al, "Information from Paleoclimate Archives," 412.

30 Ruddiman, *Plows, Plagues, and Petroleum,* 134–146.

31 Michael E. Mann, "Little Ice Age," in *Encyclopedia of Global Environmental Change: The Earth System: Physical and Chemical Dimensions of Global Environmental Change* (Chichester, UK: Wiley, 2002), 5.

32 Gavin A. Schmidt, Drew T. Shindell, and Susan Harder, "A Note on the Relationship between Ice Core Methane Concentrations and Insolation," *Geophysical Research Letters* 31:23 (2004); Simon L. Lewis and Mark A. Maslin, "Defining the Anthropocene," *Nature* 519:7542 (2015); Steffen et al, "The Anthropocene: Conceptual and Historical Perspectives." For Ruddiman's discussion of scientific challenges to the Early Anthropocene theory and his responses and rebuttals to scientific scrutiny in the five years after initial publication in 2003, see William F. Ruddiman, "The Early Anthropogenic Hypothesis: Challenges and Responses," *Reviews of Geophysics* 45:4 (2007).

33 Thomas, "History and Biology in the Anthropocene: Problems of Scale, Problems of Value."

34 Kump, "The Last Great Global Warming," 59.

35 Lewis and Maslin, "Defining the Anthropocene."

36 Eric R. Wolf, *Europe and the People without History* (Berkeley: University of California Press, 1982).

37 Kenneth Pomeranz, *The Great Divergence: China, Europe, and the Making of the Modern World Economy* (Princeton, NJ: Princeton University Press, 2000).

38 Lewis and Maslin, "Defining the Anthropocene." The Little Ice Age was already well underway by this point and Lewis and Maslin do not attribute it to population crash and reforestation in the Americas.

39 Clive Hamilton, "Getting the Anthropocene So Wrong," *The Anthropocene Review* 2 (2015): 103 and 104. For further critique of the Orbis theory of the Anthropocene, see Jan Zalasiewicz et al, "Colonization of the Americas, 'Little Ice Age' Climate, and Bomb-Produced Carbon: Their Role in Defining the Anthropocene," *The Anthropocene Review* 2 (2015).

40 Alfred W. Crosby, *The Columbian Exchange: Biological and Cultural Consequences of 1492* (Westport, CT: Greenwood Press, 1972); Alfred W. Crosby, *Ecological Imperialism: The Biological Expansion of Europe, 900–1900* (New York: Cambridge University Press, 1986).

41 Patrick Manning, *Slavery and African Life: Occidental, Oriental, and African Slave Trades* (New York: Cambridge University Press, 1990).

42 Brooke, *Climate Change and Global History*, 514–518.

43 Crutzen and Stoermer, "The 'Anthropocene'"; Crutzen, "Geology of Mankind"; Will Steffen, Paul J. Crutzen, and John R. McNeill, "The Anthropocene: Are Humans Now Overwhelming the Great Forces of Nature?" *Ambio* 36:8 (2007); Steffen et al, "The Anthropocene: Conceptual and Historical Perspectives." For an historical overview: Elizabeth Kolbert, *Field Notes from a Catastrophe: Man, Nature, and Climate Change* (New York: Bloomsbury, 2006), 183–189.

44 E. P. Thompson, *The Making of the English Working Class* (London: V. Gollancz, 1963).

45 Naomi Oreskes, "The Scientific Consensus on Climate Change: How Do We Know We're Not Wrong?" in *Climate Change: What It Means for Us, Our Children, and Our Grandchildren*, ed. Joseph Dimento and Pamela Doughman (Cambridge, MA: MIT Press, 2007), 65–99; Chakrabarty, "The Climate of History."

46 Malm and Hornborg, "The Geology of Mankind?" 66–67.

47 Jason W. Moore, "Anthropocene or Capitalocene?" https://jasonwmoore. wordpress.com/2013/05/13/anthropocene-or-capitalocene/.

48 Pomeranz, *The Great Divergence*; Joseph Inikori, *Africans and the Industrial Revolution in England* (Cambridge: Cambridge University Press, 2002).

49 Walter Rodney, *How Europe Underdeveloped Africa* (Washington, DC: Howard University Press, 1981), 219. See also: Mike Davis, *Late Victorian Holocausts: El Niño Famines and the Making of the Third World* (London: New York, 2001); Immanuel Maurice Wallerstein, *The Modern World-System* (Berkeley: University of California Press, 1974).

50 The website Gapminder World provides an accessible reconstruction of world economic history at http://www.gapminder.org. Its animations illustrate quantifiable differentiation by countries (even long before they existed as colonies or nation-states) and continents. The graph "Wealth and Health of Nations" shows "Income per person" on the x-axis and "Life expectancy" on the y-axis. When the animation begins in 1800, all countries are in the bottom left quartile with a life expectancy of less than 40 years and per capita income of below \$3,000. Over the next century and a half, the animation shows the countries of northwestern Europe and North America reaping the fruits of industrialization. They gain in income—some exceeding \$10,000—and life expectancy, even past 70 years.

51 Steffen, Crutzen, and McNeill, "Are Humans Now Overwhelming the Great Forces of Nature?" 617; Lewis and Maslin, "Defining the Anthropocene"; Hamilton, "Getting the Anthropocene So Wrong," 104.

52 Will Steffen et al, "The Trajectory of the Anthropocene: The Great Acceleration," *Anthropocene Review* 2 (2015): 81–98; Steffen, Crutzen, and McNeill, "Are Humans Now Overwhelming the Great Forces of Nature?" See also: Libby Robin, "Histories for Changing Times: Entering the Anthropocene?" *Australian Historical Studies* 44 (2013): 328–340; Jan Zalasiewicz et al, "When Did the Anthropocene Begin? A Mid-Twentieth Century Boundary Level Is Stratigraphically Optimal," *Quaternary International* (2014).

53 Zalasiewicz et al, "When Did the Anthropocene Begin?" 6.

54 Elizabeth Kolbert, *The Sixth Extinction: An Unnatural History* (New York: Henry Holt and Company, 2014); Porder, "World Changers 3.0," http://www.naturalhistorymag.com/features/232772/world-changers-30.

55 Zalasiewicz et al, "When Did the Anthropocene Begin?"

56 Luthi et al, "High-Resolution Carbon Dioxide Concentration Record 650,000–800,000 Years before Present," 2; Jean-Robert Petit et al, "Climate and Atmospheric History of the Past 420,000 Years from the Vostok Ice Core, Antarctica," *Nature* 399:6735 (1999): 3.

57 Steffen et al, "The Trajectory of the Anthropocene: The Great Acceleration," 2. One of Steffen's co-authors has been the historian John McNeill, who has written an environmental history of the twentieth century: John Robert McNeill, *Something New under the Sun: An Environmental History of the Twentieth-Century World* (New York: W. W. Norton & Company, 2000).

58 Malm and Hornborg, "The Geology of Mankind?" 64 [original emphasis].

59 Steffen et al, "The Trajectory of the Anthropocene: The Great Acceleration," 11.

60 Gapminder can be set to "CO_2 emissions" on the y-axis and "income per person" on the x-axis. As the animation moves through time, all countries increase their wealth and emissions, but the acceleration in income and CO_2 emissions since 1950 is greater among those who were the first to industrialize and who had been in advantaged positions in empire. See http://www.gapminder.org/.

61 Hamilton, "Getting the Anthropocene So Wrong," 105.

62 Brooke, *Climate Change and Global History*, 259.

63 David I. Stern and Robert K. Kaufmann, "Estimates of Global Anthropogenic Methane Emissions 1860–1993," *Chemosphere* 33:1 (1996).

64 Setting Gapminder parameters to "Children per women (total fertility)" on the y-axis and "Income per person" illustrates this. See http://www.gapminder.org/.

65 Malm and Hornborg, "The Geology of Mankind?" 65.

66 John Iliffe, *Africans: The History of a Continent* (New York: Cambridge University Press, 1995), 210–211, 38–46.

67 Tim Dyson, *Population and Development: The Demographic Transition* (London: Zed Books, 2010).

68 To illustrate these broad trends, we recommend turning to www.gapminder. org.

69 Coral Davenport, "Emissions from India Will Increase, Official Says," *The New York Times*, September 25, 2014.

70 Chakrabarty, "The Climate of History," 218.

71 J. Timmons Roberts and Bradley C. Parks, *A Climate of Injustice: Global Inequality, North-South Politics, and Climate Policy*, Global Environmental Accords (Cambridge, MA: MIT Press, 2007), 72.

72 Roger E. Kasperson and Jeanne X. Kasperson, *Climate Change, Vulnerability, and Social Justice* (Stockholm: Stockholm Environment Institute, 2001), 3.

73 Jesse Ribot, "Cause and Response: Vulnerability and Climate in the Anthropocene," *Journal of Peasant Studies* 41:5 (2014): 3.

74 Rob Nixon, *Slow Violence and the Environmentalism of the Poor* (Cambridge, MA: Harvard University Press, 2011).

75 Muhindo Emilda, "Climate Witness: Muhindo Emilda, Tanzania," World Wildlife Fund, http://wwf.panda.org/about_our_earth/aboutcc/problems/ people_at_risk/personal_stories/witness_stories/?175882/Climate-Witness-Muhindo-Emilda-Uganda; Timothy Laurent, "Climate Witness: Timothy Laurent, Tanzania" (World Wildlife Fund); Siwema Prosper, "Climate Witness: Siwema Prosper, Tanzania" (World Wildlife Fund); Monique Tombo, "Climate Witness: Monique Tombo, Madagascar" World Wildlife Fund, http://wwf. panda.org/about_our_earth/aboutcc/problems/people_at_risk/personal_stories/ witness_stories/?190801/Climate-Witness-Monique-Tombo-Madagascar.

76 Andrew K. Githeko et al, "Climate Change and Vector-Borne Diseases: A Regional Analysis," *Bulletin of the World Health Organization* 78:9 (2000).

77 Kasperson and Kasperson, *Climate Change, Vulnerability, and Social Justice,* 1 and 9.

78 Roberts and Parks, *A Climate of Injustice,* 67.

79 Ibidun O. Adelekan, "Vulnerability of Poor Urban Coastal Communities to Climate Change in Lagos, Nigeria," presented at the Fifth Urban Research Symposium, Marseille, June 28–30, 2009.

80 Michel Masozera, Melissa Bailey, and Charles Kerchner, "Distribution of Impacts of Natural Disasters across Income Groups: A Case Study of New Orleans," *Ecological Economics* 63:2 (2007).

81 Loren R. Cass, "Measuring the Domestic Salience of International Environmental Norms: Climate Change Norms in American, German, and British Climate Policy Debates," in *The Social Construction of Climate Change: Power, Knowledge, Norms, Discourses*, ed. Mary E. Pettenger (Farnham, UK: Ashgate, 2007), 24–25.

82 George W. Bush, "President Bush Discusses Global Climate Change" (Office of the Press Secretary, White House, 2001).

83 Clive Hamilton, *Requiem for a Species: Why We Resist the Truth About Climate Change* (London: Earthscan, 2010).

84 Ashley Dawson, "Climate Justice: The Emerging Movement against Green Capitalism," *South Atlantic Quarterly* 109:2 (2010).

85 Verona Collantes, "Why Gender Equality and Women's Voices Are Relevant (Even) in Climate Change Discourse," in *Outreach on Climate Change and Sustainable Development* (2014); AmazonWatch, "Cop20 Un Climate Summit in Lima, Peru," AmazonWatch, http://amazonwatch.org/get-involved/events/cop20; Brentin Mock, "Why Environmentalists Should Support the Black Lives Matter Protests," grist.org, December 8, 2014, http://grist.org/living/why-environmentalists-should-support-the-black-lives-matter-protests/.

86 IpsosMORI, "Global Trends 2014," Ipsos MORI, http://www.ipsosglobaltrends.com/index.html.

87 Leigh Brownhill and Terisa E. Turner, "Nigerian Commoners' Gifts to Humanity," Carbon Trade Watch (2006), http://www.carbontradewatch.org/archive/nigerian-commoners-gifts-to-humanity-2.html.

88 Oxfam Canada, "Gender Justice: Economic Empowerment," http://www.oxfam.ca/sites/default/files/imce/ec-gj-economic-empowerment.pdf; Abu Rakib, *Review Report on Gender and Diversity Sensitivity of Emergency Response by Der Members*, ed. DER Working Group on Gender and Diversity (London: Oxfam GB, 2006).

89 Peter Rudiak-Gould, "Climate Change and Accusation: Global Warming and Local Blame in a Small Island State," *Current Anthropology* 55:4 (2014): 365–386.

INDEX

Page numbers in **bold** refer to figures, page numbers in *italic* refer to tables.